Joint Ventures

Joint Ventures

Inside America's Almost Legal Marijuana Industry

Trish Regan

WILEY

John Wiley & Sons, Inc.

Published by John Wiley & Sons, Inc., Hoboken, New Jersey
Published simultaneously in Canada

For general information about our other products and services, please contact our Customer Care Department within the United States at (800) 762–2974, outside the United States at (317) 572–3993 or fax (317) 572–4002.

Wiley also publishes its books in a variety of electronic formats. Some content that appears in print may not be available in electronic books. For more information about Wiley products, visit our web site at www.wiley.com.

Library of Congress Cataloging-in-Publication Data:

Regan, Trish, date.
    Joint ventures : inside America's almost legal marijuana industry / Trish Regan.
      p.   cm.
    ISBN 978-0-470-55907-9 (cloth)
      1. Marijuana industry—United States.   I. Title.
    HD9019.M382.U67   2011
    338.1'73790973—dc22

                             2010054050

Printed in the United States of America

10 9 8 7 6 5 4 3 2 1

CONTENTS

INTRODUCTION

I remember the story vividly. It's one of those memories that becomes etched in your mind; it's buried deep in your database, but it's there. I was maybe five years old and had tagged along with my mother, a journalist, on one of her field reporting expeditions. We were at her friend's home, and she told me to wait in the living room on a yellow silk couch. Within seconds, she had disappeared down the hall. As I listened to hushed voices in the background, my eyes peered around the pale blue, wallpapered living room. On the polished wood side table to my left were a series of photos of a young woman with her small daughters, a woman with her husband, a woman laughing. I didn't know or understand it at the time, but the woman whom my mother was visiting, the woman smiling in the pictures next to her husband and children, was dying of lung cancer. I had met her once. I remember a white terry cloth turban tied around her head in an attempt to disguise her hair loss. The woman—a forty-four-year-old mother of four, a wife, and a close friend of my mother's—was suffering through chemotherapy treatments in an effort to save her life. She had lung cancer, and she was not going to make it.

1

Could this woman's final days have been made easier by having access to quality marijuana to help her manage her chemotherapy? Might she have responded to treatment better had she been able to regularly smoke cannabis?

That same year, my mother, wrote an article for the *Boston Globe* on the efforts to legalize marijuana in our home state of New Hampshire. It was the early 1980s, and a handful of states had made efforts to decriminalize marijuana, although it would be almost two decades before California would become the first state to legalize marijuana for medical purposes. But at that time, the tiny northeastern state known for its "Live Free or Die" motto was at the forefront of the medicinal use movement. A seventy-nine-year-old legislator named Everett B. Sackett, a Republican from the small town of Lee, had become the first to introduce a bill legalizing marijuana for state use. He told my mother, "It seems that in a state where we do so much to promote alcohol," referring to the state's monopoly on its well-publicized liquor business, "we should be willing to legalize a drug that could help people in terrible pain and discomfort."[1] Representative Sackett championed the marijuana bill in response to his gut reaction that prohibiting cancer patients from alleviating pain and nausea was somehow just plain wrong. Sackett believed his seventy-three-year-old friend, who was suffering from cancer, should not be forced to break the law just to relieve the painful side effects of his chemotherapy treatment. His friend, a former college professor, who requested that his name not be published at the time because, as he put it, "I don't like to expose myself as a law breaker," did explain that his decision to experiment with marijuana for pain came after his fourth chemotherapy treatment. "Have you ever been on a cancer ward in a hospital? You can always tell from those awful sounds coming from the room. All that vomiting and retching," he said.

Eventually, Sackett's friend asked some young acquaintances to obtain some marijuana and wrap it into cigarettes for him. By smoking one joint one hour before his chemotherapy treatment, he said he was able to ward off huge bouts of nausea. And, he added, "If I experience any nausea during the one-hour treatment, I light up another and take a couple of drags while the nurses look the other way. The nausea goes away completely."

Meanwhile, my mother's friend—the woman dying from lung cancer—suffered from massive bouts of nausea. "It was horrible. I couldn't eat anything. You can't imagine what it's like to have four different chemicals running through your body and knowing you have no control," she said. When her doctor recommended that she try marijuana, she asked him how she could obtain it. He told her that that was her problem.

It was, indeed, a problem. The woman was terrified of getting the drug because there was talk of it being laced with phencyclidine (PCP), also called angel dust. She sought out some friends in Cambridge with degrees in chemistry and asked them to secure and to test marijuana in their laboratory to ensure its purity. They did, and once she began smoking marijuana, she was able to relieve her nausea and managed to eat.

The woman's husband, a retired air force colonel, insisted that "the failure to legalize marijuana for cancer does nothing to stop the illegal drug trade. All it does is tie the hands of a competent physician in prescribing medicine for his patients and punish the people who are dying and in pain." A member of the New Hampshire state legislature at the time said that Sackett's bill was "not a legalization of marijuana bill. It is a cancer treatment bill which would allow a chemical to be used under a doctor's supervision."

When I decided to examine the underground marijuana trade for a documentary at CNBC, my memory of being in that blue living room, knowing that my mother was interviewing a woman on her death bed, came rushing back. Today New Hampshire, like the rest of the country, is still wrestling with the *same* issue. Indeed, the sad irony is that my mother's article could have just as easily been written today.

I've never smoked marijuana, and having made it this far in life without it, I don't feel a desire to smoke. But that's my decision. If I were suffering and it could help me feel better, I would want the option of trying it. Has the federal government overstepped its bounds? Are the feds contributing to a culture of violence? Might the federal government be doing the right thing by decriminalizing, or even legalizing, marijuana outright? These are the questions examined in this book. Several things are clear from my research: Marijuana is hugely popular. There is a large market for high-quality marijuana. It is difficult to succeed as a grower, in part, due to the myriad laws governing the substance.

It's disturbing to me that this many years after I tagged along with my mom on her story, I'm reporting a similar one. Nonetheless, this book isn't about why marijuana should be legalized for cancer patients. The answer to that argument, much of the country agrees, is clear. Poll numbers overwhelmingly support the use of marijuana for medicinal purposes. Rather, this book examines the groundswell sweeping the nation as state after state moves to legalize medicinal marijuana. With so many states permitting use, marijuana has reached a state of quasi-legality (although it is still illegal under federal law), and the financial rewards have been significant for some risk-taking entrepreneurs. They are, after all, risking it all for the chance to work in an industry they believe in and, more important for most of them, they may make money in.

The marijuana "industry" (and it *is* an industry, as this book explains) has changed dramatically in just the last few years. The influx of new players, for example, in the Denver market where there are now more dispensaries than Starbucks, is an example of capitalism at work. However, growers, dispensary owners, patients, and American taxpayers all suffer, to some extent, as a result of federal marijuana laws.

For a market to work properly, there must be an open, transparent system with a level playing field. Today, the marijuana industry is anything but that—creating an opportunity for outrageous profits and outrageous risk. Still, more and more Americans are vying for their chance to take part in this illegal, underground trade. It's America's Green Rush.

POTHOLES

The Challenges of the
Marijuana Business

B y some accounts, Chris Bartkowicz was living the high life. He resided in a swanky neighborhood in Denver, and he was growing pot for a living. He was self-employed, made his own hours, and had developed a steady clientele.

When the local NBC affiliate in Denver, looking to understand the newly semilegal marijuana industry, came looking for a grower to go on the record, Bartkowicz was happy to do it. He gave them a tour of his home, explaining his business, even bragging that he was living the dream. He told the camera crew that his grow was worth $400,000. The promo spot for the interview, also known as a tease, ran three straight days on channel 9. As a television journalist myself, I'm well aware of the power of a promotional tease, and this was a sexy story, tailor-made to bring in viewers. Some would no doubt watch in anger at what had happened to their beloved city, and some would watch in envy. But they would watch.

With all that talk of easy money and easy highs, it sure sounds like an easy gig. I can't tell you how many people see my documentaries on marijuana and then ask me what would happen if they quit their jobs to find a way into this "budding" industry. I remember walking across the floor of the New York Stock Exchange the morning after *Marijuana Inc*. debuted. I was bombarded with people all wanting to know more about this business. After all, one marijuana broker insisted that being a pot broker was like being a broker for any other commodity— like wheat or corn. He described the job as being a middle-man who simply facilitates the transaction. So it makes sense that his comments sparked some interest in the trader types on Wall Street.

Meanwhile, nontraders are fascinated by the growers, the so-called artists who make the industry possible. Somehow, the fantasy of packing up and moving out west to grow weed strikes a chord. Some dream mixture of Johnny Appleseed, Michael Pollan, Bill Gates, and Cheech Marin leads people to think they want to trade their lives for this one. Apparently, there's something very appealing about putting a few seeds, or small plants, into the ground and watching them grow—and then winding up with baskets of cash. After all, they say money doesn't grow on trees—but does it grow on marijuana plants?

Could your state legalize pot soon, putting you one step closer to being the Chris Bartkowicz of your neighborhood? Or is there more to this story?

Like every other profession, the marijuana business is hard work. Bartkowicz, after investing his savings in some marijuana plants and indoor growing equipment, managed to transform his $637,000 home in the well-heeled Highlands Ranch suburb of Denver into a large-scale growing operation, complete with a jungle of electrical wires and water to service the hundreds of plants filling his two-thousand-square-foot basement. "I definitely had a skill set," he tells me, a twinge of pride in his voice.

Indeed, Bartkowicz spent several years prior to starting his Highlands Ranch grow honing his horticultural skills because, as he puts it, as a patient himself (for chronic pain due to scoliosis that he developed in 2002 after being hit by a car in a crosswalk while on his bicycle), he couldn't afford to pay for pot. "I would rather sacrifice a little physical toil to circumvent a lot of those costs," he says. By the time Attorney General Eric Holder opened the floodgates on medicinal marijuana in October 2009 by saying federal agents would not target those who grew for medical purposes, Bartkowicz knew he was talented enough to start growing and selling on a large scale. He had studied his market. "There are approximately one hundred thousand patients right now on the state's registry," he rattles off. "And maybe five percent of those people would know how to grow. Five percent of *those* [are growing] maybe at A-plus levels." In other words, there's a market for this stuff. Bartkowicz wasn't alone in this realization. Since Holder issued his announcement, the pot industry in Denver has exploded. In less than nine months, the community went from roughly a dozen marijuana dispensaries to four hundred, giving Denver, the Mile High City, the dubious distinction of becoming Pot City, USA.

Still, the life of a small-time farmer is difficult, no matter the crop. "It's very labor intensive," Bartkowicz complains. "The bigger your garden, the more you're working. People think you just put a plant under a light and [give it] a little bit of water and at the end of the year you're a millionaire." But the plants need constant attention—six hours a day, every day, Bartkowicz toiled in his basement garden. He admits tending the plants got pretty lonely. "I mean, it was just me. I didn't have anyone helping me—and the business was right there, where I lived. There was no escaping it. And let's face it," he says rolling his eyes with a self-deprecating chuckle, "I spent a lot of time in my basement." So, every day,

365 days a year, Bartkowicz was on call. The occasional camping vacation with friends? Not even an option. There was no one, other than Bartkowicz, to tend and guard the pot. You can ask an acquaintance to feed your cat while you're away on a trip, but finding someone to care for your mother lode of weed is another thing altogether.

"It's just work, work, work," Bartkowicz says, waving his hands for emphasis. Meanwhile, the time he wasn't in his basement tending plants was spent distributing his product to patients and selling the surplus to dispensaries.

Bartkowicz also confronted the same struggles any small business owner faces: there's no company to fall back on, no one to issue you a weekly paycheck, no one to call when something goes wrong. Thus, the burden of failure weighs entirely on the individual. As a result he worried constantly. While lying awake in bed at night questions flooded his head: Would the harvest be strong? Did he need to improve his security? What happens if someone breaks in?

Despite the headaches, Bartkowicz knew there was huge potential in this venture. If everything went right—meaning every plant produced a maximum amount of quality bud (something growers admit rarely happens)—he could potentially make $400,000 in revenue off his business. Cash. That sounds like a lot of money, but that's just gross receipts. How much would his expenses be? Those ran him in the neighborhood of $75,000 a year. The electric bill alone cost nearly $2,000 a month. Realistically, with total sales likely to be closer to $150,000, Bartkowicz hoped to clear $50,000. "I didn't actually ever make $400,000. That's an ideal situation. A number calculated given the number of lights that I had. The reality is I was more at about $125,000, $130,000, you know, minus operating expenses."

As business models go, though, that's still an excellent return on investment. If you were to open say, a wine shop or a bagel place hoping to bring in $50,000 while fully recouping your $75,000 investment in the first year, you'd be in for a big surprise. Where do high returns normally come from, though? High risk.

And despite what Bartkowicz thought he knew about the law, he was taking a lot of risks.

You can only imagine the Drug Enforcement Administration's (DEA's) reaction when they viewed the TV promo on which Bartkowicz admitted he could make a few hundred thousand dollars from his residential grow. When Colorado's special agent for the DEA Jeffrey Sweetin saw that tease, it was the beginning of the end for Bartkowicz.

Early on the morning of February 12, 2010, before the story had even a chance to air on KUSA-TV, DEA officers approached Bartkowicz's suburban home. He and his buddy were just pulling out of the driveway. They had planned to go to a local home improvement store to buy some additional security supplies when federal officers ran up to Bartkowicz's vehicle, yanked him from the car, and asked for his consent to search his home. "I figured I'm in compliance with state laws," he said. "I didn't even know why they were here." Overwhelmed, he granted them access, signing a consent-to-search form. He was read his Miranda warnings as agents burst through his home.

Within minutes, the DEA confiscated 224 marijuana plants— 119 of which were in various growth stages, complete with root systems. The remaining 105 plants were clones or starter plants. Federal agents also found grow lights, fans, and filters—and before Bartkowicz knew what hit him, he was on his way to jail. He spent thirty days behind bars before posting bail. His life had been turned upside down, overnight.

Granted, Bartkowicz's operation was hardly a contender for business of the year—his home was a major fire hazard in a residential neighborhood. He lived less than one thousand feet from a nearby school (which makes his grow illegal even under state law). He also wasn't paying taxes on any of his pot income (which might have at least shown some good faith). Perhaps most important, he failed to keep proper documentation to prove that he was a caregiver to state residents.

Per Amendment 20 to the state constitution, state law in Colorado requires that medicinal growers maintain paper records proving they are designated caregivers for local residents. Growers are permitted three mature flowering plants and three immature plants for each medicinal card they possess. (Patients are allowed to turn over their "growing rights" for six plants to a "caregiver" who grows marijuana for them.) Given that 119 of Bartkowicz's plants were considered mature and 105 immature, to meet state requirements he should have had forty medicinal cards ready to show the federal officers. Otherwise, he had no way to prove that all of his plants were destined for medical use. But on that cold February morning of the raid, he was able to present only twelve cards to the feds. He managed to locate an additional four cards after the agents left, bringing him to a total of sixteen. But, Bartkowicz was still twenty-four cards short of the amount needed to meet basic state requirements.

Lucky for him, state law also has a clause that enables growers and patients to grow more than the specified limit of three mature and three immature plants provided the grower can prove they are needed for medicinal purposes. Although amendment 20, section 4, to the state constitution states that each patient, at any one time, may possess no more than "two ounces of a usable form of marijuana" and "no more than six marijuana plants, with three or fewer being mature, flowering plants that are producing a usable form of marijuana." It also makes clear, however, that if patients or primary caregivers are caught with more, they can attempt to prove that they need more than the law allows.

This clause creates a gray zone that permits an indefinite number of plants provided a grower can prove a medicinal need, a defense to which Bartkowicz is clinging. As he puts it, "If it's medically necessary, I can have that much. The law clearly states, if you need more [marijuana], and it's medically necessary, *that* is legal."

Regardless of whether Bartkowicz was in violation of state law, the DEA would argue that state law is irrelevant and does not matter in a federal court. Although being in compliance with state regulations may have generated some goodwill with the Denver public, the reality is that even if Bartkowicz was in compliance with state law, what he was doing was still 100 percent against federal law. Period.

Bartkowicz's biggest mistake was his inability to grasp that what he was doing was still, in the eyes of the DEA, illegal. He didn't (and still didn't when I met him) seem to comprehend that the federal law contradicted Colorado state law and he was therefore, in the eyes of the feds, running a criminal operation.

Despite sporting a goatee, couple arm tattoos, and a few extra pounds, Bartkowicz looks more like twenty-eight years old than thirty-six. He greets me at the front door of the small track house where he's staying on the outskirts of Denver, Colorado. Under house arrest (after posting a $10,000 bond), he sports an ankle bracelet under his jeans that prevents him from venturing beyond the three cement steps at the entrance of the house. Several yards ahead, a low chain-link fence encloses the tiny front lawn. I suggest we talk outside, but moving just four feet into the sun—even on a beautiful summer day—means his ankle bracelet will set off an alarm and he'll be back behind bars.

Staring down at the beige shag carpet in the dim living room of the house, Bartkowicz runs his fingers through his short brown hair and sighs as he surveys the room. It's clean but barren. Seventies-style fake wood paneling adorns the walls. Loosely motioning at the few mismatched pieces of worn furniture, Bartkowicz shrugs. "Nothing here is mine," he explains to me. "My house is gone. All my possessions—gone. They took everything." "They" refers to the feds. Bartkowicz is living with a friend because everything he owned—except the clothes on his back (a dark T-shirt and jeans when he and I met)—was confiscated by the DEA.

He did the local TV interview, he claims, because he hoped to demonstrate that the pot business was a real business—that growing pot can be done safely and that medicinal producers serve a purpose in the community. Still, Bartkowicz was naive in assuming that if he could just show the public that pot producers live in real homes and "a lot of us have clean, safe, electrical wiring," people would appreciate all he was doing to legitimize the business. The reality was that his willingness to come forward was probably too much for local DEA officials, who were likely embarrassed by the television promo. Special Agent Sweetin told local media, "Four hundred thousand dollars a year goes beyond 'I'm just a caregiver for sick people.'"

Bartkowicz argues that since he was providing *medicinal* users with marijuana, the DEA should have taken into account the Obama administration's change in policy. Just months prior to Bartkowicz's arrest, Eric Holder, the attorney general for the Obama administration, shocked the country by announcing that the Justice Department would no longer raid medicinal marijuana clubs that are established legally under state law. In a statement, Holder said that drug traffickers and people who use firearms will continue to be direct targets of federal prosecutors, but that on his watch, "it will not be a priority to use federal resources to prosecute patients with serious illnesses or their caregivers who are complying with state laws on medical marijuana." It was a major departure from the policies of any previous administration, and many marijuana enthusiasts and medicinal growers, like Chris Bartkowicz, believed that this statement effectively shielded them from federal arrest. One of the constant themes in my conversation with Bartkowicz was that he had taken the federal government at its word. He believed that as a result of Holder's assertion, he had effectively been given a green light to operate. Bartkowicz insists he should be cleared from any federal wrongdoing in part because "Holder says, if you're violating state *and* federal law, then we're looking for you. But because no state charges have been levied against me and no state investigation was conducted, why would I even have a hint of fear of the federal government? I was not worried about the feds coming after me." He should have been.

What Bartkowicz failed to understand is that although Holder may, in effect, be sanctioning medicinal use and production, the DEA still has the authority to invoke federal law and most definitely has the blessing of Holder's office when it comes to arresting what it considers to be "traffickers." Bartkowicz's operation, due to its size, was in the eyes of the DEA a trafficking operation. In addition, although the administration might discourage medicinal marijuana arrests, there are different interpretations of what is medicinal and what is not. Critics regularly argue, for example, that medicinal marijuana is simply an excuse for recreational users to gain access to the drug. Further complicating the issue, it's difficult to separate the "totally necessary" users from the "possibly useful" users.

In addition, there are internal divisions about whether medical marijuana should be permitted, and some DEA holdovers do not appreciate the Obama administration's lenient policy toward the drug. Regardless of what the president and his appointees say, the majority of DEA officials in various communities across the country stress that it is their duty to uphold the law when it comes to pot. And U.S. law clearly states that marijuana is a Schedule I drug and is illegal.

Bartkowicz's case has sparked debate in dispensaries, cafes, doctors' offices, and restaurants throughout the Denver community. The raid and subsequent arrest is making the many pot growers, brokers, and dispensary owners in Colorado increasingly nervous. They had assumed that their activities were essentially sanctioned by the federal government as a result of Holder's assertion. Although Bartkowicz had permission from the state to smoke pot and grow it both for himself and other patients, U.S. prosecutors maintain that even if he was following state guidelines, the drug is still illegal, and therefore they have the right to prosecute, regardless of the Obama administration's relaxed policies.

Meanwhile, Bartkowicz is facing a daunting sentence. After turning down a plea deal that would have meant two years in prison, he's potentially facing as many as sixty years behind bars (in part due to two prior convictions for marijuana possession). Why not take the deal and plead guilty? Bartkowicz's answer is tinged with a political undertone. "[It would] give the federal government more confidence and comfort in terrorizing sick people," he tells me. "By rolling over and taking it, it would do more harm to the community at large that I don't even know—the elderly lady that has cancer or the seventy-year-old man with arthritic pain that's beyond measure."

That "community at large" is left in a state of bewilderment, laced with fear, as a result of the DEA's charges. With conflicting state and federal laws, they're left asking, who's in charge? DEA agent Sweetin wants to make sure they know *he* is the chief regulator. Yet, even he has admitted to local reporters that he's not in the Rocky Mountain region to be the regulator of medicinal marijuana. Still, he's inundated with daily phone calls and e-mails from community members demanding that he crack down on neighborhood dispensaries. Nonetheless, it's clear where the U.S. Attorney for Colorado stands on this issue. In a brief filed in Bartkowicz's case, U.S. Attorney David Gaouette writes that regardless of what voters in Colorado voted for, no grow operation will be tolerated by the federal government. He writes, "Colorado's state drug law does not, and cannot, abrogate federal drug laws." Federal attorneys assume their power to prosecute marijuana users and growers primarily as a result of the commerce clause—article I, section 8, clause 3 of the U.S. Constitution—which states that Congress shall have the power to regulate commerce among the states.

Interestingly, and perhaps fearing a backlash from residents and important people in the Obama administration, Gaouette did reference state law in the initial press release from the DEA arguing that "in this instance the defendant had in his possession more plants than state law allows." In the same release, Gaouette even points out that his office is in full compliance with a Department of Justice memorandum issued on October 19, 2009, by Deputy

Attorney General David W. Ogden, since according to the memo, medicinal marijuana growers' actions must be in "clear and unambiguous compliance with existing state laws." Gaouette concludes that Bartkowicz was not in compliance with state law and that "the U.S. Attorney's Office will continue to focus on large-scale marijuana traffickers."[1]

Colorado's Democratic U.S. representative Jared Polis criticized Bartkowicz's arrest in a letter on February 23 to U.S. Attorney General Holder, referring to his state's marijuana approach as "both practical and compassionate." He asked Holder to clarify how federal drug authorities plan to address marijuana growers, but he has not received a reply.

I bet that marijuana is probably the only issue on which Polis, the openly gay and liberal Democratic representative from Colorado, and conservative Supreme Court justice Clarence Thomas, actually agree. Thomas, true to his conservative roots, believes in the limited powers of the federal government. In his view, the feds have no right to interfere in a practice a state considers legal. Polis, as a liberal, sees nothing wrong with marijuana usage and would like to see it legalized at the state level. He has cosponsored three marijuana bills in an effort to push states' rights when it comes to pot. This is an issue on which the extremes of both parties actually agree: keep the federal government away from state decisions.

Regardless of politics, the bigger question here is: is the business of marijuana a real one? The answer, as this book explains, is yes. Is there real money to be made? Yes. Will the industry spread beyond Denver and the West Coast? Without a doubt. However, as long as marijuana remains in a quasi-legal environment, in which the feds have the ability to throw users and producers in jail regardless of state law, the marijuana industry will continue to attract violence and wreak havoc on communities while providing massive profit margins to the few entrepreneurs and criminal rings that are willing to engage in the trade. Meanwhile, the people who need marijuana as medicine are still struggling to secure their doses.

Many critics argue that marijuana legalization will result in a massive increase of pot use among the general population to the detriment of society. Meanwhile, state governments and entrepreneurs alike are all asking: can real money really be made on these ventures? Given the developments in Colorado and California, as well as the experimentation with legalized drugs in Portugal, it's possible to make some pretty educated guesses as to the outcome of legalized marijuana. Still, as U.S. laws on pot usage and production continue to change, there are plenty of questions surrounding the business of marijuana. Perhaps there is one thing of which you can be assured: things are about to get very interesting.

2

The Mile High City

An Emerging Market of Pot

Just weeks after the feds raided Chris Bartkowicz's house, the local police raided a grow belonging to Wanda James and Scott Durrah, located in a suburban business park north of Denver. Police claimed it was the biggest medical marijuana grow operation they had ever seen. The North Metro Drug Task Force said that there were marijuana plants everywhere and that they found 536 plants in different stages of growth. The police raided the grow facility, they said, in response to complaints from neighboring businesses that were concerned about the smell.

But these were local police—not the feds—bursting into James and Durrah's grow house. All James needed to prove was that she was not in violation of any state laws. She says she did. According to James, she met the state requirements with one caregiver card for every three mature plants on the premises. She also stresses that she had no intention of hiding her business from authorities and that her lease clearly states she is growing marijuana in the facility.

Recalling the raid, James insists it's critical to keep detailed records because proving that a dispensary is operating within the state's guidelines is critical to its survival. "I don't worry about the police breaking into my restaurant and confiscating all my liquor, but I do worry about it [a police raid] with my dispensary."

Local authorities were able to verify all of her cards, and as a result, no charges were brought. But because the industry is so new, James complains that she is constantly forced to educate people—even the authorities like the police officers who raided her property. "We had to sit down and talk to them about why this is a legal grow, why you can't raid us, why you can't take our plants," she says. She remembers how the local SWAT team burst in and broke though her windows, only to find out that she was legal. "They said they were sorry and moved on," she says, shrugging.

Wanda James may be in the same industry as Bartkowicz, but it's hard to find anything they have in common beyond that. For starters, her primary business isn't growing cannabis; it's selling it. She and her husband, restaurateur Scott Durrah, are co-owners of the new Apothecary of Colorado, a marijuana dispensary at 1730 Blake Street in the heart of downtown Colorado.

While Bartkowicz appears disheveled and underprepared for the onslaught of attention as a result of his arrest, James is beautiful, articulate, a former naval intelligence officer—and a perfect spokesperson for the marijuana movement. A forty-six-year-old African American woman, James is tall, slim but shapely, with wavy dark hair that falls just under her chin. She has a magnetic smile, emphasized with a hint of shiny gloss on her lips, and an enthusiasm that makes her instantly likable. Her polish reflects her background as a political consultant, having run campaigns, including Jared Polis's successful Democratic bid for U.S. Congress. (Polis has become a major advocate for medicinal marijuana, joining Representative Barney Frank in pushing for the legalization of marijuana.) As a member of President Obama's National Finance Committee, James was a major fundraiser for the president in Colorado and thus she is tapped into the community's most prominent social and political circles. With her husband, a former marine and current chef, she co-owns the popular 8 Rivers Caribbean restaurant, located just a few blocks from her dispensary's headquarters.

James is rattled by the DEA's action. "At the end of the day we're not very different," she says, referring to Bartkowicz and herself. "The same thing could happen to me. A lot of people are terrified about a federal indictment."

So why would she take the risk of growing marijuana, if growing can be so risky? To maximize profits. To really make money in this industry, dispensary owners need to have their own grow operation because the costs are too high to purchase marijuana from outside growers.

For example, it may cost $1,000 to grow a pound of high-quality bud indoors. The climate in Colorado means that, unlike somewhere such as California, marijuana growers in Colorado need to concentrate on indoor strains that require more equipment, including special lights and watering systems. One grower I met actually spends $500 a gallon on ultra-high-end fertilizer and uses expensive meat-eating "predator" bugs, instead of pesticides, to prevent vegetarian bugs from eating all of his marijuana leaves.

With $1,000 of built-in cost per pound, growers can then sell their product at the retail level (to their own medicinal clients) for between $4,000 and $6,000 per pound. If they sell to another dispensary, the wholesale price hovers around $3,400 per pound. So if a dispensary has the ability and know-how to grow, it is best served by growing its own product because the profits are significantly higher. In addition, by growing marijuana themselves, dispensary owners can maintain their own quality control. In fact, beginning in July 2010, new laws required dispensaries to grow 70 percent of their own product. It's an attempt by state government to better regulate the industry. The thinking is that by having the dispensary and grow operation under one owner, the paperwork will be easier to track. When I visited Denver in late June 2010, dispensary owners were scrambling to partner in joint ventures with various growers in a last-minute attempt to comply with the new laws.

Driving down Broadway, through the heart of Denver, you might think—just for a minute—that you're in the center of Amsterdam. Nestled among the dozens of specialty clothing shops, coffee shops, and hip bars and restaurants are the city's newest ventures: medical marijuana dispensaries. Since Attorney General Eric Holder announced that the federal government would not seek to arrest and punish medicinal marijuana users, the Denver marijuana industry has exploded. Overnight. In the last year, hundreds of dispensaries like the one James and her husband run have opened their doors in the region, and marijuana advocates have proclaimed Denver, Mile High City, "America's Cannabis Capital." Dispensaries are so plentiful that locals have dubbed this part of town "Broadsterdam" (a play on Amsterdam), and much like its counterpart in the Netherlands, many of these businesses market their stash with large, green marijuana leaves on their signs. Colorado is at a crossroads. Some equate the new marijuana boom in Denver with the Criple Creek gold rush of 1899. Modern-day forty-niners are piling in, anxious for their chance to cash in on the Colorado's new Green Rush.

Call it U.S. capitalism at work. Demand for marijuana is skyrocketing, and suppliers are happy to oblige. Eighty thousand Colorado residents currently hold medicinal cards enabling them to purchase or grow their own marijuana, and according to state officials, that number is growing at a rate of four hundred applicants per day. Suddenly, everyone in Colorado seems to have developed some type of ailment, and entrepreneurs are rushing to fill the market's need. Denver is now home to the most dispensaries, per capita, in the country with one dispensary for every 1,500 residents. (Second place goes to Los Angeles, where the ratio is one for every four thousand residents, although laws are being developed to significantly reduce the number of pot shops on the West Coast.) At this writing, there are currently nearly one thousand dispensaries in Denver. There are actually more dispensaries in Denver than there are Starbucks or even liquor stores, while in the crunchy granola haven of Boulder, Colorado, there are more dispensaries than Starbucks and liquor stores combined.

With so much demand for marijuana, Wanda James says the medicinal marijuana business is, plain and simple, a good business. Although she intends to advance her politics through her entrepreneurship, she also wants to make money. Despite its potential, however, marijuana is still a business like any other and therefore vulnerable to all of the normal pitfalls—and then some.

It's not uncommon for top medicinal clinic owners to pour $100,000 to $300,000—or even more—into their dispensaries. That doesn't even include the labor and supplies for growing the product. Meanwhile, the high number of dispensaries means competition is fierce, and any new outlet has to monitor not only for changes in the law but also changes in price and the popularity of strains as well.

James's business has existed for more than six months, but she still hasn't managed to turn a profit. "We're almost there," she promises. "We started the dispensary and the marijuana grow at the same time. It's the same as starting any other kind of farm. We had to get the initial plants, the lights, the hydroponic systems, the grow spaces. Even the rent on this place," she says, stretching out her long arms and looking around her dispensary, "is expensive." And the growing operation costs even more.

Unable to turn a profit so far, James has been using money from her restaurant business to invest in the dispensary. You read that right: she's financing her supposedly "can't miss" marijuana business with her profits from the notoriously risky restaurant business. If James is having a tough time, you know this business is complicated.

Despite their proliferation, marijuana growers are increasingly unwilling to discuss their businesses, as *New York Times* reporter David Segal experienced when researching his reported in his

June 25, 2010, article, "When Capitalism Meets Cannabis." He writes of the marijuana entrepreneurs: "Many have a long history with marijuana, and they remain [reluctant] to share their names . . . none of the owners offered a look at their 'grow,' as indoor, hydroponic crops are known. On that subject, everyone became bashful."

Indeed, the community is nervous. Nonetheless, after having spent over two years reporting on the subject, I did develop sources that were willing to walk me through their grows. They trusted me enough to share their business plans, to explain the intricacies of the business and even their names. A common question I ask them: If growing marijuana is risky both as a legal proposition and as a business venture, why go into it? For James, growing and distributing marijuana is not just a business opportunity but a political calling.

Nearly twenty years ago, while living in Los Angeles, she and her husband became outraged by the number of young African Americans being sent to prison due to the possession of small amounts of marijuana. They publicly fought against the jailing of young black men for selling marijuana at a time of widespread jail overcrowding. "It was the mid nineties, early nineties, when L.A. County started letting out rapists early because of overcrowding in L.A. county jails," she tells me. "People that were actually committing real crimes we're letting out of jail early so that we can make more room to lock up people who were using marijuana? This became *absurd* to me."

After several family members were arrested for marijuana possession, James and Durrah set out to help change the stereotypes surrounding the substance, to remove the stigma, and to work toward legalizing marijuana. "This is a political job," she tells me, her melodic voice filled with conviction and determination.

As a marijuana user herself, James explains that pot alleviates her hip pain while helping her husband with his constant back pain caused by a herniated disk. "When we came out"—she refers to her and her husband's public acknowledgment that they smoked pot as "coming out," a common term I hear from many area growers—"we felt like it gave other people permission to come out. Permission to say, 'You know what? Let's change what we think about the person who smokes marijuana is all about.' The person who smokes marijuana doesn't sit on their sofa all day, doesn't not have a job. Many people who engage in smoking are highly effective people, CEOs, business owners."

She knows her marijuana history, and she believes that she and her fellow dispensary owners in Colorado will have a place in the history books. "We're at the beginning of, or maybe the end of, a movement," she says, predicting that marijuana will be legal at the federal level in five years. "Nineteen thirty-seven was when this became illegal. One of the first people arrested for using marijuana was jazz artist Louis Armstrong. This whole marijuana prohibition actually started out of severe racism. Over the last seventy years, we've been locking up black and brown kids by the boatload for the amount of pot they may have on them." She is convinced it has to—and will very soon—end. Public perception and the realization that pot "isn't so bad" will help the movement toward legalization.

James is right about the role of racism in marijuana politics during the twentieth century. You need to look only to the man who was effectively the drug czar for the U.S. government long before it was an official title: Henry Anslinger. As the head of the new Federal Bureau of Narcotics (FBN), a position he held from 1930 to 1962, Anslinger's livelihood depended on being able to police a substance (really, *any* substance). That meant he needed the public to want to prohibit *something*. When it became clear that Congress would need to repeal the Eighteenth Amendment (as negative attitudes toward alcohol waned), Anslinger was a realist. He knew that the key to his success at the FBN would be based on the country's commitment to fighting drugs.

Anslinger launched a campaign against the substance he believed was most easy to target: marijuana. In speeches and in writings, he stuck to two dominant propaganda themes—blacks and Hispanics were the worst abusers of marijuana and that marijuana bred violence.

Anslinger embraced the country's racism and catered to white Americans' fears. The FBN released a series of propaganda films, including the infamous *Reefer Madness*, in an effort to reinforce the public's fears. It wasn't hard for Anslinger to find sympathy for his cause: already, twenty-four states had outlawed marijuana.

Anslinger died in 1975, but he would be proud that much of his groundwork is still alive. Through a tenure that lasted five administrations, he worked hard to perpetuate his view that marijuana breeds violence, and the connection between the drug and violence is still being discussed today. In a 2010 interview I conducted with the administration's drug czar, Gil Kerlikowske, he told me that there is a direct link between marijuana and crime. In everything from shoplifting to homicide, he says, marijuana is most often involved. "People [who are] arrested, regardless of what they are arrested for . . . [there's] an association with drugs. Not just marijuana but certainly a very very high association."

Wanda James has her own mission: to tear down Anslinger's decades-long push to stigmatize marijuana and minorities. Her hope is to advance her politics through her business, and so far, her plan seems to be working.

I meet James at her dispensary early one Saturday morning in May 2010. I am surprised when my driver pulls up outside a new four-story office building and I am told the shop is inside. "Are you sure you have the right address?" I ask the driver. "This is it." He confirms, double-checking his paper. Standing outside, I glance around at the spiffy, new brick buildings lining the street. I could be standing outside a downtown law firm as easily as a marijuana dispensary. Indeed, the Apothecary of Colorado radiates a dramatically different vibe than some of its counterparts in California. That's, in part, because dispensaries in Colorado do not permit patients to smoke on the premises. Rather, they're only allowed to purchase products. It's also because this is the image James and

Durrah have chosen to convey. Denver is still home to some stereotypical "pot shops," the kind with flashing green neon marijuana leaf signs designed to attract a young demographic, but The Apothecary is focused on an older, more conservative clientele.

As I walk down the hallway toward the elevator, I can still smell fresh carpet—not marijuana. There's a sun-filled atrium with a courtyard in the middle of the building, so even on a Saturday morning, the building is well lit and doesn't rely on dreary fluorescent bulbs. On the fourth floor (the building's top floor), I get out and make my way toward a glass door and venture inside. The dispensary itself consists of three rooms: the reception area (similar to a doctor's office); a large, conference-style room with a couch and sizable table; and most important, a room in the back that houses all of James's products.

We chat for a while as the camera crew prepares the lights for a sit-down interview. I ask her how much a typical sale might be. Instructing the receptionist to get her some "Blueberry," she promises to show me.

Twenty-something-year-old Grant, one of her "bud tenders," runs to the back room and comes back with a glass jar filled with marijuana. James cracks open the jar and a faint, minty scent emanates from the glass. She pulls out a small portion of the pale green bud with faint highlights of blue and purple, and holds it up. "This is an eighth of a gram," she tells me, "and that's what most people will buy." Reaching back into the jar with her other hand, she pulls out some more bud. "That's an eighth of an ounce," she explains, "and that would go anywhere from forty to sixty dollars."

An eighth is enough for a few days or a few weeks, depending on how often the patient needs to smoke. One joint, for example, uses about a gram of marijuana. James recommends patients smoke their pot via a pipe rather than roll it in a traditional joint. Due to the quality and high tetrahydrocannabinol (THC, the key chemical that gives cannabis its psychoactive powers) counts in marijuana today, patients need smaller hits.

Still, the potency of the marijuana, as James explains, is subjective because it affects different people different ways. That potency is primarily determined not only by a plant's genetics but also by the person growing the plant. Just like tomatoes, it all comes down to the gardener.

Although prices for marijuana vary widely depending on the quality, the grower, and the dispensary, the drug still doesn't come cheap in Denver. For example, a patient might buy a quarter of an ounce for about $100 to $200. There are about twenty-eight grams in an ounce, so if a person put a gram in each joint and smoked four joints per day, that pot might last one week. Thus, a month's worth of pot can run $400 to $800.

Even though Colorado legalized medical marijuana in 2000, James opened her dispensary less than six months before our first meeting, making her a relative newcomer to the field. As a result, she's struggling with some significant internal politics within her marijuana community. Some of the holdovers (people that she says have been working in the industry since the sixties) resent her and her husband trying to burst in on the scene and capitalize on the marijuana momentum. But she says that regardless of how long someone may have been in the industry, it's a competitive business. With four hundred dispensaries in town, it's clear that many will not survive. "I think we've created an atmosphere that our client base appreciates. Because of that, we're doing very well. We offer phenomenal strains. We are superior growers that offer a superior product."

Meanwhile, she must cope with trying to educate patients, some of whom call up assuming they can waltz in and buy some pot. "I'm like, 'Mmm, not so much.'" She laughs. But she will refer them to a doctor who can issue them the proper paperwork.

James's patients at the dispensary are older—mostly baby boomers. But it was not the age of her clientele that most surprised her, but rather the gender of her customers. Older women make up roughly half her business. "That's the group that I did not expect to see," she tells me. Moms, grandmothers, even ladies on their way home from church. "This group of women is really interesting," she muses. "I think women may be the pivotal piece that changes the legalization of marijuana. It's hard to look at a professional woman or at a grandmom or at a lady in a cooking class learning to fix marijuana in her food and say, 'You're just a stoner. You just want to get high. And you belong in jail.'"

A group of fifteen of these women are frequent visitors to her husband's Cooking with Marijuana class that he offers for $25 per person (for legal reasons, no tasting allowed) at their restaurant on the third Saturday of every month. On the morning I visit the class, there are at least forty students, and it's standing room only. The majority of participants are between fifty-five and seventy-five years old (though I did spot some in their twenties and thirties), and there's a consistent motive for why they're in the class: they tell me they suffer from severe pain but don't like to smoke. One woman is president of her condo association and a grandmother; another woman is a recent retiree. I also meet a Vietnam veteran and a former vice president of an established greeting card company. All are hoping to pick up some tips so they'll be able to cook up their own remedies.

James's husband, Durrah, is high energy. With his quick laugh and big smile, he reminds me of a thin version of Emeril Lagasse. His cuisine specialty is primarily Caribbean, and he's able to draw on his Jamaican background for many of his signature recipes, like jerk chicken. The restaurant is small with bright yellow walls and a large bar showcasing seventy high-end rums—perfect for Caribbean-style drinks.

Durrah's cooking platform, similar to a stage, is positioned in the back of the restaurant. As soon as he begins talking, it's clear—Scott is in his element. A fast talker, with a thick Boston accent and a quick sense of humor, he stresses one theme over and over: Marijuana can make you feel better. It can help you manage your pain, and the best way to manage that pain is to always have some level of marijuana in your system. "Levels are critical," he tells the class, as students scribble notes in their notepads. The biggest challenge, he warns, is knowing how to properly medicate since the effects of marijuana are slower when ingested through food. On the menu today: marijuana quiche and marijuana-infused shrimp scampi. His food, he promises, is nothing like the bad brownies you may have sampled in college, with all those twiglike things mixed into the batter. The key to his cooking is in his marijuana-infused butter and marijuana-infused olive oil. I ask if the drug "cooks off" similar to alcohol, and he promises me that it does not. In fact, the heat is what activates the THC and other cannabinoids.

Cannabinoids are the chemicals in the plant that bind to cell receptors in the brain. They cause the release of dopamine, which produces the "high" effect that marijuana users desire.

When the cooking class ends, dozens of students make the short walk over to the Apothecary of Colorado, where James greets them with a big smile and helps them select their latest meds. She's a little like an old-fashioned pharmacist, listening to their ailments, nodding her head in sympathy, and then promising she has just the cure. She asks what the pain is, whether they suffer from nausea or if they're struggling to sleep at night before suggesting different marijuana strains. "It not just about the potency of marijuana," she tells me, "it's also the strain of the marijuana. What it's going to do to you and how it's going to affect you. We try to tailor your symptoms to all the different types of marijuana that we have." James maintains files on all of her patients in order to keep track of their response to various strains. "So, if they really like the Bubble Berry, we'll continue to grow that strain." James proudly tells me she has tried every kind of marijuana available on her store shelves, and she has her preferences. She's a fan of Bubble Berry, but her favorite is Nectarine. "It gives me the right amount of up. It makes me really joyous and really happy. And it relieves a lot of hip pain." Excited, she claps her hands together, adding, "But it keeps me mellow all day. I don't crash. I don't feel tired. It doesn't knock me out."

Developing an understanding of the different strains, how to grow them, and how they may help people is a job in itself. It's another reason James echoes Chris Bartkowicz when she says she gets frustrated by the number of people who assume that you simply "open your doors and a million people come in and then two days later, you're a millionaire. That's just not the case."

In fact, the dispensary business uses basic business practices like any other, James explains, and an understanding of accounting and marketing are critical. There are also employee issues. In fact, there are all of the same things and issues that she confronts in her restaurant business—and then some. "It's ridiculously harder than it looks, because law enforcement doesn't always know what they're doing so we're always on edge about what's going to happen."

Between the potential busts on one side and the taxes on the other, James's bottom line will remain hard to predict for a while. "Every couple of months, the city, the state, or *somebody* comes up with some large fee that we need to pay to stay in business."

Indeed, as state and local officials try to contain this dispensary explosion in Colorado, they're also trying to ensure they get a cut of profits. The state has imposed a 2.9 percent sales tax on all medical-marijuana-related purchases, enabling it to collect $631,000 in revenue from 199 dispensaries in less than a year (from July 2009 to February 2010). Meanwhile, according to Treasury records, an additional 201 shops that applied for a sales tax license haven't paid anything yet. In Denver itself, where the number of dispensaries is the greatest, there's $5,000 in licensing and registration fees charged to every pot shop operator. With 279 owners paying that fee, the city stands to collect nearly $1.4 million. Between 2000 and 2008, the state issued about two thousand medical marijuana cards to patients. That number is expected to reach one hundred thousand. Considering the state charges a $90 fee for a registration card, Colorado could collect an estimated $9 million from patients. It's a lot of money, and it's also essentially found money for a community that is trying, like the rest of the nation, to weather a severe downturn in the economy.

3

PURPLE KUSH

Lessons from a Successful Business

The cappuccino machine buzzes in the background, and the baristas greet me with a warm smile from behind a large glass case filled with pastries—but, let me warn you, this is no Starbucks. This is Blue Sky, one of California's many medicinal pot clinics.

Weed is the third most popular drug in America, after alcohol and tobacco. By some estimates, the U.S. marijuana market is worth as much as $100 billion a year, although conservative studies argue it might be less. (Because it's an illegal substance, the size of the market is difficult to determine.) What is known is that one hundred million Americans admit to government survey takers that they've used pot, with nearly fifteen million acknowledging use in the past month. Translation: the number of pot users in the United States is extremely higher than the number of Americans who will buy a car. (According to the U.S. Department of Transportation, 7.67 million passenger vehicles were purchased in the United States in 2006.) So, yes, it's a big market. A major part of this market stems from the quasi-legal, or at least locally sanctioned, medicinal pot clinics sprouting up across the country. The dispensaries in California and Colorado, where marijuana is legal for medicinal purposes, generate the bulk of their pot supply via their own grows. This is, in part, due to economics; it's cheaper for dispensaries to grow their own marijuana rather than purchase it from a variety of suppliers. Meanwhile, because many dispensaries simply don't trust the quality of the marijuana for sale on the open market, they are reluctant to buy directly from growers.

In Colorado, dispensaries grow their own weed not only for market-driven reasons but also because of legal requirements. The state mandates that dispensary owners grow 70 percent of their product in an effort to better control the supply chain. The remaining 30 percent is often purchased from growers whom a dispensary owner trusts.

In California, where there are no requirements for dispensaries to grow their own product, retail pot shops often purchase excess product from a steady supply of vendors with whom they maintain relationships. In most cases, they may be well acquainted with anywhere from six to twelve growers, depending on the size of the operation. Generally, these vendors operate small grows, not even big enough to be thought of as farms, and they work for the same dispensaries on a regular basis. Interestingly, these growers rarely sell their *best* product to retail outlets, in part because medical clinics rarely pay the best price. Most often, individual growers prefer to work through a broker who connects them to a buyer, because that buyer tends to pay a higher premium.

As for illegal weed trafficked into the country via Mexico, or so-called stinkweed grown on U.S. parklands, it's highly unlikely that this marijuana ever shows up at a reputable dispensary. Like any other small business owner, dispensary owners make an effort to serve their clientele to the best of their ability while also turning a profit. Much of the dispensaries' business depends on repeat customers. Thus, it's not in their interest to give their customers poor-quality marijuana. While this kind of product may wind up on street corners and may often be funneled through murky supply chains to end users, it's rarely for sale in state-sanctioned dispensaries, which cater to a group of buyers who are, for the most part, trying to do things the "right" way—complete with a doctor's note for marijuana as a medical treatment.

Although it's a clandestine operation, the marijuana market is a competitive one like any other. The bottom line is: you get what you pay for. Of course, since this business is illegal and growers are taking on major risks to cultivate marijuana, you're going to pay way more than what the product would be worth in a federally legal environment.

Richard Lee, a self-made, full-fledged marijuana entrepreneur, has mastered the art of knowing what his customers want. Better than anyone else I've met, Lee has managed to maximize the profitability from this industry and seems to have developed a set of rules that have served him remarkably well.

In California, where medicinal clinics got their start, retail pot outlets have morphed into a multi-million-dollar industry—and are still growing. With a four-year head start on Colorado, California is also in the middle of a major boom as a result of U.S. Attorney General Eric Holder's declaration that the DEA will no longer raid medicinal clinics. Applications for retail medicinal outlets are surging in the Golden State; in Los Angeles alone, estimates suggest nearly 1,000 clinics are operating, up from about 180 just a few years ago. "Certainly, after Holder made the announcement, there was huge growth in 2010," Dale Gieringer, president of California's National Organization for the Reform of Marijuana Laws (NORML), tells me. The spike in marijuana dispensaries has even angered some established medicinal businesses, since more outlets mean more competition. At the same time, the community is frustrated because the clinics, they argue, attract unsavory characters. Meanwhile, some Americans who dominate Northern California's supply chains tell me they don't want to do business with the Los Angeles dispensaries because there are too many Russians and Armenians working their way into the trade and "they don't play by the same rules." Thus, for a host of reasons, the increased popularity of clinics has become such an issue that the Los Angeles mayor is trying to close down new shops. The city hopes to eventually limit the number of dispensaries to seventy, although it plans to "grandfather" in over a hundred preexisting cooperatives. It's an ambitious directive because, to a certain extent, Pandora's box has already been opened in L.A. and limiting participants now is extremely challenging.

Competition aside—does the retail outlet business model for pot in California work? Lee, an Oakland marijuana entrepreneur on the front lines of the legalization battle, tells me, without a doubt, "Yes." His success so far seems to stem from five things he's focused on, and throughout this chapter and the next, I'll highlight his lessons.

I met Lee while working on my documentary for CNBC in the summer of 2008. He doesn't look like the kind of guy who runs a multi-million-dollar marijuana empire, nor does he look like a political activist for pot. But he's both. Very thin, pale, with large, rather eighties-style silver-framed glasses, Lee is forty-five years old but could pass for ten years younger. His thin, brown hair is stick straight and hangs just above his eyes.

For twenty years, Lee has been in a wheelchair due to a spinal cord injury—and for twenty years he has smoked pot every day to alleviate his pain. Although he needs the drug for his condition, Lee believes everyone should have access to marijuana whether for pain or recreation. His first business was called the Hemp Store, in Houston, Texas. "Back then, in the early nineties, we were about promoting hemp," he explains. "Now you can find it in health food stores everywhere. You know, even Whole Foods has hemp soymilk! There's lots of hemp clothes, hemp soaps, shampoos. None of that existed back in the early nineties. So our mission was to promote the hemp and get it grown in other countries, then import here."

By the mid-nineties, Lee was ready for a bigger challenge. When California introduced its medicinal clinic law, Lee packed his bags and headed west. The area he came to in Oakland is now known as Oaksterdam—a deliberate play on Amsterdam. It's one of Oakland's tonier sections of town, home to a pricey grocery superstore, two new specialty grocery stores, *and* Lee's marijuana businesses.

"I heard about Dennis Peron and the San Francisco Cannabis Buyers Club," he tells me, referencing an early pioneer in the legalization battle. "They were operating in San Francisco in the early nineties. He's the guy who was working to get 215—" Lee stops, perhaps remembering that I'm not as familiar with the lingo as he is. "Proposition 215 passed," he repeats, with emphasis, referencing the ballot proposition that started it all.

Proposition 215—also known as the Compassionate Use Act of 1996—was a statewide voter initiative, a ballot proposition from California voters permitting the medical use of marijuana. It passed with 55.6 percent of the votes in favor and 44.4 percent against. As a result of Prop 215, patients with a valid, written doctor's "recommendation" (it is purposefully not called a "prescription" so as to sidestep conflict with federal law) can possess and grow marijuana for personal use. The original proposition has since been expanded to enable a system of cooperative distribution and is the source of much angst for antimarijuana activists as well as those who believe federal law trumps that of state law. Lee came to Northern California to be on the front lines of the movement, and he had it right. Northern California gave birth to a medicinal marijuana movement that even critics admit may prove unstoppable as it sweeps the country, picking up states one by one. His activism even extends to scolding me for my choice of words.

"You keep calling it marijuana," he says, the disdain evident in the tone of his voice.

"Well, what do *you* call it?" I ask, eyebrows raised. (After all, I thought I was being polite by not calling it pot.)

"Cannabis," he says, with emphasis. "It's the Latin term. That's the scientific name. To me it's like alcohol and booze. You know, firewater, jungle juice? You wouldn't be taken seriously if you were doing a report about Budweiser and you kept calling it, you know, firewater."

Lee and I reach a truce on the terminology, at least for the length of the interview. It's hard to imagine the public has a negative connotation for one term and a positive one for another, so, as the reader will notice, I use them all interchangeably in this book. If cannabis becomes legal across the United States, it won't be because activists stopped calling it marijuana.

Lee took me on a tour of his operations, including the Bulldog, his older café/dispensary. Like Wanda James, he thinks keeping a low profile is an advantage, making customers and neighbors more comfortable.

"It's very rough," he continues, somewhat apologetically, referring to the decor. "I was looking at maybe buying the building, and then we could remodel and everything. But right now, it's, uh, it's nothing compared to the Blue Sky, the new place. We spent a lot of money on the decorations there," he says, referring to his newest venture just down the street.

"It's nice. It's really nice!" I assure him. It is. "If I walked in here I'd have *no* idea there was actually anything other than coffee available."

He nods his head. "We had people who were going and getting their cannabis from nearby places, and then they'd come here and get coffee, and they didn't even know we had the dispensary in the back!"

But that's the way Lee wants it. Unlike the majority of medicinal clinics, which display pot as easily as coffee shops display pastries, Lee modeled his café on the marijuana coffee shops of the Netherlands. "It's what I've taken from the Amsterdam business model," he explains, referencing the famously tolerant city. "They'll have a coffee bar in the front, and they'll have a bud bar in the back. The coffee and drinks go together well with cannabis. People get the munchies and so they need a snack or a drink to go with it. It's kinda like a pool table in a bar, they just kind of go well together."

I take a deep breath but notice that all I smell is, well, *coffee*. That's because the Bulldog has special ventilator in the back room designed to keep the smell of marijuana from permeating the rest of the café. That ventilator helps preserve the Bulldog's image as a café rather than a marijuana dispensary.

Keeping a low profile, I soon realize, is Lee's lesson number one. Although it seems counterintuitive for any business to operate under the radar, the reality is Lee doesn't need the whole world knowing what he's up to, just the people who need his service. They have ways to find him.

"Okay, but Richard, you need customers," I insist, still a little caught off guard by the fact that no one (myself included) would know there was marijuana for sale at this establishment. "How would anyone even know that they could get cannabis here?"

"There are a lot of new cannabis publications," he says as he edges toward the counter and picks up a thin magazine with a giant marijuana leaf on its cover. "You see, *this*," he opens to the back of the magazine, "has a list in the back. Right here," he points, "you can see pages and pages of listings. Here are the Oakland Clubs, San Francisco, and then you start going to L.A.—that's where you've got hundreds and hundreds of clubs. So that's one resource." Consider it the yellow pages for marijuana dispensaries in California.

A marijuana magazine? Later in the book, we'll take a look at some of the start-up businesses connected to pot, many of which may end up being more profitable than growing or selling. It's important to consider it now, though, only to put the numbers I've been throwing out about the industry in context. Remember, they don't include the profits generated from magazines, real estate agents, garden supplies, or, as we'll see, how-to classes.

Lee looks at his watch. It's Friday and just after lunchtime. The Bulldog is packed. "People are getting their weekend supply," Lee tells me. "Come on. If we go in the back, I'll show you the bud bar." We push our way through a small crowd, inching our way toward the action.

Pulling back a thick velvet curtain, Lee reveals a tiny room, not more than about 250 square feet. Stepping into the room, I realize that now I can smell the pot. A cloud of smoke envelops us. It's dark, and a small group is seated in a corner, smoking. Behind a wood bar, on the left side of the room, is a young man, about twenty-five, with a winning smile. Lee introduces us. "Hi, Trish, I'm the budtender," the kid tells me. Of course, the *bud*tender. This is the half-pharmacist, half-bartender salesperson who helps patients choose their pot.

I want to see the menu, so the budtender pulls out a thick, black binder. In it are dozens of clear folder pages, and each page contains about four sealed pockets, each filled with marijuana. He points a small flashlight at the envelopes so I can read the white, handwritten labels that distinguish one product from another. Each is marked with a price. Some pockets are significantly more expensive than others—and it's like any other market.

"Different prices for different quality. It's like there are lower grades and premium brands of alcohol," Lee tells me.

Lee charges patients, on average, about $150 an ounce—a markup (from what he pays) of 25 percent. After expenses and overhead, Lee claims his profits are closer to 10 percent—or $15 for every ounce sold. Lee proudly points out that his prices are 10 to 20 percent lower than his competitors', meaning less profit on the margin. Still, what he lacks in price he makes up for in volume. Lee owns one of the busiest dispensaries in the neighborhood, thereby making him one of the highest grossing.

As I question Lee about the business, he explains how marijuana is trafficked among growers, dispensaries, and end users. Although he supplies some of his cafés' marijuana through his own grow house, much of his pot comes from a chain of growers in Northern California, including the big producing regions such as Humboldt and Mendocino counties.

Each week Lee restocks his cafés with a fresh supply—but he refuses to tell me by how much. "That's kinda getting into a little sensitive area, as far as trying to put numbers on that."

"Why?" I ask innocently.

"I'm not sure I feel comfortable with that." He looks me directly in the eye.

"Why?" I repeat. I don't realize, at this point, how important keeping a low profile is. It's not what you do that gets you into trouble, it seems, it's how much everyone knows about it.

"It just—kind of goes into the area of taunting the DEA. We're about promoting the business model and stuff, but I don't think we need to get into exact numbers."

"Why does talking about how much marijuana you're serving taunt the DEA? I mean, hey, you've got a café right here." I keep pushing.

Lee sighs. "For one thing, it's a confession. They can use this in court against us."

"But," I continue, "haven't you already confessed by telling me that you serve marijuana?"

Lee smiles. "It doesn't mean I need to do it again."

Here's what he would admit: he works with roughly a dozen marijuana brokers and growers. They present their product to him weekly, and his relationship with them, he tells me, is critical. In the restaurant industry, a relationship with suppliers (like wine or meat providers) is essential. It's the same in the marijuana dispensary business. A clinic owner needs to know that he or she can trust the producer (or vendor) of the product. Because marijuana is illegal, relationships with suppliers are even more critical. A trusted supplier will make sure a marijuana clinic owner receives good pot (determined in part by the taste and the high the marijuana produces), uncontaminated pot (remember, a lot of marijuana grows in the wild and can fall victim to bug infestations or *E. coli*), and receives it all at a fair price.

"Do you pay a pretty fair price?" I ask.

"We try," he tells me. "But we're also trying to get the price down. There's a conflict there. On the one hand, the growers are at great risk. Right? They risk being locked in jail for a long time. So it's hard to put a price on that. But on the other hand, we're trying to get the price down for the customers."

One way to get the price down would be through full-on legalization. As long as marijuana is illegal on the federal level, pot brokers and producers are susceptible to arrest. As a result, prices are higher than what they should be. Consider the markup: it costs about $400 to grow a pound of marijuana, yet that same pound costs $2,400 at the Bulldog dispensary and up to $6,000 on the street. The bottom line: consumers must pay a price for the risk growers take.

Shifting my attention back to the budtender, I glance down at the two nearly identical-looking packets of marijuana in his hands. "So, what exactly is the difference between this and this?" I ask, pointing to each bag.

"They're completely different," the budtender tells me, as though stating the obvious.

Lee interjects, trying to help. "Think of it like red and white wine."

"Oh, *that* different?" I ask, somewhat incredulous.

"Here, tell for yourself," the budtender says as he pulls one of the marijuana bags out, opens it, and then lifts it toward me. I lean in and take a deep breath.

"Now this one," he says, holding a different bag toward my nose. This one has a much sweeter smell.

The first one, Purple Kush, is popular thanks to its grapey taste. Its pain-relieving effects are said to be immediate, and it's good for anxiety and depression.

This is lesson number two: offer your customers variety. Some are connoisseurs, some are picky, some are price sensitive, and some may just get bored from time to time. Selling cannabis isn't like selling aspirin tablets; it's not an interchangeable commodity like it is where pot is still totally illegal. Consumers will become regular customers only if they like the options, the prices, and the service better than anywhere else.

For those in the know the following information will come as no surprise—but the reality is, each strain of marijuana has a different taste and a different high. For example, marijuana with higher THC counts, provides bigger highs and is priced accordingly. The DEA's Javier Pena, who was a special agent in charge of the Northern California region from 2004 to 2008 (when I met him, he had recently been reassigned to the Caribbean), told me the marijuana being created today is extraordinary. "The potency," he tells me in his light Spanish accent, "is something. We're not seeing that kind of marijuana from the eighties, you know that stinkweed as they used to call it. This is high-potency marijuana. The good stuff." He says today's product has THC counts of 18 to 20 percent, meaning, "It's a lot of high. It's very strong."

Whether that's true or there has always been high-potency pot available, the semilegal cannabis market means you're a lot more likely to find the good stuff if you're willing to look for it—and pay for it. For example, on marijuanastrains.com, a Web site that sells seeds to prospective farmers, the types of pot available (and the highs they create) are described in great detail. The site touts White Widow marijuana as "the strongest weed in the world. White Widow marijuana buds have so much THC on them that it is hard to see the bud at all. The White Widow marijuana high is extreme and the taste divine. The buzz is powerful and energetic, yet social. White Widow marijuana seeds have won more Cannabis Cups than any before."

The Cannabis Cup is an award presented at the annual Netherlands festival, started in 1987 by *High Times* editor Steven Hager. Thousands gather to pick the best strain of marijuana—the so-called Cannabis Cup winner. As you can imagine, it's a huge deal in the pot community, and the winning strain gets a big bump in value.

Lee likes to compare the marijuana business to the wine business, telling me there are "different flavors and tastes. People don't want the same thing day in, day out. It's not just like any old can of Budweiser." Hell, no. Especially when strains have names like Purple Kush and White Widow. "It's more like the wine industry," he says, "where there are specialty small vineyards."

Lee's Purple Kush is one of these specialty lines. Smelling the leaves again, I note that the Purple Kush is, in fact, fuller. And I've always been more of a Cabernet fan than a Riesling wine drinker.

"So, what else have you got? What if I don't want to smoke?" I ask the budtender.

He ducks down, reaching below the bar, then pops back up, a basket in his hands. "We've got everything," he declares. "Marijuana cookies, cakes, brownies, olive oil, lemonade, salad dressing, lozenges—"

I interrupt him, laughing: "It's like a pot supermarket!"

I survey the stash (the peanut butter cookies look pretty good) before thanking the budtender. We make our way out of the café, pushing ourselves through the small crowd. Lee wants to show me his newest shop, Blue Sky, just around the corner from the Bulldog. Blue Sky is a little shinier than its predecessor. It has outdoor seating (think Parisian café meets a pot bar) and is humming with activity. As we walk in, I spot a child about seven years old sitting alone by the window, sipping a can of soda from a straw. I'm a little disturbed by the sight.

"You allow kids in here?" I ask Lee.

"Yes, but only in front," he tells me. "They can wait there while their parents smoke or buy in the back." To Lee, this is the advantage of his Amsterdam model because it allows children to be shielded from the marijuana while their parents can still secure their supply of the drug.

Scanning the room I note the diversity of Lee's customer base: There's the father of the seven-year-old boy, some artist-musician types, several businessmen in navy blue suits, and a couple of the preppy, country club set. One woman, about fifty, attractive with blond hair and blue eyes, is dressed more like she's about to go play tennis than buy pot. She tells me she stops by Blue Sky every week for marijuana to help alleviate the arthritis in her hands. Another man, clean-cut, dressed in a blue, pin-striped suit and dark red tie, tells me he works in finance and is making a quick stop at the café before heading back to work.

I do have to point something out about the clientele, though. As readers have probably guessed, I am in favor of people who need marijuana as a medicine getting it as easily as they can. Nonetheless, as a pure, unbiased observer, I notice that the people frequenting this café on a Friday afternoon are probably the healthiest sick people I've ever seen. A DEA agent told me later that he always noticed the same thing. Still, realistically, who am I to judge? Some of them really don't look that much different from the people I see in line at the local pharmacy.

Meanwhile, although the café goers know I'm a journalist, they're happy to talk. There's no embarrassment—rather, they seem anxious to promote their pro-pot message.

I ask Lee if he has ever considered combining his cafés— making them into one larger location to control costs. He tells me no, that he likes the smaller, more intimate feel of his individual cafés. "That's part of the Amsterdam model," he explains. "A bunch of small places instead of one big, you know, Walmart, mega operation."

But it's not just atmosphere (or his anti-big-business agenda) that motivates Lee's belief in small medicinal businesses. Rather, Lee is a realist. Smaller is better because then "the government can't come in, the DEA can't come in and just close everything by closing down one place." Point taken.

4

CANNABUSINESS
Those Who Can, Teach

Fifteen million dollars in annual sales? Not bad for a business that hasn't even been open two years. That's the number that Harborside, the largest marijuana clinic in Oakland, California, reported for its yearly sales in 2008. Harborside may be the big time, but its smaller counterparts aren't doing so badly. It's estimated that each California dispensary brings in between $3 to $4 million in annual sales revenue. Although Richard Lee refuses to tell me how much marijuana he sells each week ("It's a matter of having a little respect for your opposition," he says, referring to the DEA), he does admit that he pays $300,000 in state and local income tax and *double* that in federal income tax. He also pays payroll taxes, workers' compensation insurance, and unemployment insurance.

"How do you pay federal income tax when you're selling marijuana?" I want to know.

"Actually, the federal income tax law says that you have to pay taxes on your income, no matter what your income is from. So they don't really care whether it's from cannabis." (Of course, Lee doesn't mention cannabis on his tax return; instead, when it comes to official documentation, he runs a coffee shop.)

Oakland is an example of a community that has imposed its own system of taxation—dispensary owners must pay the city $30,000 a year for a license to operate. On top of that, they pay the city $18 in tax for each $1,000 in sales. But Lee and his competitors are not the only marijuana retailers contributing to government coffers—California currently collects about $18 million in sales tax from medicinal marijuana dispensaries throughout the state, and nationwide the revenue generated from dispensaries is even larger. It's one reason some California lawmakers are taking the pot debate a step further—endorsing a regulated, government-approved marijuana trade that would enable residents to buy marijuana much like they buy cigarettes.

It was a spring day in May 2009, at a fire-safety event in Davis, California, that Governor Arnold Schwarzenegger made head-lines by calling for a large-scale study to show the possible effect of legalized, recreational marijuana. Although he says he's person-ally opposed to legalization (and he was very outspoken against Proposition 19, which aimed to legalize marijuana for recreational purposes in the Golden State), Schwarzenegger did admit to reporters that it was time for a debate. "I think all of those ideas of creating extra revenues—I'm always for an open debate on it. And I think we ought to study very carefully what other countries are doing that have legalized marijuana and other drugs. What effect did it have on those countries?"[1]

While critics suggest the governor's comments show his des-peration over the state's $20 billion deficit, marijuana advocates consider Schwarzenegger's invitation for debate a significant development in their crusade. Ethan Nadelmann, executive direc-tor of the Drug Policy Alliance, told the *New York Times*, "What stands out about Governor Schwarzenegger's comment is not that he thought it, but that he said it. There has been enormous fear at the political level about saying out loud and on the record that we should think about this."[2]

One reason the governor is willing to consider the issue is that California voters (like the nation) show an increasing willingness to support legalization. According to a field poll taken in April 2009, just weeks before the governor's comments, 56 percent of the state's registered voters said they support the legalizing and taxing of marijuana for recreational use to fill some of their state's budget deficit.

California's division of the National Organization for the Reform of Marijuana Laws (NORML) predicts that a legally regulated market for marijuana would be significant to the state's bottom line. A legalized marijuana market in California is estimated to be worth $14 billion, and NORML predicts legalization could yield the state at least $1.2 billion in annual tax revenues and reduced enforcement costs—at a time when California is in dire need of cash. Here's the math: an excise tax on pot of $50 per ounce, or about $1 per joint, translates to $770 to $900 million per year, plus another $240 to $360 million in sales taxes. Moreover, an estimated $200 million in enforcement costs (arrests, prosecutions, and prison) for marijuana offenders would be saved. Additional benefits would include increased employment and spin-off industries, including coffeehouses, tourism, and industrial hemp. The total economic effect, according to NORML, would be $12 billion to $18 billion. In simpler terms: If the marijuana industry were just one-third the size of the wine industry, it would generate fifty thousand jobs and $1.4 billion in wages, along with additional income and business tax revenues for the state. In other words, there is real money at stake.

Richard Lee sums up NORML's study on marijuana profitability and what he calls "business politics" and agrees with what NORML considers an economic reality. "The hundreds of cannabis outlets are already paying millions in sales tax in California," he tells me, "and it can be so much more. My goal," he says, "is to have the business push the politics. Show everyone a working model."

Part of that model includes a university. Well, more like a storefront, devoted entirely to the cultivation, processing, and distribution of pot. Lee is the president and founder of Oaksterdam University, the first formal school for marijuana in the United States. He told me he got the idea a couple of years ago after returning from a trip to Amsterdam, home to the thirty-year-old Cannabis College.

Which brings us to Lee's lesson number three: diversify. It's difficult to make money running a business in a highly competitive market. It's much easier to make money serving all of those businesses in a highly competitive market. A magazine is one direction an entrepreneur could go, and a school to teach people how to start growing is another.

In a $250 weekend seminar, students can learn to grow, trim, harvest, and sell marijuana. In addition to an introductory course in horticulture and "bud tending" (the art of picking the best cannabis buds), Oaksterdam University offers courses titled Retail Management, Starting a Business, and Packaging and Distribution. Students can even elect to take a full, traditional semester program with thirty-two hours of class work. They all receive an overview of the political, economic, and legal issues surrounding pot, and if they attend all of the classes and complete all of the course work, they "graduate" with a diploma complete with a cannabis leaf seal.

"But, what you're doing is illegal. You're violating federal law," I tell Lee. I think back to my father telling me stories about his days as a young lawyer in the JAG (Judge Advocate General) program in Vietnam. He would regularly deal with soldiers who had been arrested for smoking pot, and he'd tell them, "If the government outlawed peanut butter sandwiches, you couldn't eat peanut butter sandwiches. It's that simple. The law's the law." But for Lee, and the millions of other pot smokers in America, it's not that simple. "We're teaching them [the students] how to change the laws," Lee explains, "how to be involved in the politics and to pay taxes and obey regulations."

Indeed, the curriculum at Oaksterdam University includes all you need to know about growing and selling pot. An excerpt from the university's course book includes classes like Horticulture 101:

Learn how to grow cannabis from start through harvest. This course covers everything needed to get going and produce a harvest. Instructors will detail the basics of watering, lighting, ventilation, cycles, and equipment options. Even experienced folks can learn from this presentation about cuttings, pest control, smell abatement, security, pH balance, and drying/curing.

Lee says that an aspiring grower can just put a few seeds in the ground and hope for the best or that grower can get serious and "do it right." Would you have ever guessed there's so much that goes into achieving a good yield?

For those with culinary aspirations, there's even a cooking class called Methods of Ingestion: Cooking 8501. Here's the course description:

Hundreds of alternatives to smoking cannabis are now available, including: confections, cheesecakes, salad dressings, beverages, and more. Learn how to cook with whole plant medicine and extracts, regulate and titrate dosages, proper packaging, food safety, and how to make cannabutter step-by-step. Learn from long-time cannabis cooks and professional chefs.

While some of those classes may sound entertaining, one of them could turn into an entire degree as this industry becomes more complex and spreads across the country. The practicalities of running a business are addressed in Cannabusiness 7401: Legal Business Structures:

For learning about many opportunities in the cannabis industry; whether it's a commercial grow, dispensary, cannabis edibles company, clone provider, delivery service, Measure Z club, or any of the numerous cannabusinesses still to develop in this industry. The process to obtain city, county, state permits and licenses are covered in detail. Legal Business Structures, and standard business issues such as payroll, sales tax, workman's compensation, health insurance, and other requirements for operating a business are covered. The instructors share firsthand experience and knowledge. Current political issues and local politics are explained, including reference to the Attorney General Guidelines.

Perhaps most important, Know Your Rights, a workshop that helps students navigate the gray areas of marijuana law, offers this course description:

Unlock justice and secure your freedom during police encounters! This class includes skits that simulate encounters with law enforcement. Students will see the knowledge learned in Legal 101 & Civics 101 applied in action. Experienced instructors teach examples of common encounters and teach you specific wording. Most people give up their constitutional rights during encounters with law enforcement. These mistakes are avoidable and costly! For everyone in the cannabis industry, this class is essential to know your legal rights and explore the "gray areas" in order to do risk analysis and make informed decisions. This class is a must for anyone in the cannabis industry.

Oaksterdam University first opened its doors in November 2007 with twenty-two students. These days, it's standing room only, as more and more want-to-be growers gravitate to the business.

When my documentary team visits the Oaksterdam classroom, it is packed with nearly fifty students ranging in age from their early twenties to early sixties. Instructor Joey Ereneta paces back and forth the front of the classroom as he explains the intricacies of how to grow the best plants. It's clear this is more art than science.

"These are commercial cannabis trimmers." Ereneta holds a pair of agricultural scissors up to a packed classroom. "When you get cannabis out in the garden, it grows. It'll look like this with the leaves on it," he says, showing them a leafy, overgrown plant. "And you want it to look more like this, without all those larger fan leaves, or sun leaves on it." He points to another freshly trimmed marijuana plant. The students crane their necks to view the finished product.

Fifty-four-year-old Mona Clausnitzer is also a student at Oaksterdam University, but Clausnitzer is looking for a little more than a backyard garden as a result of her course work. She says she hopes to grow enough marijuana to sell to a dispensary. For thirty-five years, she has worked as a dental assistant, and although she doesn't intend to give up her day job, she does hope to make enough money growing marijuana to create some retirement income. "I have no retirement. I'm going to have to work 'til I'm seventy. And you get burned out. Maybe my hands won't be so good, dental assisting, so I'll need to do something. I'm hoping that it [growing pot] will ultimately supplement my retirement. At the same time, I can help others who need it."

Laurie Strand is another of these students. She's also a mother to three young boys, ages five, seven, and nine. "My husband is a contractor, we have a dog, a Dalmatian, I mean, we're just very normal." Strand spends most of her days working as a real estate agent and carting her young boys to school and swim practice. ("My husband's with them at the swim meet right now because I'm here at class," she tells our documentary team.) She speaks on camera in part, she tells us, because, "I want to put a normal face on this. I'm not a hippie addict. I'm a person who lives in an affluent area. And there are a lot of cannabis users in the affluent area where I'm from." Her reason for enrolling at Oaksterdam University? She hopes to grow some marijuana in her vegetable garden. You could call her the living, breathing version of Mary-Louise Parker's character on the hit Showtime series *Weeds*. Indeed, when you spend a little time around Northern California, you quickly realize that the *Weeds* series, about a widowed suburban mom who begins selling marijuana to her neighbors to help support her upper-middle-class lifestyle, isn't entirely that far-fetched.

The desire to grow pot and help others by providing them access to medical marijuana is a common theme among students at Oaksterdam U. Yet, while helping others is quite noble, growing aspirations are not entirely fueled by altruism. Most are looking for a potential income stream. There is a huge economic incentive to growing pot. (Just revisit the numbers. It costs $400 to grow a pound. That pound retails for upward of $2,000. There are few businesses as lucrative as this one.)

Lee knows that. He tells me he plans to create a nonprofit entity so that he can pour his money into his cause. But, as of now, he's simply pouring his profits back into his empire. Across the street from the university is Lee's Oaksterdam gift shop, where he sells everything from Oaksterdam University T-shirts to bongs, vaporizers, commercial growing equipment, hemp clothing, and pretty much anything else you can think of related to pot.

"This is hash-making equipment," Lee shows me. "It works basically like a little mini washing machine. And over here," he spins his wheelchair across the room, "you have vaporizers. Let me show you the Volcano." The enthusiasm is all over his face, and his voice gets a little louder. "This is the latest five-hundred-dollar model." Vaporizers are becoming increasingly popular among marijuana users as they seek new ways to absorb the drug, and its effects, without smoking. A vaporizer like the Volcano heats the marijuana to a temperature that is hot enough to vaporize the cannabinoids (the sixty or so compounds that are unique to marijuana, some of which are believed to have therapeutic effects) but not hot enough to trigger combustion. The vapors are captured in a balloon and inhaled, thereby providing a user with, Lee says, "the good effects but not the bad effects." Indeed, vaporizing is becoming increasingly popular. It's so in vogue that some dispensaries like the Green Oasis in Los Angeles, which opened in May 2009, now offer on-site vaporizing lounges. A vaporizing lounge offers prospective customers the ability to get high without needing to smoke and while diffusing the costs. "It has an advantage over eating [pot]," Lee explains. "You might think eating it is best 'cause there's no smoke. But it takes a lot longer to take effect so it's harder to control the amount you take." The benefit to smoking is that a user feels the effects almost immediately.

"So, you're gonna say, okay, I've had enough?" I ask.

He nods, "You'll stop. But with the brownies, you eat one, you wait half an hour, nothing happens. So you eat another one. And then, about an hour later, the first one kicks in, then the second one, and by then, you've had too much." That's in part because it's difficult to orally inject THC, whether it be from pot-laced brownies or a synthetic pill version.

In 1986, the Food and Drug Administration (FDA) approved a synthetic version of THC. The hope was that by isolating the key ingredient in pill form and simplifying the way a patient absorbs that drug (orally as opposed to individuals smoking the ground-up leaves of a highly variable plant), Americans would have access to the benefits of pot without ever needing to light up. After rigorous testing, the FDA found THC to be safe and effective for the treatment of wasting diseases, nausea, and vomiting. Marinol, a legal, Schedule II capsule drug, was created.

But there's one problem: as Lee already pointed out, THC cannot be absorbed as effectively when it is eaten as when it is inhaled. The American College of Physicians concluded this in a 2008 report, in which it wrote, "Oral THC is slow in onset of action but produces more pronounced, and often unfavorable, psychoactive effects that last much longer than those experienced with smoking."[3]

Back at the Bulldog, I flip through that marijuana magazine. I notice that along with dispensary listings (or "compassionate care clinics" as some medicinal enthusiasts prefer to call the shops), it contains a series of ads for doctors offering marijuana "recommendations." To purchase pot at any of Lee's dispensaries, or any other clinic in California, an individual must have proof that there is a medicinal need for the product. This proof comes in the form of a marijuana ID card, and to get the card, a doctor's note recommending marijuana is needed.

California doctors have the latitude to prescribe marijuana for pretty much anything. Although California law suggests doctors recommend marijuana for patients over the age of eighteen who are suffering from a specific set of diseases, the law also includes a provision allowing pot for "any other illness for which marijuana provides relief."[4] So the reality is, anyone who wants pot can get a "recommendation" for marijuana. Headaches, anxiety, trouble sleeping, you name it. Moreover, at a time when doctors are increasingly struggling with penny-pinching insurance companies and a poor economy, recommending marijuana has become a thriving business in and of itself, as the multitude of doctors' advertisements in the back of the pot magazines' "yellow pages" suggest. Doctors typically charge a $200 consultation fee, and I've never heard of anyone being denied a recommendation. There are currently an estimated four hundred thousand medicinal marijuana patients in the state.[5]

In the back of Lee's marijuana gift shop is a business that one of his friends, Jeff Jones, started: the Patient ID Card Center.

This is lesson number four: Lee knows he must create an easy and reassuring environment for the customer. The industry is new enough that most potential customers don't really know anything about it. So Lee is making efforts to simplify the process and make everyone feel at home.

The IDs Lee and Jones create in the card center are part of SB240, sometimes called the Medicinal Marijuana Program Act. SB240 helped clarify Prop 215 (though some would argue it's created more legal complexities by allowing counties to be as liberal as they want in allowing medicinal usage). SB240 called on counties to create a voluntary state ID card system. Lee says it's akin to the Department of Motor Vehicles. Medical marijuana patients can bring their doctor's recommendation here, the ID Center verifies the doctor's legitimacy, and then for $35, issues the patient a card with a twenty-four-hour hotline number on the back. This way, if a patient is stopped by the police, the authorities can call at any time to verify that the recommendation is legit and that a user is indeed a medicinal marijuana patient.

If all you have is a recommendation, then the police "can't call a doctor up at three in the morning and wake him up." But they can call the Patient ID Card Center. The other advantage to the card is that it's a practical, sturdy, laminated, small card that fits well in any wallet. It's similar to a driver's license as opposed to a piece of paper that gets folded and refolded.

Lee introduces me to Chad, a young man who, like Lee, believes in the cause. Chad works at the Patient ID Card Center registering users and has been with the company for five years. He is also a medicinal user. "I believe that what we're doing is worth my time and effort, no matter what kind of money I'm making. I can at least support my rent . . . [but] I would work here for nothing, if I could."

I tell him the story of a woman I met recently in Humboldt County. In her twenties, she's still in school for her bachelor's degree and working part time as a hair stylist. The woman, very pretty, with dark hair to her shoulders, told me that when she first met her boyfriend (a marijuana grower), she was devastated, because she liked him so much—she just wasn't thrilled with his career choice. Eventually, she got over that—enough to move in with him. Because the rules in his county allow each individual with a recommendation to grow up to ninety-nine outdoor plants within one hundred square feet, he wanted her to get a medicinal recommendation so they could grow more plants on the property. I met her just after she returned from the doctor's office, waving the recommendation.

"So was it difficult?" I asked.

"Not at all," she told me, shaking her head and smiling. "He [the doctor] did ask me why I needed the recommendation and I told him I got headaches, which wasn't true, I just needed to say something. And that was that." A couple hundred dollars later, she had her recommendation, enabling her boyfriend to grow up to 198 plants within two hundred square feet.

"So here's someone who doesn't actually need marijuana for medicinal use," I tell Chad, referencing the young woman. "Do you see a lot of that at the ID Center?"

He admits that the system sees some abuse. "But in anything, people can abuse. People are people." Abuse, he insists, doesn't change his view that marijuana should be available to those who need it. One point made by medical marijuana advocates: how many doctors overprescribe Big Pharma's products?

The ID Center, combined with the clinics, gift shop, and school, goes a long way toward normalizing an industry once considered taboo. That normalization of the industry is something Lee has helped create and of which he is proud.

"You're going public with this, in a very big way," I tell him. "I mean, here you are, talking about your coffee shops that serve marijuana. Talking about your school that teaches people to grow marijuana." I push him. "Why are you doing this?"

"The politics," he responds. "We've been doing it for over twelve years now in Oakland. We're showing that it works."

"But, how is it that you can have these coffee shops, that you can have a school that's teaching people how to grow marijuana, right here on Main Street, and not get busted by the feds?"

Indeed, when I speak with Javier Pena from the DEA, the special agent who had been in charge of the area where Lee operates his businesses from 2004 to 2008, I ask him how it was that someone could operate as openly and brazenly as Lee—that there was even a pot university on Oakland's main drag.

"We are very familiar with that," Pena says curtly, a crisp, slightly agitated note creeping into his normally lilting voice. "I cannot talk about pending investigations. We are very familiar with Oaksterdam. We are very familiar with its founder. We know what he is doing. I can truthfully tell you that we are very familiar with that situation, and let me also mention that it is against the law."

But Lee says his ability to operate comes down to local support. He's certainly supported by local rules, pointing out that "the city council has issued permits for cannabis dispensaries and we have a permit signed by the mayor and the police chief."

"Yes, but still, if you're violating federal law, you're violating the federal law." I push back in an attempt to understand how Lee can be so blatant about his work.

And herein lies the answer: "We have strong juries here in the Bay Area that would refuse to convict," Lee admits.

Bull's-eye. I remember that a friend of mine who had worked as a district attorney in Manhattan once told me he dreaded getting a marijuana possession case because even though pot was still illegal in New York at the time, it was rare that a jury (or a judge for that matter) wanted to punish someone and put him or her away for years for what most people consider a harmless crime—and that was New York, this is California. *Oakland*, California. A bastion of (pot-smoking) liberals.

"So you don't think if the feds came and arrested you, that you'd be convicted?"

"Betting everything on it," Lee grins.

And here's the final takeaway from Lee: set up in a supportive location. You're going to run into a lot fewer problems if the locals have no problem with what you're up to and, even better, wouldn't convict you if they were put on a jury.

Lee hopes that his example will prove to others that marijuana can be mainstream. "People need to see a working model. For years, we've heard 'Well, they can't legalize it. It'll be mayhem.' You know, dogs sleeping with cats and craziness. But we've been doing it, and you can see there are no problems. If anything, we've improved the neighborhood and we're helping to revitalize this part of Oakland." It's a valid argument. Oaksterdam has seen its property values soar in the last decade, storefronts are being rebuilt, and the community's vibe is upscale urbane, not drug-infused slum.

"Look at Amsterdam," he insists, "where they've been selling pot for thirty years. They bring in hundreds of thousands of tourists, millions of dollars of tax revenue, and they create jobs. That's what we're trying to do here in Oaksterdam."

5

GREEN RUSH
The Towns with Backyard Billions

In Iowa, they grow corn. In Kansas, they grow wheat. In California's Emerald Triangle they grow—weed. Lots of it.

Mendocino County covers a sprawling 3,510 square miles of coastal mountains, redwood forests, and beaches. It became the poster child of the Northern California marijuana movement through its adoption of Measure G, which went further than California state law in determining how much pot could be grown in the state. Measure G was the first national piece of legislation to allow pot to be grown for recreational purposes. Yes, *recreational* purposes.

So far we've looked at Denver, with its nascent marijuana industry, and Oakland, which has embraced medical marijuana for a long time. But what happens to towns and cities when growing pot becomes not just semilegal, but astonishingly widespread? That's Mendocino in a nutshell, and the results are surprising.

Driving up a winding dirt road, I glance at the car's dashboard—103 degrees. It's the height of the California summer growing season, and the sun is blazing. It's desolate here. Not a home in sight, no cell phone service, not even an occasional telephone pole. Turning right onto an unmarked road, I spot my destination: a small, white ranch house, nestled in the middle of a vast vineyard. Its paint is peeling, and its window shades are drawn tight. The only sign of life emanates from a small red geranium in a clay pot, perched on the corner ledge of the front porch. My eyes wander from the geranium toward a twelve-foot high, weathered gray wooden fence attached to the right side of the house. I'm in the heart of Northern California's Emerald Triangle. Instinctively, I know exactly what's behind that fence.

Rolling hillsides, a rocky coastline, vineyards that stretch for miles— at first glance, the Emerald Triangle seems to be a picture postcard of the Far West. But beneath its tranquility lays a controversial, complex, and increasingly problematic commercial enterprise: the marijuana trade. Dan Offield, a twenty-year veteran of the DEA, tells it like it is, "This is ground zero for marijuana. Nobody produces any better marijuana than we do right here."

Pot is growing in homes, backyards, and on parklands. From housewives hoping to earn some under-the-table cash from their backyard gardens; to growers with large-scale indoor and outdoor operations; to Mexican drug cartels setting up grow areas; to members of the *real* economy who service the growers, including gardening shopkeepers, real estate agents, restaurant owners, and car dealers—an increasing number of people are raking in huge sums from an illegal pot boom that's sweeping the region.

Slamming the car door shut, I brave the short walk on a brick pathway toward the house and knock on the door. Within seconds a man in his late twenties greets me. "Hey Trish, I'm Eric. Come on in."

"No dogs?" I smile, eyebrows raised.

"Nah, not yet." He laughs somewhat nervously, ushering me into the house. Eric Sligh is not used to reporters, but he agreed to do the interview because he believes the marijuana industry should be "out in the open" and recognized for its contributions to the local economy. "But we *are* going to hire some dogs for protection during the harvest," Sligh assures me. The dogs are a major line of defense against thieves looking to steal marijuana from backyard gardens.

Inside the house, the air conditioner hums in the background, a welcome reprieve from the oppressive valley heat. Referring to the dogs again, Sligh warns, "You can't take any chances here." He's right. During harvest season, robberies are common.

I'm in the Emerald Triangle to interview Sligh for my CNBC documentary on marijuana. Six feet tall, with short, dirty-blond hair, a trimmed goatee, and hazel eyes, Sligh looks more like a grad school student than a one-time marijuana grower and broker. But, as I soon learn, no one here *seems* as though they're involved in the drug trade. A small-town newspaper man, a former police officer, a former politician, and the rest of the growers I meet tell me the same thing: they grow pot because it's the best way to make a living in this part of the country.

Sligh agrees. He used to work as a substitute teacher (before transitioning into the growing and brokering of pot), but now he devotes all of his time to an offshoot of the marijuana trade, as editor of *Grow* magazine. Dressed for gardening in a navy blue T-shirt, cargo shorts, and flip-flops, Sligh leads me through the house, past a small living room with a beige shag carpet, down two stairs, and into a sunroom. A large black-and-white television screen, divided into quadrants, is positioned in the corner of the room. "For security," Sligh offers, noting my interest. "There are outdoor cameras on every side of the house. You can monitor everything. You have to."

He swings open the sunroom door. The hot air blasts us as we step onto the blue slate patio, and there it is: a massive garden of pot plants. The biggest plants I have ever seen. I take a deep breath. The distinct, some might say sweet, smell of marijuana permeates the air. "Just wait until harvest time," Eric warns. "That's when you'll really smell it. Everywhere. The whole town reeks of pot during harvest."

Dozens of lush marijuana plants, or rather trees, since they're enormous—about eight feet tall—are scattered across the yard, rooted in giant black containers or planters. Leading me through the garden, Eric informs me that Mendocino County marijuana plants can actually grow up to twenty feet tall, depending on conditions. "These," he explains, his neck craned back as he squints his eyes for a better view of the plants, "can't get too much bigger than this, or they'll grow taller than the fence and attract attention. So part of the key is growing them big, but not too big."

That's the fine line growers here must walk—growing as much marijuana as they can without triggering a crackdown from law enforcement. They can do that because authorities are overwhelmed by the sheer number of growers and hampered by conflicting state, federal, and county laws governing marijuana in Northern California's Emerald Triangle.

Sligh says he couldn't imagine the region without marijuana. When I ask him what it would be like, he shrugs, admitting, "I don't know. I think we'd all be selling Amway. You know, I think we'd all be going door to door trying to sell each other trinkets and bracelets. I mean, what else are people doing up here? This is just normal. It's what we do."

The Emerald Triangle is considered ideal for growing marijuana, both in terms of its weather and its politics. Named for the green bud it produces, this region of Northern California is the spot where three marijuana-friendly counties—Humboldt, Mendocino, and Trinity—meet. While the possession or growing of marijuana is completely illegal under federal law, growing marijuana for medicinal use became legal under California state law in 1996, when voters passed a referendum known as Proposition 215. California residents are permitted to grow up to six mature plants or twelve immature plants. Meanwhile, for years, parts of the Emerald Triangle maintained county laws that were even more permissive. Beginning in 2000, Mendocino County residents were allowed to grow up to twenty-five pot plants for medicinal, even recreational, use. In 2008, the law was brought back in line with the rest of the state in part because residents feared too many large-scale producers, with major grows, were putting smaller "mom and pop" growers out of business while overtaking their community. Nonetheless, it is still considered legal to grow in the Emerald Triangle, and local police are instructed to make marijuana enforcement their last priority. With few up-front costs and a nearly zero percent chance of facing jail time as a pot producer (since juries in this neck of the woods are reluctant to convict marijuana growers, sellers, and users due to their tolerance for pot), weed enthusiasts are honing their horticultural skills for a chance to cash in on America's biggest cash crop, worth an estimated tens of billions of dollars. It's a new kind of Gold Rush— the Green Rush. A chance to strike it rich in America's biggest underground industry.

Pulling a plant toward us, Sligh points to its bud, which resembles a small pineapple. "You see these, what we call nodes, up here?" he shows me. "Those are gonna push out what's called a bud. These are going to create a larger bud that could weigh anywhere between three grams, five, ten grams." It's those buds that are later trimmed (a process known in the industry as "trimming bud"), harvested, dried, and chopped up into the marijuana that is sold on the street. The money is in the buds.

"So how much do you think this garden is worth?" I ask Sligh as we weave ourselves through the plants, pushing back branches from our faces as we walk.

He tries to dodge the question. "Well, we don't really like to talk numbers so much. You know, the media is always emphasizing how much money people make. But we consider it kind of distasteful to talk about. Part of growing is having an appreciation for creating the best kind of marijuana."

"Yeah, yeah. But I mean for my research purposes, I just want to understand what a typical pot garden could yield."

Sligh grins and gives in. He knows exactly how much the plants are worth. "Okay, well, you've got about twenty plants here," he says, his hazel eyes taking a quick survey of the garden. "A plant like this," he points to the leaves, "assuming that it's gonna yield about two pounds, it would be worth about five thousand dollars. With twenty plants, assuming all the marijuana is harvested, the garden could be worth a hundred thousand dollars."

What happens to a town where backyard gardens could be worth more than a regular day job or two? It may not be possible to become chemically addicted to using cannabis, but here's a whole area of the country absolutely addicted to growing it. If the Emerald Triangle ever tried to quit cold turkey, the results would be devastating. A county-commissioned study found that pot accounts for up to two-thirds of economic activity in the region. As one grower puts it to me, "I don't think there's anything more important in this economy. To take this out would be a major blow. I mean it'd be no different really than an earthquake or a tsunami hitting this area, economically speaking. Pot is the life-blood of this county, and it has been for more than thirty years."

Sligh says the opportunities for making money are seemingly limitless. "You have a lot of young people making forty, fifty, one hundred, three hundred K cash. Just depends on how aggressive they are. And they're living that fast-paced kind of lifestyle in a very rural area."

A walk through any downtown in the Emerald Triangle provides evidence of the so-called high life. For a community with seemingly no source of commerce, there are an awful lot of young people driving BMWs, Mercedes, and tricked-out trucks. Local fast-food restaurant owners complain they can't find high school students willing to work in their restaurants because there's so much more money to be made in the marijuana trade. Javier Pena, the DEA special agent who oversaw this region from 2004 to 2008 tells it like this, "Pot is the money maker. It's hard to get the young kids to work at fast-food places because they're out tending to these marijuana groves. They're cutting the plants. They're seeding. They're trimming the buds. They're driving around in forty-thousand-dollar, fifty-thousand-dollar vehicles.

They're seventeen, eighteen years old and already have twenty-five K in the bank—and it's all because they're helping with these marijuana grow operations."

If you live in a town that makes all of its money on soybeans, textiles, or oil drilling, every local business comes to depend indirectly on the money that main industry pulls in. The same is true for pot. While most estimates of the economic activity connected to weed only include sales of the actual product, talk to people in Mendocino and you see how it turns the wheels of commerce, especially in related businesses such as garden centers and real estate.

Real estate agent Dick Selzer of Ukiah, California, runs Realty World, Selzer Realty, Selzer Home Loans, and Selzer Property Management, all located in the infamous Emerald Triangle. He's been in business thirty-plus years and admits the real estate industry in this part of the country is "a little bit different." To say the least. "Agriculture is our big industry here, and you have another industry that . . . ," he pauses and lets out a hearty laugh, "people just don't talk about." Of course, marijuana cultivation is technically agriculture, too.

The significance of the marijuana economy is evident in house and land values, with the most desirable properties here being the most remote. Indeed, real estate is counterintuitive in the Emerald Triangle when compared to the rest of the county. "Normally," Selzer explains, "if you had a forty-acre piece of property, all else being equal—same topography, same exposure, that kind of thing—if everything else is the same, the closer that parcel is to a population center, the higher its value." But here? "A piece of property at the *end* of the road, which is further out and may even be a little less desirable in terms of topography and exposure, has a greater value because there are fewer people driving by it to complain about the smell or to report illicit growing." According to Selzer, there's another benefit: "The person who is growing gets a little more warning if the authorities are coming."

The premium on land in marijuana country is significant. A forty-acre parcel of land in Mendocino can costs between $400,000 and $600,000. However, if you were to take marijuana out of the equation, real estate agents in the region estimate that same forty-acre parcel would be worth an estimated $100,000. The reason for the markup, according to Selzer, stems from "the amount of money that you can make growing marijuana." (Selzer is well acquainted with these figures. As one of the community's top agents, he must understand property valuations, and in the Emerald Triangle, a property's worth is entirely dependent on its marijuana-growing potential.) So, to be successful in Emerald Triangle real estate, you must understand the marijuana business.

And what a business it is. Consider the math: Growers tell me one large marijuana plant requires roughly twenty square feet of land. One acre provides 43,560 square feet of land. So, in theory, growers can plant up to 2,178 plants on each acre. (In reality, however, most growers plant far fewer due to the quality of the soil and other topography issues.) So, to play it safe, assume a grower plants just 1,000 plants per acre. That means on a forty-acre parcel of land, the grower could be cultivating 40, 000 plants. If grown properly, each plant may yield $5,000 worth of marijuana (two pounds at $2,500 a pound wholesale). One acre of land could potentially yield $5 million worth of pot, while a forty-acre parcel of land might gross an ambitious grower as much as $200 million. Yes, $200 million. Is anyone growing that much anywhere? Not that I could find. Still, there's not a farmer in the world growing food that could touch a return like that. No wonder property values in the Emerald Triangle are skyrocketing.

The town of Mendocino itself (there's a distinction between the town and the county) is charming. Settled by New Englanders in the mid-1800s, Mendocino was once a fishing and logging village. It's about as close as you'll get to Maine on the Pacific Coast.

In fact, the area looks so much like New England (and I can say that as a New Englander myself) that the TV show *Murder, She Wrote*—which was supposed to take place in Cabot Cove, Maine—actually filmed its episodes on location in Mendocino.

The town is tiny, just seven square miles with about eight hundred permanent residents. Quaint streets filled with low-level, small, white-and-red painted colonial-style wood buildings, along with magnificent views of the Pacific Ocean, have made the village popular with weekenders from San Francisco. It's jammed with cozy bed-and-breakfasts and restaurants serving organic food. The crisp air and semipermanent blanket of fog hovering over its coast adds to the town's mystery.

The county of Mendocino, however, is vast, spanning an area of nearly four thousand square miles. Nearly one hundred thousand people live in the county and, according to government officials, 60 percent of them are directly involved in the marijuana business. The county has become the most notorious region in the Emerald Triangle, and it's notorious for one thing: the best pot in the world comes from Mendocino.

Eric Sligh was born in Oakland and raised in Mendocino County. "Sometimes I feel like I'm in a bubble," he muses as we stroll through the garden, "because I don't . . . I just really don't know what it's like *not* to grow marijuana."

When he was growing up, most of his friends' parents grew pot in their backyards. He recalls neighbors getting busted for illegal grows; he remembers being told not to go near certain houses; and most of all, he remembers being simply fascinated by the *business* of pot. "When you're fourteen, fifteen years old, you know, you're not really trying to be an upstanding citizen so much as you're trying to be like a pirate or an outlaw. So, as a kid, listening to gansta rap, I thought it was pretty hip to be an outlaw. I mean, come on," he says with emphasis, his arms extended. "Johnny Depp and the *Pirates of the Caribbean* movies? I mean, he's a hero! He just runs circles around the law." And so did Sligh, for a time.

Sligh was a marijuana broker—the kind, he says, with "two phones to his ears at all times," constantly trying to connect a marijuana grower with a marijuana buyer. It was "kinda like being a commodities broker on Wall Street," he says. "There's a developed, sophisticated system of brokering marijuana that exists all throughout California. These are people that specialize in connecting the two parties."

He recently gave up the brokerage business to publish *Grow*, a magazine filled with graphic pictures of pot plants and meant for readers to gawk at with envy, like teenage boys with *Playboy*. The magazine enables him to benefit from the marijuana boom without having to directly engage in illegal behavior.

We head back to the sunroom to cool off for a bit. As I gulp down a glass of ice-cold water, Sligh shows me some of the highlights from his magazine, including pictures of a huge commercial garden that provides harvests four times a year. "It takes a team of like five to ten people to run this level of growing," he explains, referencing the pictures. "They might make up to half a million dollars, possibly much more on an annual basis." Flipping through the pages, he points to several articles offering advice on how to grow as well as those that tackle some of the legal and sociological issues facing local growers. "For people who live in this area, marijuana as a topic deserves a larger forum." Apparently a popular book store chain thinks so, too, because *Grow* magazine was just added to store shelves.

Flipping through the magazine, I ask Sligh the question I would eventually be asked over and over while working on my documentary and this book: "So, how does it happen? How do you actually become a successful marijuana broker?"

"You kinda fall into it. Somebody might just know where the marijuana is grown . . . and they know someone who wants to buy it . . . and it's that simple. You're just putting two people together." Some brokers, Sligh tells me, never even touch the product.

In Sligh's case, he would buy his marijuana from nearby grows in Ukiah, then sell to brokers in San Francisco and Los Angeles. In turn, those brokers would sell the pot to other brokers (the term *dealers*, I'm told, is passé) or individuals. At each level, the price of the marijuana increases as brokers claim their slice of the profits.

Typically, brokers work with several growers. Although some sell their product to medical marijuana dispensaries (legal under state law), dispensary selling is not considered the most lucrative. Dispensaries, while dependable, pay the least for the drug. Brokers quickly learn that the highest prices are paid on the open, *illegal* market.

Another reliable, and profitable, way for brokers to sell their product is through what's called a pot clearinghouse. Brokers bring their pot to a location where other brokers come to preview, test, and buy. There are clearinghouses in every town in California, from Eureka to San Diego. Sligh offers a simple, albeit unusual, comparison. "You take your cow to the fair, and you auction it off. In a clearinghouse, you have buyers that come to bid on the pot. The highest bidder gets the product. Simple." Generally, it's the broker who sets up a clearinghouse event— most often with a buyer from out of town. A good buyer tells his broker the type of marijuana he wants, and how much of it he wants. A good broker makes sure his buyer is oversubscribed. "It's just like the airlines," Sligh explains. "Airlines oversell their seats to make sure they have a full plane. The broker brings more growers with more pot than a buyer actually needs because this way, the broker ensures that he'll get a cut of every dollar his buyer has to spend." It's not unusual for a buyer who is in town to purchase one hundred pounds of herb to have five hundred pounds from which to choose.

On the day of the event a buyer shows up at a house (generally late). The buyer sits, sometimes on a couch in a broker's home, while growers wait in line with plastic tubs filled with fifteen to twenty pounds of weed. Most often, buyers in the Emerald Triangle are visiting from Atlanta; Washington D.C.; New York; and Boston. By traveling to California, they'll get a wholesale price for the pot and can therefore stand to make a lot of money. If they buy it at $4,000 a pound (a typical price at a clearinghouse event), they can sell it back in New York for upward of $5,000 a pound. (One trader at the New York Stock Exchange, whose "dealer" provides him with California grown herb, pays $400 an ounce, or the equivalent of $6,400 a pound.) The challenge for the buyers is getting the stash back across the country without landing themselves (or whoever may be driving the goods) in jail. "He's taking on risk," Sligh sums it up. "But let's face it, in the marijuana game, that's what you get paid for. Risk."

Growers tell me they like the division of labor between growing and selling. Most say, "It's easier this way," because it enables people to specialize. Indeed, most seem more interested in farming than in selling their crop. Think of it like this: in the Emerald Triangle, the grower is the "artist" while the broker is the "businessman." Each needs the other. One grower, ironically a former member of law enforcement, told me, "Trish, without someone to sell this stuff to, all you've got is a whole lot of pot. And as good as that may be, let's face it, you just can't smoke it all." He told me of marijuana that was rotting in grow houses and being infiltrated with mice. "Growers," he said, "are only as successful as their brokers. You need to get your product from point A to point B, and the broker accomplishes that."

6

CASH CROP

Moving from the Woods to the Mainstream

Ukiah Morrison lives up to his "artistic" reputation as a grower. Morrison (who shares the name of the Mendocino town of Ukiah, California) is a Mendocino County local who once ran for county supervisor. He grows eleven mature plants, more than California's legal limit of six. In his late thirties, tan, clean-shaven, with short, dark brown hair, Morrison insists that "growing marijuana is as natural as, well, growing corn" to him.

Every day, he checks his plants to see if they need water or fertilizer. He prunes and trims them himself. "It's important to prune," he explains, because the plants need to be "evenly placed. The nutrients rise to the top. And the best of the best is usually in that top third of the plant."

"It's actually quite a lot of work," according to Morrison, his sunglasses shielding him from the sun's glare as he examines his grow. "So it's very important to understand that you have to create, or recreate, the perfect environment to optimize growth. You have to understand humidity. You have to understand pH, electrical conductivity, you must know to dissolve solids. You must understand how to prevent infestations of bugs or mold."

Morrison represents one of the biggest open questions about the future of cannabis: will big commercial grows push out small artisans like Morrison? Will legalization bring with it an industry like most agricultural products, with small farmers crushed by huge factory farms, or like the market for alcohol, which mixes high-end specialty brewers and vintners with international conglomerates?

A sophisticated gardening technique is one reason the Emerald Triangle is known for exceptional pot. After all, the area has been honing its expertise since the sixties when the region first became a haven for people using marijuana. Driving into Ukiah, I was struck by the multitude of huge gardening store billboards scattered along the side of the road, advertising the best fertilizers, sophisticated irrigation systems, and pretty much anything else you can imagine to help your "plants" grow. County officials tell me, per capita, there are more gardening shops in the Emerald Triangle than in any other part of the country. (Be forewarned, though, never say "grow" in a gardening store—let alone pot, marijuana, mj, weed, or any other term referring to cannabis. Do so and you'll be sent straight to the exit. Everything is sold with a wink, wink. So, if you're looking to prevent infestations of bugs on your marijuana plants, just tell the sales clerk you're trying to protect your garden. They'll know what you're talking about, and they'll make sure you get the right stuff.) Growing is both an art and a science, and it's nearly been perfected here.

Indeed, the community almost seems to embrace marijuana. Not only are there gardening stores on every corner but there's also a sociology course at Humboldt State University that focuses on "the growth of the marijuana economy," and a Ukiah clinic that prescribes medical marijuana stands next door to the recruiting offices for the U.S. Air Force and the Marines.

Jim Wattenburger, the chairman of the Board of Supervisors for Mendocino County, is stout, in his late fifties or early sixties, balding, with some rosacea creeping into his cheeks. He is a larger-than-life personality. His booming voice and hearty laugh make him seem more like a good ol' boy from Texas than a lifelong resident of Mendocino County. But Wattenburger grew up here and has become an outspoken critic of marijuana. He believes the industry has grown too fast, too soon, and he is actively trying to limit the amount of marijuana that can be grown in Mendocino. It's a position that makes him increasingly unpopular with some growers. When I met him, he had already received four death threats thanks to his efforts to regulate marijuana, and he told me he carries a gun with him six out of seven days a week.

Wattenburger says he knows why his community has gone to pot, so to speak, and it all comes down to one thing: economics. "We used to have timber," he tells me. "We were the timber king in Redwood for the last hundred and fifty years." But that industry has been nearly decimated. "When I was a kid here," he reminisces, glancing up toward the ceiling of the county office, then back at me, "we had thirty-three operating lumber mills of various sizes in this valley. We now have a total of three mills for the entire county."

Plenty of towns lose their lumber mills (or the local equivalent) to overseas competitors, but those towns don't become world leaders in pot production. So why here? "We're the fifth-largest geographically sized county in California. We are one of the most sparsely populated counties. So you have vast areas where you have no people. Out of sight, out of mind." Wattenburger makes a convincing argument. Driving through Mendocino County, you can go miles without seeing a soul. It's both beautiful and eerie.

The community's natural resources also make it a prime area for growing. As Wattenburger points out, there is "lots of water and a great climate." He stresses the diversity of agricultural products grown here. "We have a Japanese maple tree nursery that ships all over the world. We have award-winning grapes. We have alfalfa. We have cattle. We have more organic acreages under cultivation in this county than anywhere in the United States!" He's getting excited now, almost patriotic, and waves his hands for emphasis, as though he's making a campaign speech.

"How much is all that worth?" I ask, trying to put it in context.

He sighs. He knows where I'm going with this, and I've just burst his bubble. "Well, all the *legal* agricultural products, wine, raw crops, timber, livestock, about $2.4 billion."

And how much is the marijuana worth?

"The conservative estimate for the county, in 2007, was $12 billion." In other words, about five times the legal agricultural products—and that figure, according to Wattenburger, is just the tip of the iceberg.

"Honestly, Trish," he looks me square in the eye, "I think it's more than that. People are going to say I'm full of hot air if I say fifteen to twenty billion. But I actually think it's around that. This is an illegal industry that reaps huge profits off marijuana. I'd say if marijuana was to be eradicated, this county would become destitute. The small mom-and-pop grocery store, the agricultural supply store . . . they're making ninety percent of their annual budget off marijuana [customers]."

Wattenburger is caught on both sides of the law in Mendocino. On the one hand, he's obligated to uphold county law (which, when I interviewed him, still permitted the growth of up to twenty-five plants but has since been amended to allow just twelve), but on the other hand, he's vehemently opposed to a marijuana economy. Further complicating his position, he is friends with many of the area's top growers.

"I grew up with some of them," he tells me. "They were members of my class of high school graduates at Ukiah High."

Regardless of friendships, Wattenburger is actively trying to rein in the rampant growing of marijuana in his county.
A believer in medicinal marijuana, he resents that his community has been overtaken by "out-of-staters" looking to make some
fast cash. "Some growers have become so successful they now
own three or four homes in our community and have brought in
other relatives from Washington, Oregon, Nevada, Utah, to par-
take in this gold rush. The family members are put to work in a
family operation. It's a family business, and everyone is makin'
money at it."

Like many in the Emerald Triangle, Wattenburger wants marijuana production to be the way it used to be—a backyard garden or two is permissible, but a full-fledged, multi-million-dollar
operation is another thing entirely.

His goal now—and he doesn't pull any punches, the determination seeping from his sharp, baritone voice—"I'm here to
eradicate the greedy bastards and the scum that have infiltrated
my county and, unfortunately, made it nationally known as a producer county of," he stops and shakes his head, "good marijuana."

Why the surge in production? Wattenburger has a theory.
He says the word has spread about Mendocino's tolerance. *High
Times*, a popular marijuana magazine, wrote about the Emerald
Triangle region in 2006. Shortly after, he claims, hundreds of new
growers flooded his community. "I took a flight over the county in
2006 with a marijuana eradication team. We looked at a specific
area and counted forty gardens. I took the same flight in 2007 and
I quit counting at four hundred gardens."

On a recent trip to a county supervisors' convention in
Fairbanks, Alaska, people said to him, "Hey, you're from
Mendocino County? Did you bring the good stuff with ya?" "It's
embarrassing as hell," he tells me. "I'm ashamed that we're known
for this."

Ukiah police chief Christopher Dewey is not just ashamed his
hometown is known for marijuana, he's concerned about the effect

it may be having on the community's youth. A tall, clean-cut, forty-something-year-old man with a baby face and soft-spoken voice, Dewey says his community has been overtaken by pot, and young people are increasingly turning to an illegal business, in part, he believes, because they have no choice. Chief Dewey moonlights as the coach of the local youth football team, working with boys between the ages of thirteen and fifteen. He sees sports as a way to help keep kids out of trouble, but more often than not, in Mendocino County, he complains, the trouble finds them.

To illustrate his point, Dewey tells me the story of his most talented player, who missed a week of practice. "When he came back," he says, "I asked why he missed a week. I mean, it was really important for him to be at practice. He was our star player. And he said, 'Look, I needed to help my parents.' I said, 'Well, what were you doing?' And he says, 'Well, I was helping my parents trim their bud, so they can package and sell it.'"

"This is a kid," the chief continues, "that had already been in trouble and was playing football to stay out of trouble. Now, he's trimming bud, so he's back involved in criminal activity." And he told the chief of police? That wouldn't necessarily be my first choice for the confession.

"It's really hard. You're wearing a hat that says police officer, but you're also wearing a hat as a coach. The idea is to keep the kids out of trouble. I want him on the football field, not trimming bud."

Still, when a community—and in this case, a family—depends on marijuana for its livelihood, the lines between right and wrong can quickly blur, even for the chief of police.

"You know, day in and day out, we arrest people. But when you have a kid telling you, 'Hey look, I need to help my parents. This is how they make a living,' then you suddenly realize this is serious. We really have a problem here. Are we sending the message to kids that drugs are okay? They're forced to make these ethical decision at such young ages."

More and more young people are facing this kind of pressure because more and more residents are turning to marijuana as an income stream. "People that never grew marijuana before have decided to start growing for profit," he says. It's a new phenomenon. "In years past, marijuana was grown in the hills. It was grown out of sight, away from people. But over the last few years, it's moved into residential communities."

In the middle of our morning interview, Chief Dewey gets a call. "Sorry," he says, looking apologetically at me as he scrambles to grab his cell phone. "Hello? Hi, Bob. It did? Where are you at? 4681? Okay, we're on our way."

Putting his phone down, he yanks off his microphone. Adrenaline in his voice, he says loudly as he stands up from his chair, "They've hit one house. They're at a second house. If you want to get it, come now!'

"They" refers to the Mendocino Major Crimes Task Force led by Bob Nishiyama. Every week, Nishiyama and his team head out on a series of raids in an attempt to clamp down on the commercial grows now permeating the community's downtown.

Chief Dewey scribbles an address on a piece of paper and hands it to me. "See you there," he shouts at me as he rushes out of the room.

Less than an hour later, the chief and I are standing on a cul-de-sac outside a pale blue town house. There are about a dozen town houses on this street, and each house looks the same. In the front of each property sits a tiny front lawn—some with bright yellow daffodils adorning stone walkways. In one driveway, I spot a small red tricycle with blue and silver streamers dangling from its handles, blowing in the soft breeze. This is a quiet, family neighborhood—but, according to Mendocino investigators, it's also home to a significant commercial grow operation.

Guns in hand, the officers bang on the door. Pulling out a loudspeaker, they demand entry into the town house. No answer. They bang again. Nothing. Drawing their guns, they hoist themselves against the door to gain entry. I'm watching from behind, and as soon as that door swings open, the smell hits me. It's pungent. Overwhelming. I hold my hand up to cover my nose and shield myself from the stench. This is not like Sligh's outdoor grow. This is far more concentrated. It's like nothing I've ever smelled before.

As the police storm in, their guns pointing ahead, I stand in the doorway, peering into what would be the house's living room. It's dark (every shade is drawn), and all I can see are rows of enormous plants. They're each over seven feet tall and grazing the ceiling. After getting an "all clear" signal from one of the officers, I inch my way into the house—there is barely room to move, because the plants are so close to one another. Everywhere I look—the living room, the hallway, the kitchen, and the dining area—all I see are marijuana plants. Every inch of this town house is being used for growing purposes.

Chief Dewey is standing on the stairs. "Come on, it's clear. There's more upstairs," he yells, motioning for me to follow him. Upstairs I spot three small bedrooms and a bathroom. In the bathroom, the showerhead is hooked to a hose. It's providing a simple irrigation system for the grow operation. Dewey leads me into one room filled with tiny plants. This is a clone room where the growers are creating small plants in hydroponic beds. They're essentially creating a root system on the stem of each plant, Dewey explains. The second bedroom serves as a holding room for the plants' intermediate stage. "They're growing them up in here," Dewey says, his eyes fixed on the dozens of small potted plants in the second bedroom. Meanwhile, in the third bedroom are fifteen large plants, similar to the ones I saw downstairs, all about seven feet tall with mature buds. The chief tells me these buds "have budded" and are ready to be harvested. We finish surveying the property and make our way back downstairs toward the garage. It's empty, but evidence remains scattered on the floor: some empty pots, a few lights, and some trimming equipment. "They just finished a harvest," Dewey tells me, folding his arms and shaking his head. "This is a *commercial* operation," he says emphatically. "This house was rented for one purpose, and that's to grow marijuana." I ask him how he knows it isn't a medicinal operation. "If you were growing for medicinal purposes, you would be growing the two or three plants you need, not *that* many plants," he says, gesturing back to the main part of the house.

The money being generated from an indoor grow operation like this adds up. "That one room that was ready to be harvested," Dewey says, his eyes looking up at the blue sky as he computes the math, "was probably worth about twenty thousand dollars." The room they already harvested was "twice the size. So it could have been forty K," he estimates. "And then, they had two more cycles on the way, probably at twenty K each."

The beauty of the indoor operation, as commercial growers see it, is that plants can be grown and harvested every ninety days, affording them four major cash opportunities a year.

But the problem, Dewey laments, is that this kind of bust has become too typical. "What used to happen out in the woods— large commercial operations—just made its way into our neighborhoods."

According to the Mendocino Major Crimes Task Force, this commercial grow was a family-run operation involving six individuals, including a seemingly upstanding citizen: the city government reporter for the *Ukiah Daily Journal* paper was allegedly connected to the case. Authorities allege the reporter and his fiancée rented the town house (along with other locations) while the fiancée's brother covered $2,000 a month electric bill. The fiancée's parents were allegedly involved in the scheme as well. Authorities confiscated eighty plants and twenty-two pounds of marijuana, which they claim the ring was selling for $3,000 a pound to local cannabis clubs. It's great money—until you're caught.

Law enforcement and most residents would probably agree that some grows are too big, too commercial, but the question is, Where do you draw the line?

I meet a team of growers—a newspaper reporter (not the one busted in Ukiah), a former police officer, and a former elected local politician at dusk one spring evening at a quaint, oceanfront café in a small town along the Emerald Triangle's coast. All are in their early sixties, all have families, and all requested that their names not be used. Tall, thin, with a baseball cap covering his head, a ruddy complexion, and a deep baritone voice, the former politician told me over red wine and pizza that his daughter, while she was growing up, hated pot and everything for which it stood. He remembers a fateful day when she was a teenager and came home from school with some friends only to find the smell of marijuana had permeated their house (he had just smoked a joint, he tells me sheepishly). She was furious, he said, and swore she would never have anything to do with marijuana. But that was ten years ago. She's now an adult, and she recently chose to move back to the area after finishing college. The hard reality of making a living has set in, her father says, and she recently approached him for some guidance on developing a small grow. "How else can someone make fifty K, cash?" he asks. "It's expensive to live here and there are no jobs. She really doesn't have a choice," he insists, "if she wants to be in this area."

When he first moved to Mendocino County thirty years ago, he says there was actually no economic incentive to grow pot. At that time, "It wasn't really commercial. People were just giving it away. It was the hippie days. It was just a nice thing to do. It wasn't about money."

The turning point, all three of the growers conclude, came in the early eighties, when law enforcement began cracking down on pot due to the Reagan administration's "get tough" drug policies. "Suddenly, the price started going up from there, and it went up and up and up until it became obvious that you were able to make a decent living growing pot," says the local reporter.

With my camera operator and producer, we leave the restaurant and head to the former police officer's home to film an on-camera interview. (We bring special lights and other equipment including, believe it or not, a fog machine to help disguise their identities.) It is late at night, and they each light up a joint upon my arrival. They offer me some of their "good stuff," but I laugh, assuring them I'll probably get my fill of a contact high just by interviewing them. (The shoot goes most of the night, and I head straight to the airport that morning. I am nearly convinced one of the drug-sniffing German Shepherds is going to stop me as I go through security. Fortunately, that doesn't happen, although my fellow passengers on the plane may wonder about me, as I'm confident my clothing must reek.)

The former politician tells me he gave up growing during his political tenure because he didn't want to deal with the potential embarrassment of getting arrested. But he recently returned to his craft due to an adjustable rate mortgage that had reset higher, costing him much more money than he could otherwise afford every month. Without the ability to grow pot, he tells me, he would have been forced to foreclose on his home. The former police officer is now retired and says he grows just enough pot for himself and has a little income on the side. All three are adamant about one thing: marijuana is the lifeline of the local economy. Without it, the former police officer insists, "The economy would crash. It would tank." The former politician offers an analogy—it would be as if "Apple closed [its] plant in San Jose."

According to the journalist, "This is the reason that it [pot] is so accepted. It's not because so many people think it's so great. Even though a lot of people do. It's because *everyone* knows how important it is to the economy." The three insist the entire community gets a cut of the action. "Even the sheriff's department counts on seizure money," says a grower. "There's a whole industry in enforcement! It's all part of the game. Everybody's making money one way or another on this. So nobody wants to talk about it."

But these guys *do* want to talk about it—albeit anonymously. They tell me they're tired of marijuana's bad rap. "Everyone focuses on the bad guys, the people who *aren't* involved in the community," says the former police officer. But what about "that single mom raising kids without welfare because she converted the bedroom into an indoor grow operation?" he asks.

"You have a friend that did that?" I ask, intrigued.

"I know *many* people that are *doing* that," he tells me.

The journalist sums up his community's economic dependence on marijuana this way, "If you wipe out the marijuana crop, it would be catastrophic. You might as well turn off the Sacramento River."

The three pride themselves on being "gourmet" growers—after all, between them they have seventy-five years of growing experience. One grows several different varieties of pot, telling me he likes to dabble in a bit of everything. "Whether it's indica, sativa, or any combination thereof. That's fun. That's what makes it different. It's like having different vegetables at your table," he smiles.

When I ask what they're seeing the most demand for now, they insist it's the indoor stuff, especially Kush varieties. "Kush," the former cop tells me, "is an indica sativa cross. The sativa will grow a lot of very slender flowers that lay along the stem. And when you cross those, then you get lots of different combinations of how the flowers will grow. And indoor, especially, some of the flowers are just absolutely weird!" (He means that in a good way. I think the joints are taking their effect.)

How can these guys grow pot, enter their products in marijuana "competitions" where taste testers choose the best weed, sell their bud to neighbors and dispensaries, and *not* get caught? "There are thousands and thousands of little producers all over the place. They're working independently and entering the marketplace on their own, like us," the newspaper man says.

The key is to "stay small. Stay off the radar," they add, practically in unison. The former cop (who after all, should know how to avoid the authorities) warns, "You get too big, you're gonna be sitting in jail some place." The journalist reminds me of a story in the local paper that morning about a grower who got busted. "The guy had three or four properties. People were living on them, growing, and they just arrested all of them. He was too high profile." He pauses for a moment to think, then sums it up like this, "You drive a fancy car around, it's going to come back to you."

There are more problems that come with all of this money than calling attention to yourself by driving a fancy car. It's not that hard to spend a few thousand dollars in cash without being noticed. But once you start talking about tens of thousands of dollars, it gets complicated.

Indeed, it will come back to you if Richard Adams, a money-laundering expert and a special agent for the IRS's Criminal Investigation Division, is on your trail. Adams has been following the money trail for twenty-six years, and his favorite cases are marijuana investigations in the Emerald Triangle. Marijuana is the most profitable drug in the world—and its profits, he claims, are the most traceable. Although there is money in cocaine, heroin, and meth, the "overhead" for those drugs is significant and cuts into profit margins. Take cocaine, for example. It's profitable, but it's also riddled with expenses. "You need to pay all the people. The smugglers, the trans-shippers, the growers, the processors, the subdealers." It adds up. After all, if you pay $22,000 for a kilo of cocaine, a very large percentage will end up going back to Colombia or Mexico." But with marijuana, there is a much higher return on investment. Expenses are low, profits are enormous, and the money generally stays within the domestic economy, making it, from an investigator's viewpoint, much easier to track.

At some point, Adams promises, marijuana growers are "gonna make mistakes. They're going to buy things. They're going to buy the toys. They're going to spend it on their houses. And it just makes it easier for me to follow."

Eric Sligh agrees that dealing with all of that cash can indeed be a problem for those in the marijuana trade. After all, you can't walk into the bank and deposit tens of thousands of dollars without a few eyebrows being raised, nor can you walk into a real estate office with a briefcase full of cash trying to purchase some land. He knows growers who have actually buried thousands of dollars in their backyards rather than make deposits at the bank. He also knows growers who have established sideline businesses to help "cleanse" their dirty money.

Speaking of money, the garden Sligh and I were touring may well yield some serious cash. In eight weeks, when the temperature cools, the small pineapplelike buds we've been examining will have grown into huge buds. "When they reach that point," he tells me, "it's time to cut'em down." But how much money the grower makes will depend on market conditions. When security tightens along the U.S.-Canadian border, less marijuana from British Colombia is able to make its way into the country. As a result, the Emerald Triangle quickly becomes flooded with brokers from Seattle and Portland, all trying to get their hands on some of Mendocino's finest. Similarly, when security increased along the Mexican border after 9/11, brokers saw an increase in demand for California pot. For example, when border patrol strengthens (along both the Mexican border and the Canadian border), prices, naturally, go up.

"It's hard to tell how much the marijuana is going to sell for on the open market," Sligh tells me. "Is that price going to increase because of less supply? Is it going to be decreased because there is more supply? You know, it's hard to tell how much marijuana is out there."

It's the basic law of supply and demand. A normal part of life for marijuana growers in the Emerald Triangle.

7

SEED MONEY

Making Money Supplying
Suppliers

B en Holmes has big plans for his fledgling company. Another entrepreneur hoping to make a name for himself in the marijuana industry, Holmes is neither a generation-Xer looking to make money nor a political activist. He is looking to form a major company and believes marijuana will be the next major boom business—like the Internet was in 1999.

Holmes is actually one of the last people you'd expect to begin a venture in the marijuana business. A former banker who managed to strike it big by selling his independent research firm ipoPros.com to TheStreet.com in the heyday of the tech boom (when everyone was super hungry for IPO research), Ben is a fifty-something, preppy family man with a wife (who doesn't approve of his marijuana venture), two young boys, and a dog. He created a startup company to manufacture and distribute not marijuana, but marijuana *seeds*. He has a few employees and hopes to turn a profit this year (his second year in business!). His ultimate goal? He's thinking big. He wants to take his company public on a major exchange.

If there's anyone in this industry who could take his venture public, it's Holmes. After all, researching whether a company will succeed in a public offering is his business. He provides stock market research and analytics to institutional investors and has been involved in the U.S. IPO market for over twenty years. Holmes began his career in the brokerage industry with Merrill Lynch & Co., and later worked as a position trader at Buttonwood Asset Management. He is the founder of Protégé Funds, a private asset management firm, and has even been interviewed a few times on CNBC for his expert investing advice. But *seeds*?

In 2004, Holmes received his first medicinal card to possess pot. At the time, there were no dispensaries and there were no seed sources. He didn't know anyone who grew pot, so he was pretty much on his own. He began combing through the back pages of *High Times*, the popular marijuana magazine, where companies from Amsterdam, the United Kingdom, British Columbia, and South Africa advertised their seeds for sale. They weren't cheap (and still aren't), running anywhere from $90 to $200 for a pack of ten seeds. As for the quality? "Terrible," he says, shaking his head in disgust. "The overall genetics that have been developed in these places, like Amsterdam, are fantastic. The problem is that the seed supply is stale. It's mislabeled. It comes from intermediaries that might be making knockoffs. From Amsterdam to the U.S., it doesn't translate into good product, and we have no recourse if it's not good." After all, you can't call up the seed company in Amsterdam and say, "Hey, my seeds were bad." First, they don't really care and second, it's illegal to be buying the seeds in the first place. Holmes learned this through his own experience. He sent a check in the mail, and a few weeks later a package of stale seeds arrived via U.S. mail. (Yes—the United States Postal Service.) But as far as the company is concerned, your transaction with them "never happened," according to Holmes, and thus, "there's no recourse."

Holmes spotted a business opportunity. "It's pretty simple. There's demand for this, but no market." So he's now devoting all of his free time (when he's not managing money) to managing his new seed business. He plans to sell seeds for $45 to $55 per pack (roughly half the price of European seeds), and unlike his foreign competitors, he'll guarantee that they'll grow—or your money back.

Like other pot entrepreneurs I met, Holmes stresses that while it may look easy, his business is actually incredibly difficult. "It's a job," he tells me. "Most people wonder about the money being made, and they think, it's easy money, that this is a gold rush. And the truth is, it's work. And we're doing well because we work at it."

Holmes's business doesn't require as much growing equipment as a dispensary like Wanda James's requires—in fact, when I meet him at his company, a large warehouse on the outskirts of town, complete with a coffee room, a small office, and a conference room, I only see about six plants and a small amount of growing equipment. Instead, Holmes's seed company requires plenty of "know-how"—the intellectual capital that enables him to know whether it makes sense to cross one strain of marijuana with another. When I ask him what his biggest up-front cost is, I get a one-word answer, "Time." That is because, as he puts it, "The education required to do this well takes time. You must read everything. You need to talk with other people." Ben learns a lot online, he confesses, but any way you slice it, you've got to do your homework. Laughing, he admits, "It's the equivalent of a graduate degree. Really!" For a first-time grower? Ben predicts it might take someone at least two years to get to the point where they could grow some decent stuff.

Becoming very serious, he looks me in the eye and says slowly, "It's a four-hundred-dollar-per-ounce commodity. If it could be done easily it would be. It requires effort and it requires a specialized knowledge." It's something I'll hear over and over. People earning a profit, or on the verge of it, tell me pot is expensive because it's a lot of work. Others watching from the outside or just getting involved say it's from the risk.

Every morning Holmes wakes up by five-thirty. He heads straight to his warehouse where he spends about an hour or two (before heading to his day job) dabbling with the plants, germinating them, feeding them, and watching them grow. He monitors the progress of his plants—checking to see whether they're rooting well. He pollinates them, leaving small ribbons on the branches so he knows which ones have already been done. To do this, he takes the pollen into a closed room, sprinkles pollen on the female plants, then five weeks later has his seeds. Pointing to a plant, he shows me the seeds, explaining that this is an example of "low intensity pollination," but it will still produce a few hundred seeds. He'll grow some of the seeds and see how strong the plant is before offering those seeds for sale. It's essentially a test phase.

Holmes sees similarities between marijuana prohibition today and alcohol prohibition in the 1920s. "It's a states' rights issue," he tells me. "It's plain and simple, just as alcohol was. Alcohol prohibition was repealed one state at a time by a group of lawyers who worked and lobbied at each state in the country until, eventually even Utah, turned over. And then, it was repealed at the federal level." Already, fifteen states have made moves to legalize medicinal marijuana, and Holmes predicts more will follow. "It represents a real source of income. And it's a double gain because we give up the liability of policing [marijuana], which is very expensive. It's a net win for the state."

He points to Colorado's history of entrepreneurship—Crocs, the successful shoe company, began its business in the Rocky Mountain state. "Their first year in business, they did twenty-four thousand dollars in sales. I'll pass them in the second quarter of this year," he states with pride. (He's just over a year into his venture.) "It's not a big number. I may stall out at that number. But my hope is that eventually, we have the ability to sell these seeds into other medicinal states." And therein lays his biggest opportunity.

In the meantime, Holmes has slowly begun marketing his product. In fact, he even has a salesperson on his staff, a young, blond, blue-eyed, attractive girl who recently finished her degree in business at the University of Colorado. Similar to a pharmaceutical sales rep, she travels the city, introducing dispensary owners to the various marijuana seeds and strains. For now, Holmes sells only in Colorado because state law permits him to operate in this area. But, as I remind him, every day he's taking a risk.

"Why take that risk?" I ask. I'm always struck by marijuana enthusiasts' willingness to shrug off federal law. "You're someone who has a clean record; you're in the investment business and have had no run-ins with the Securities and Exchange Commission for your trading practices, so why risk it all?" I ask him and get an answer similar to many in this field. At the end of the day, he and his counterparts see an inherent flaw in the system that they want corrected. But his motivations are not just business. "I've known my entire adult life that these laws are wrong," Holmes tells me, his blue eyes staring straight into mine. His voice is measured and deliberate. It's clear that, like Wanda James, he is passionate on this issue. "They're hurtful, and they're harmful to our society. Set the plants and your beliefs on the drug aside. Since I was born twenty million Americans have been arrested on marijuana crimes. Twenty million." Including some of Holmes's friends, such as a physician in California who is close to finishing a two-year run in prison for writing prescriptions. "It's just wrong. But it's a simple thing to fix." In the meantime, if he delivers his seeds to clients in Colorado then he's committing a major offense—by sending marijuana seeds in U.S. mail.

These are risks he's willing to take. Holmes's hope is that the economics will influence lawmakers to move toward legalization, and he believes Colorado, more than any other state, is best positioned to serve as a template. He compares his state to California, the traditional bastion for all things pot related. The problem with California's effort, as he sees it, is that the state built the marijuana business from the bottom up. One county, one municipality at a time. As a result, when you drive down the freeway, the rules change at each mile marker. That's the last thing a growing industry wants to deal with. In comparison, Colorado developed a statewide mandate permitting medicinal marijuana use so there's one law governing the state. Holmes wasn't the first to stress this model with me. It's popular in Colorado. Residents here like to emphasize that it became legal in the *entire* state. All at once.

But not so fast. Just weeks after I first spoke with Holmes, Colorado's governor, Bill Ritter Jr. signed two bills into law in June 2010 in an effort to improve the oversight of the state's medical marijuana industry. The new regulations are similar to California's in that they enable municipalities, through elected officials or voter initiatives, to ban dispensaries outright. Meanwhile, doctors must also conduct a physical exam of any patients they prescribe marijuana to and are prohibited from having a financial relationship with a marijuana dispensary. The dispensaries are facing a new, sixty-page list of requirements and regulations—including a mandate that they must grow 70 percent of their product in-house.

The regulations are designed to help appease a growing chorus of Coloradoans who are questioning what the onslaught of dispensaries, without proper regulations, will mean for the state. Colorado attorney general John Suthers is one of them. He believes the amendment to the state constitution that allowed the new businesses is inherently flawed, and in an October 2009 statement, he said, "Colorado has seen a rapid proliferation of medical marijuana dispensaries and patients since the Justice Department earlier this year announced it would not actively prosecute medical marijuana businesses—despite the fact that marijuana remains an illegal drug under federal law."[1]

State Senator Chris Romer, a Democrat whose south Denver district includes the popular "Broadsterdam" area, has told reporters that "right now it's easier to get a medical marijuana license than it is to get a liquor license."

Medicinal marijuana advocates are concerned that local governments will ban dispensaries and large growing operations altogether. Already, several city councils have begun the process of outlawing dispensaries, among them the posh ski resort town of Vail. "We thought that this ran counter to the marketing and all the things that we've done," Vail mayor Dick Cleveland tells NPR. "We're primarily a destination resort."[2]

But Brian Vicente, executive director of Sensible Colorado, a nonprofit organization working for effective and humane drug policies in Colorado, fires back, arguing, "We think a community should have no more right to ban a dispensary as they should to ban pharmacies. We are talking about access to medicine for sick people, and we don't think communities should be able shut that off."[3] Advocates also are threatening to challenge community bans in court.

Regardless of the outcome, it's clear Colorado is heading for a rocky future as communities debate whether they want to embrace the growing number of marijuana dispensaries. At the same time, they must tackle the broader question of whether they want to sanction businesses that are in direct violation of federal law. At the end of the day, it may come down to money. With fees for start-up dispensaries and new patients adding to the municipalities' bottom lines, it may be the money rather than a perception of morality that does the talking.

You don't have to sell pot, or even seeds, to make a living from the marijuana industry in Colorado. The onslaught of dispensaries has created an entire subculture of service industries—from legal experts, lobbyists, and gardening equipment consultants, to real estate agents specializing in the best grow warehouse spaces—they're all ready to capture their share of the action. There's even a "university" devoted to marijuana cultivation in Colorado. Similar to Oaksterdam University in Berkeley, California, Colorado's version is actually accredited by the state and boasts that it is the first school for cannabis in the country to have secured a blessing from state officials to function as a vocational college.

But perhaps the most original and innovative of the sideline start-ups is Full Spectrum Laboratories—a company that tests the

quality of marijuana and promises to be the future of the industry. It's not a bunch of guys sitting around smoking and ranking
their favorites. The owner, a thirty-six-year-old, tall, clean-cut,
academically trained biochemist who dropped out of medical
school to pursue this venture, says he gets teased about that a lot.
Instead, Full Spectrum uses a form of scientific testing that promises to tell clients the exact chemical makeup of a particular marijuana sample.

According to the company's Web site, Full Spectrum is "the
nation's first independent botanical testing laboratory providing
innovative quantification, certification, and product safety testing
to the emerging medical cannabis industry."

Until now, strain name, species, smell, appearance, and anec-
dote have been patients' primary tools for selecting the best medicine for their individual symptoms. Today, with the services
provided by Full Spectrum Laboratories through participating
dispensaries, patients have the ability to know that their medicine is both free of contaminants and most appropriate for their
symptoms. The bottom line is that Full Spectrum can tell you
how good your pot is by testing the "potency" of the marijuana
bud. Although the company can also determine whether there are
any pesticides, fungi, or hard metals present in the cannabis, the
majority of growers and consumers these days want to know
the answer to one question: how much THC is in this product? "I
get that question all the time!" The company's CEO and founder,
Bob Winnicki, laughs as he walks me through his lab, housed in
an old warehouse in North Denver. "The other thing I get is, 'Oh,
wow. That's some job you've got. Going to work and testing pot
all day. How can I get a gig like that?'"

His answer? Through hard work. His business, he says, is no
joke. One of the biggest challenges to consumers of marijuana is
a lack of quality control. Although the majority of caregivers in
the state of Colorado have good intentions, there are still about
5 percent, he says, who might be "playing games," and knowing
there's someone "out there that can actually call them on their she-
nanigans, well, that will make most of them step up their game

and raise the levels of ethics in this industry." Hundreds of thousands of cancer patients ingest cannabis every year. Given their suppressed immune systems, these patients are highly vulnerable to any opportunistic bacteria and fungi growing on the marijuana bud. Although the majority of microbiological hazards associated with cannabis are unlikely to affect healthy humans, there exists a subset of opportunistic plant pathogens associated with "post-harvest" or "storage" decay of marijuana.[4] These organisms may infect people with compromised immune systems. Moreover, many opportunist organisms on plants produce dangerous toxins and can generate allergenic reactions when inhaled. While these infectious bacteria are most commonly found in low-quality Mexican "weed" or "grass," they can exist in any plant.

Contaminated weed was an issue General Barry McCaffrey viewed as a major reason to prohibit medical marijuana. In 1999, when Maine voters approved ballot Question 2—a controversial plan for medical marijuana use, General McCaffrey wrote in the *Maine Sunday Telegram* that the proposed law was "unnecessary and dangerous." He argued that marijuana's psychoactive component, THC, was already available in its synthetic form via the drug Marinol. "Just as people who are ill don't grow their own penicillin from moldy bread," he wrote, "individuals can't guarantee the purity and dosage of THC by growing crude marijuana." Bob Winnicki's company hopes to appease General McCaffrey's concerns by ensuring that marijuana is not the penicillin equivalent of moldy bread. Ultimately, Winnicki believes Full Spectrum Laboratories would become the "seal" of approval that informs a potential customer about the quality of the marijuana.

Quality control is so haphazard that Winnicki says customers have no way of even understanding what it is that they may be buying. For example, if a grower says he's selling you Sour Diesel (a particular strain) and is promising a certain kind of high from a specific THC level, there's no way to know if what you are buying is in fact Sour Diesel. That is, unless you go to Winnicki's lab.

Winnicki states, "Other than smell, taste, and visual appearance, there's very little way for someone to determine what a strain is. Someone can call something Blueberry. They might think they really have Blueberry, but you could put five different strains of Blueberry on a table and three of them might look very similar, the other two might not look anything like the first three and, they might not be Blueberry at all. Eventually, we'll be able to say, 'Well, we've seen this strain called Blueberry a hundred times and it all has this DNA profile.'" People are not above changing the name of something because it might sell better if they bill it as a very popular strain. Then again, people may not know whether something is what they think it is. This often happens when providers run out of a particular strain. For example, a customer may return to a dispensary trying to buy a certain strain, like Blueberry. That provider may reach out to another grower to replenish his or her stock, and the customer may come back wondering why Blueberry no longer seems to do the trick.

"The reason," explains Winnicki, "is the two strains often have very different cannabinoid profiles." He's trying to identify what (genetically speaking) characteristics make up various strains. He equates it to DNA testing among dog breeders, a process in which owners run a test to determine what a dog's makeup is. "Our work is based on that technology. It's a mix of the technology they're using there and forensic criminal science technology, so that we'll be able to sit here and say, 'Ah, yes. This has Blueberry in it. And this is actually a clone that we've seen three other times that has this other unique cannabanoid profile.'"

To do that, Winnicki is developing a set of "markers." "There are thousands and thousands *and thousands* of strands of marijuana. But no one knows for sure what constitutes a particular strain. Through my research, I'm able to determine the basic properties that certain strains, like Blueberry, which is hugely popular here in Denver, possess . . . and this way, when someone comes in with something they haven't seen before, I'll be able to look at the genetics and say, 'This is a cross between Blueberry and Sour Diesel.'" Teasing him, I suggest it's akin to the human genome project, only for pot. He smiles and lets out a hearty laugh. "I am in no way, shape, or form sequencing the genome for cannabis. What we're doing is trying to get a commercial application of sequencing technology to apply to this industry. And there is some sequencing that is done, but we are not sequencing the entire genome. I don't have enough money to do that!"

Winnicki left medical school in his third year at the University of Colorado to start Full Spectrum. He got the idea for his company after one of his buddies, who owns a dispensary in town, asked him if there was any way to test bud to know what the actual psychoactive ingredients were and how much there were of them. "I knew it could be done," he tells me. "I'd been testing other products in similar ways since I was an undergrad at U Michigan." Bob wears a white lab coat, his name embroidered in navy blue thread on the right breast pocket, over a pale blue collared shirt and tie. His complexion is a little ruddy, and he seems almost boyish, with short brown hair and a bright smile.

"But you *left* medical school?" I ask.

"I just couldn't see myself becoming a doctor. I was far too interested in being an entrepreneur," he tells me.

With his savings from the sale of his first company (at twenty-eight, Winnicki had started a biotech company in Massachusetts while pursuing a doctorate in biochemistry) and a little help from his family, he got his fledgling business off the ground in August 2009. Ten months in, he's still not yet profitable, but he's close. In the meantime, he and his employees are having fun.

Leaving school to start a marijuana testing company? Wasn't that decision a little out there? "Well, that's what my ex-girlfriend thought," he says, laughing, shaking his head, and rolling his eyes. "She didn't quite go for the whole dropping out of med school thing to start a cannabis testing company, but this has major potential."

The potential, he believes, lies in consumer demand for safe marijuana. For $75, a dispensary owner can have a small sample (500 milligrams) tested via an advanced form of chemical analysis called high-performance liquid chromatography—or HPLC for short. The test determines the psychoactive components of the plant by measuring the amount of THC and other cannabinoids present. This way, a pot buyer needn't rely entirely on his broker, dispensary owner, budtender, or grower to find out how high a particular substance might make him feel—instead, the consumer can gain confirmation through scientific data.

Pointing at some equipment lined up against the far side of the room, Winnicki tells me these machines are the heart of the operation. He picked some of them up on an online auction site. "They were broken, but I was able to put them back together," he offers. (That undergrad work in engineering comes in handy.) The remainder of the equipment he purchased from either companies that were closing down or replacing their machines. "It's the exact same equipment I was using back in grad school. We bootstrapped this business into existence, which means everything was done with cost on our minds."

Pointing to a small tube, Winnicki explains how the machines take a tiny sample of the plant's cannabinoids, run it through a series of tests, and within minutes, determine the exact cannabinoid mixture of the plant. An analysis appears on the monitor of a nearby computer. The charts are read by one of the lab technicians and simplified into laypeople's terms so that someone is aware of how much THC is in the plant (3.9 percent in the sample Winnicki is running for me), what other cannabinoids are present, and whether there are any molds or other fungi in the sample.

Looking at the computer screen analysis, Winnicki points to a chart in the middle. "See this?" he asks me. I nod my head. "This shows that there is a lot of CBN." Although dozens of cannabinoids have been isolated from the cannabis plant, the most prevalent are tetrahydrocannabinol (THC), cannabidiol (CBD), and cannabinol (CBN). While THC is considered desirable, CBN tends to make an individual feel lethargic and is therefore most often consumed before bedtime. "That's the typical stoner, kind of 'out-of-it' high that people think of," Winnicki explains. Interestingly, it's created by exposing the plant to heat, and for that reason, it is most heavily associated with Mexican "ditch weed," or low-quality cannabis that's grown outdoors. Looking back at the computer screen, he shows me the spike next to the letters CBN. "This was an edible [like a cookie or a brownie] that was dropped off at the lab. What you see here is there is no THC acid and a bigger CBN peak. There's no acids from the plant material left because it was heated and all converted to the active form." Winnicki's data reveals something more. "This sample probably was heated a little too much." He comes to that conclusion by looking at the high amount of CBN in the sample. "THC acid, upon heating, turns to THC. If you heat it even more it turns into CBN. So what this tells me is this person probably baked this in the oven a little too long."

Growers, and even bakers, are flocking to Winnicki because they want to perfect their products. Bakers may want to ensure their CBN levels are not too high, while growers may want to develop higher and higher THC counts (23 percent is the highest Winnicki has seen) or possibly match the THC count with other cannabinoids to create a different kind of high. One technician in Winnicki's lab, a twenty-two-year-old recent college kid who passed up a job teaching high school science to work at Full Spectrum, told me he prefers a 7 to 8 percent THC count with other cannabinoids mixed in.

Although the equipment looks formidable, it's not the machines that do the heavy lifting. According to Winnicki, it's just him and the other scientists. "These machines are kind of like computers. They can do a lot of different things. But they need programming to do it. That's what we've developed here. A very specific method for separating cannabinoids and finding out their exact amounts. That's the art form of this science." And it's what makes his company unique. His techniques are his trade secret. "We're treating them right now as a trade secret because if we were to patent them it would be very easy for someone to take them, replicate them, and use them in their own laboratory. Whereas if we keep them as a trade secret, it allows us to have some degree of competitive advantage over other laboratories. This is not something someone could go out in their garage and do."

Winnicki's company is also working on developing an at-home test kit that would be, he says, the most scientific test of any other on the market. From a business standpoint, what is the best part about the at-home market? Although marijuana use is against federal law, the test kit contains no marijuana. There's nothing illegal about ordering a chemistry kit off the Internet and shipping it to your house.

The company's already considering new ventures, such as a certification process for marijuana growers (think of it as the marijuana industry's Good Housekeeping Seal of Approval), a "street scale" to help patients decipher the proper level of potency, and a high-caliber marijuana edibles business.

Although Winnicki's business is not yet profitable, it has certainly taken off. The company is testing over one hundred samples a week, and Winnicki has been adding to his staff. It's him, a few lab technicians, a marketing manager, and two salespeople. He promises results in twenty-four hours. "We're working around the clock right now," he says. He's running his lab with the same regulations and codes as any other, "which means," he says, smiling, "everyone who works here is subjected to random drug testing. Even me! Once a week, someone has to test."

Still, the marijuana Winnicki has on his premises is a Schedule I drug, and according to federal law, he could be arrested for having the substance. Indeed, he already had a small run-in with the law after applying for what's known as an analytical license with the DEA. He had originally planned to operate as a federally sanctioned research company and wanted the ability to handle DEA-exempt material. This material can be purchased and handled only by labs with a DEA analytical license—but, as Winnicki found out, "You can't test medicinal cannabis in the United States with a DEA analytical license." So he applied for the license, but after receiving his application, the DEA paid his lab a visit—or rather, they raided his lab. Winnicki was at the state capitol that day, preparing to testify about state senator Chris Romer's new bill to strengthen the relationship between doctors and medical marijuana patients. Shortly before he could speak, he received an

e-mail letting him know the DEA had descended on his lab. He
rushed back to his facility, where DEA agents spent the next few
hours gathering up all of the marijuana samples they could locate.

Agents confiscated the marijuana material on site—even test
tubes filled with extraction fluid that are run on the machines.
Full Spectrum's customers didn't lose out, because all of the samples had already been tested. Meanwhile, Winnicki says the company was fortunate that the DEA didn't seize his equipment.

Still, it took some time before the lab's personnel learned that
they wouldn't be arrested or charged with a crime. Such are the
hurdles Winnicki and his employees must face.

8

MODERN-DAY PIRATE
The Price of Prohibition

They called him the Marijuana Kingpin. A knack for organization, combined with a complete disregard for the law, made Bruce Perlowin a multimillionaire by the ripe old age of twenty-eight. He had $16 million in bank accounts from the Cayman Islands to Luxembourg and was spending millions of dollars more on his "business" every month. A nice boy from a conservative, middle-class family in Florida, who happened to have a penchant for smoking pot after class in high school, Perlowin grew up to create what would become the largest drug-smuggling operation in West Coast history.

It was the late seventies—decades before the U.S. pot business exploded in Northern California and long before Mexican drug cartels would develop a presence in the region. At this time, huge amounts of the drug were being smuggled into the United States from Latin America via a few select, well-financed drug trafficking operations. These smuggling rings were not only illegal and dangerous, they were highly profitable. No one was better at this business than Perlowin.

"At a certain point, I wanted to be a big marijuana smuggler," he tells me, his arms stretched out to emphasize his point, "and I wanted to bring in *as much* marijuana as I possibly could." As for the small problem that marijuana and smuggling were actually illegal? He smiles, the excitement spreading across his face. That was the best part. "I'm an *outlaw*!" he says, laughing, his blue eyes twinkling. "We saw ourselves as modern-day pirates."

At about five foot nine, with unruly, combed-over gray hair, glasses, a little extra weight around the middle, pasty white skin, and light eyes, Perlowin looks a whole lot more like an eccentric college professor from the northeast than like Johnny Depp in *Pirates of the Caribbean*. Nonetheless, the story of Perlowin's smuggling operation is filled with all of the intrigue and drama of a blockbuster Hollywood movie. "You just don't magically become the King of Pot and the largest marijuana smuggler in West Coast history. It's a process," he explains. Indeed, it is.

For Perlowin, that process began rather simply. When he was a teenager, he peddled nickel bags ($5 bags of marijuana stashed inside small, square matchboxes) at his high school in North Miami in 1968.

"In the beginning—in high school," the fifty-seven-year-old former drug trafficker reminisces, "most of [the marijuana] was coming from Mexico in these bricks with colored paper around them. Red bricks, orange bricks, green bricks, and the quality wasn't that good." Still, he (and millions of other Americans) smoked it anyway. "We were experimenting with everything. New music, new drugs, new lifestyles, new political views, new religious views, new *everything*." He pauses to take a breath, then, speaking slowly for emphasis, adds, "There were *a lot* of drugs back then, and everybody wanted them. Everybody was selling 'em." And soon, so was he. If one were the entrepreneurial type, which Perlowin was, marijuana was an easy and lucrative opportunity.

Perlowin's first taste of profit came shortly after high school when a friend offered him a little extra of his stash to sell.

Perlowin was promised a profit of $10 a pound for as many pounds as he could peddle. "This is easy," Perlowin thought, and it certainly seemed doable. Within two weeks, he had sold fifty pounds and pocketed $500. Suddenly, pot was worth more than just an after-school smoke. "*That's* when it became a business. And the lights started really clicking." And they kept clicking. Perlowin was on his way to becoming the Marijuana Kingpin.

America's introduction to marijuana was equally small time and innocent. The early colonists were major producers of hemp, the fiber cultivated from cannabis plants (now illegal to grow in the United States). In fact, in 1619 American colonists in Virginia were required to grow hemp for making paper, garments, sails, riggings, caulking, and other products. It was so valued that colonists even exchanged hemp as legal tender. By 1762, Virginia actually imposed penalties on those who did *not* produce it.[1] Even Betsy Ross's first American flag was made from hemp fabric.

Eventually the cotton gin and other machinery made hemp less relevant, and the cannabis plant began to take on a new significance in the United States—as a medical cure-all for pretty much anything. You name it, marijuana could help.. Cannabis sativa continued to make its appearance in *The Pharmacopeia* until 1942.

In the mid to late 1800s, the most common form of marijuana ingestion was not through the smoking of the substance but rather through unregulated concoctions, known as "patent medicines," mixed and sold by local pharmacists. Think Coca-Cola, Dr. Pepper, and all of the variations on those once not-very-soft soft drinks.

A lot of these pharmacist-concocted potions contained marijuana as well as more powerful, addictive drugs like cocaine, morphine, and heroin. Patented medicines were heavily marketed under lively brand names like The People's Healing Liniment for Man or Beast (now, doesn't that sound like it could cure pretty much anything?) or Dr. Fenner's Golden Relief, and they grew significantly in popularity.[2] In fact, by the late 1890s, an estimated

2 to 5 percent of the U.S. population was actually unknowingly addicted to morphine, a popular "secret ingredient" in various elixirs.[3] The ease with which these harder, addictive substances could be purchased—without consumers having any idea what they were buying—is startling. For example, Mrs. Winslow's Soothing Syrup contained 65 milligrams of morphine per fluid ounce: "for children teething," the advertisement advised customers. The Lloyd Manufacturing Company sold cocaine "toothache drops," and the 1890s Sears, Roebuck and Company catalogues—which were distributed to millions of American homes—offered a syringe and a small amount of cocaine for sale.[4] Interestingly, some of those originally patented "potion" brands still exist today, albeit with different ingredients. Some well-known names include Luden's Cough Drops, Bayer Aspirin, and Coca-Cola (sold today with less caffeine and, of course, no cocaine).

It was clear by the early 1900s that a growing number of Americans were becoming addicted to the substances they assumed were safe. Hundreds of thousands of people were using heavy drugs as medicines. Thus, in an effort to temper American addictions, the government introduced the Pure Food and Drug Act in 1906, thereby creating the Food and Drug Administration. While the Act didn't apply to the regulation of marijuana, it did enable the government to better control the distribution of opium and morphine. For the first time, the U.S. government was demanding the regulation of chemical substances.

Eight years later, the government made another attempt to control drug usage through its Harrison Narcotics Act of 1914. Although it again chose not to include marijuana in the act, it did make an attempt to regulate the recreational use of opium, morphine, and cocaine and to earn revenue by taxing the production, importation, and distribution of opiates.

Less than two years after selling his first tiny stash, Perlowin was consistently pulling in $10,000 a week *cash* selling pot—and this was in the seventies. In today's dollars, Perlowin was making more than $35,000 a week. Perhaps the most pivotal moment for the young outlaw came after a friend "did a smuggle" from Jamaica.

The friend motored from Miami to Jamaica, loaded his boat with tens of thousands of pounds of pot, and then, upon docking back in South Florida, offloaded the weed into motor homes on trailer wheels. Perlowin had arranged to secure a trailer for himself filled with seven thousand pounds of pot. He and his partner packaged the weed according to the orders they already had received. Sleeping in shifts in a rundown motel room, they guarded their stash. One would sleep while the other worked. "We worked around the clock; we were delivering ten pounds, five pounds, two pounds. To eat up seven thousand pounds of Jamaica, you know, it took a lot of individual buyers of small amounts," he recalls.

Perlowin's customers were friends from high school along with distributors and other contacts he had met along the way. Even though it was a rare and hard-to-come-by commodity, there is still a sales skill involved in peddling marijuana, and Perlowin certainly had it. He had a base of demand—and even if some customers only wanted small amounts, he still serviced them. "You must develop and nurture contacts," he advises. "You know, like any industry. If you are selling jewelry, you develop jewelry buyers and distributors. Same thing in the marijuana industry," he says, matter-of-factly. As he and his partner rushed to fill orders and make deliveries, they managed to keep their operation running twenty-four hours a day. The demand was insatiable. You could never fill it. Within ten days, Perlowin had sold all seven thousand pounds and made $100,000 in profit. By the time he had hit his heyday in California, seven thousand in ten days would seem like nothing. He would eventually be smuggling thirty thousand pounds at a time into the country and have it distributed and gone within forty-eight hours. But, in Florida, the "Jamaican deal," as he dubbed it, would turn out to be his biggest deal yet.

At the time, Perlowin was already making initial inroads in California; he tells me about the suitcases of marijuana that he flew from Miami to the West Coast on commercial airlines. "I'd just stuff it in some suitcases, check the suitcases, and fly to California." Laughing, he adds, "I'd pick 'em up at the baggage claim and walk out. I could usually get about a hundred pounds in three suitcases."

He was willing to take risks most people never would. It's who he is, he says, his arms making a large, swooping gesture to help emphasize his point. "I'm a Z personality," he tells me. "A Z personality craves excitement and adventure. You can become a race car driver. You can become a skydiver. And you can become a criminal." Perlowin chose option three.

Meeting Perlowin now, I'm struck by his near inability to understand that, in fact, he *was* taking on risk. It's almost as though he was like a child who wanted to ride a roller coaster over and over again, just because it was fun. He actually enjoyed the business and the thrill of smuggling, but at the same time, he seemed overly optimistic that he could circumvent the law indefinitely.

"It was a rush." His voice is a little louder now as he tries to convey the adrenaline he felt as he carried his suitcases full of pot onto commercial airlines. "I was taking a chance," he says definitively, then pauses adds, "But, I wasn't stupid. They didn't have dogs. They weren't searching luggage. They weren't sniffing for marijuana back then. It was so early on in the movement that it was just a normal route." As much as he enjoyed the rush, he soon began contracting out the trips. Not because he was fearful he'd be caught, but because there was just so much dope to smuggle and he was just one person. He had dozens of people, primarily women, who would fly west with his suitcases. He paid $1,000 per trip, and women were lining up by the dozens to fly marijuana to the West Coast.

How did he find women to take that risk? "Remember, the risk-reward ratio," he says. "If you got caught, it was your first-time offense. So, the risk wasn't that great. But, it's interesting," he muses, "nothing bad ever happened on those trips."

. . .

Two main ingredients fueled Perlowin's rise, and it wasn't female mules and ingenuity. The two things that keep so much money sloshing around America's drug market are one group's insatiable desire to get higher and another group's insatiable desire to keep them from getting high. For more than a hundred years the long arm of the law and the long draw of the pipe have combined to make smuggling possible.

By the turn of the twentieth century, smoking marijuana for recreational use had begun growing in popularity, in part, thanks to the sultan of Turkey who, in 1876, gave marijuana (smoked, recreational marijuana) to the United States to celebrate its centennial. By 1880, Turkish smoking parlors were opening throughout the metropolitan northeast. In 1883, H. H. Kane, writing anonymously in the November issue of *Harper's Monthly*, wrote of a hashish house in New York City on Forty-second Street near the Hudson. This is his impression of the club's entrance: "A volume of heavily scented air, close upon the heels of which came a deadly sickening odor, wholly unlike anything I had ever smelled greeted my nostrils. A hall lamp of grotesque shape flooded the hall with a subdued violet light that filtered through cremated disks of some violet fabric hung below it."[5]

Kane writes that for two dollars, he received a small pipe filled with potent marijuana. With his companion, he retired to one of the many smoking rooms that were filled with divans and pillows. He recalled, "As I smoked I noticed that about two-thirds of the divans were occupied by persons of both sexes, some of them masked, who were dressed in the same manner as ourselves. Some were smoking, some reclining listlessly upon the pillows, following the tangled thread of a hashish reverie or dream."[6]

In the early 1900s, as a result of the Mexican Revolution, immigrants began pouring across the border into the southwestern United States looking for work. Much like today, white Americans were hardly welcoming of their neighbors to the south. High unemployment combined with the immigrants' willingness to take jobs at lower wages than their American counterparts breadresentment. White Americans were determined to separate themselves from the influx of immigrants crowding "their" country. Mexicans' use of marijuana became an expedient way to criticize and stereotype immigrants. In fact, the actual word *marijuana* comes from the Mexican word *marijuango*, which means "intoxicant." The word *pot* is a shortened version of the word *potiguaya*, another Mexican term for marijuana. A *roach*, meaning a marijuana cigarette butt, is derived from the Mexican folk song "La Cucaracha" (the cockroach), which depicts Pancho Villa's soldiers running out of marijuana.

Thus, the seeds of racism had been planted. Government officials in the southwestern states of Texas and California insisted marijuana "incited Mexican immigrants to violent crimes, aroused a lust for blood and generated superhuman strength."[7] Similar stories circulated throughout the Deep South, with New Orleans newspapers depicting marijuana as most prevalent in African American communities, popular with jazz musicians and prostitutes.

In 1915, local laws began criminalizing marijuana. By 1937, more than twenty states had passed antimarijuana laws. Some states aimed to stop former morphine addicts from turning to marijuana, while others were overtly taking aim at minority populations. Despite the antimarijuana and anti-immigrant campaigns across the country, marijuana use continued to increase— most significantly with the arrival of Prohibition in the 1920s as Americans began seeking new methods to secure a high. After all, in most states, it was far easier to secure marijuana than to secure alcohol. As a result, marijuana "tea pads" similar to the hashish parlors of the late 1800s began opening their doors. These tea pads were essentially low-priced speakeasies where weed could be bought, sold, and consumed. By the early twenties, there were roughly five hundred of them in New York City. Though the Eighteenth Amendment and the Volstead Act of 1920 attempted to curb Americans' "addiction" to alcohol, Prohibition actually resulted in an increase in marijuana use for recreational purposes.

In addition to driving thrill seekers to marijuana (and far harder drugs like opium), Prohibition brought a major unintended consequence—a surge in violence. It's well known that in the Roaring Twenties, the mass production, importation, and distribution of alcohol were controlled by the criminal gangs of the underworld rather than by legitimate businesses. Gangsters, like Chicago's notorious Al Capone, generated massive profits through trade in the illegal substance. These crime organizations became deadly as they worked to defend their territories at any cost, much like the Mexican drug cartels of today.

The similarities between twenty-first-century marijuana prohibition and twentieth-century alcohol prohibition are striking. For example, both substances had widespread use despite their illegality. In addition, just as the public shows a tolerance for marijuana today (in October 2009, 44 percent of Americans favored outright legalization of marijuana for recreational or medicinal use), alcohol was accepted by the population at large in the twenties, despite Prohibition. Speakeasies became popular among the "respectable" classes, while cocktail parties became a fixture in high society—indeed, the "cocktail" itself was popularized during Prohibition, since mixing alcohol with other products could hide the taste of inferior alcohol. Another similarity worth noting is that the complex laws governing marijuana production today are much like the laws allowing the home production of alcohol (known as moonshine) in the 1920s. Indeed, section 29 of the Volstead Act permitted the production of two hundred gallons (the equivalent of about one thousand 750 milliliter bottles) of "nonintoxicating cider and fruit juice" to be made at home each year—effectively legalizing the home production of liquor.[8] Sounds a little like the state sanctioned medical marijuana growing that is now permitted, in some variation, in fifteen states and Washington, DC. Finally, doctors were able to "prescribe" whiskey for their patients much as doctors can "recommend" marijuana today.

By 1933, it was clear that Prohibition was no longer popular. Alcohol was increasingly accepted socially, and Prohibition was leading to widespread disrespect for the law as well as the growth of violent organized crime. Prohibition simply wasn't working.

• • •

In the early 1970s, prohibition of drugs wasn't working any better. Most made their way into the United States from Latin America via Miami. As heavier drugs—primarily cocaine—sped across the border, the violence level amid South Florida's drug rings spiked. It's for this reason, Perlowin says, he stayed clear of the harder drugs. "We never dealt cocaine because of the violence," he confides. "Cocaine brought with it a violent nature of people. The people who smuggle it, the people who sell it—they're all nuts. When I say 'nuts,' I mean they're violent. They want guns, they get guns, they get high, they get crazy."

Shaking his head, as if in disgust, he says, "If anyone ever had a gun around me, they were gone." Perlowin, who insists his group was nonviolent and "just a bunch of hippies smuggling marijuana," left Miami for California due to escalating violence. He insists his team never used guns. At the time, the marijuana trade had very few players on the West Coast, other than Perlowin. As a result, he wasn't competing for turf with rival gangs. He operated under the assumption that there was no need to have arms because his only enemy was the police, and "if the police are going to come after you, they're going to win. Right?" Still, on some of his teams' runs to Thailand to pick up marijuana loads there, he did insist that they be heavily armed. "There's a section that you had to go through, which is known for pirates. So they had LARS rockets with them, rocket launchers and machine guns. It's the only way to protect yourself against modern-day pirates in speedboats that come up and try to board your boat and steal your boat, your load, and your money."

But as much as it was violence that pushed him out of Miami, that was just one of the reasons. The other? Money. Profits had the potential to be much fatter on the West Coast—if brought via boat, thereby eliminating the airline flight and any additional overhead costs associated with moving drugs from Miami to Los Angeles. Meanwhile, the feds hadn't entirely caught on to the drug trafficking on the West Coast, and Perlowin knew that. He had done his homework, and the market was ripe for the taking.

His goal was simple—smuggle as much marijuana as possible into the West Coast by boat, much like he had in Miami. The only question: which ports would he be least likely to get busted in? Thinking more like a CEO than a drug peddler, Perlowin hired a research firm to analyze the strength (and more important, the lack thereof) of the feds in various ports along the coast. "I told them I was writing a book on smuggling," he says, mischief brewing in his blue eyes. He's clearly pleased with his ingenuity. "The research company compiled this entire project for me." What Perlowin discovered from that research was that the majority of the busts occurred in Coos Bay, Oregon, or down in San Diego along the two borders, the border of Canada and the border of Mexico, respectively. But there was no heat in San Francisco. San Francisco Bay was wide open. The extra benefit was that, at the time, no one would have ever dreamed of a marijuana smuggler cruising into the country under the Golden Gate Bridge. The San Francisco Bay Area was the opposite of Florida. While in Miami the feds assumed a fishing boat was smuggling marijuana, in San Francisco they assumed a marijuana smuggling boat was carrying fish. Perlowin had found his home for ground zero of what would become a massive drug trade operation. It was a billion-dollar operation that smuggled more than 300,000 pounds of marijuana into the United States. As Chuck Latting, the FBI special agent in charge of investigating Perlowin, told CNBC, "He was really big. He was, at that time, the largest that we were aware of in the FBI. By far."[9]

As Perlowin got rich off his smuggling operation, the U.S. government was stepping up its efforts to curb drug usage, primarily among the nation's youth, through its brand new Drug Abuse Resistance Education program, also known as D.A.R.E., and "Just Say No" campaigns. Each week, young students across the country would receive a classroom visit from a uniformed

police officer who would spout off about the dangers of drugs.
The program was an attempt by the Reagan administration to
resurrect President Richard Nixon's "war on drugs" (a term that
Nixon had popularized in 1971).

During the Carter administration, critics insisted that a weak-
ened drug policy (part of President Jimmy Carter's campaign
platform included decriminalizing marijuana and ending federal criminal penalties for the possession of up to one ounce of the
substance) had enabled violent Colombian drug cartels to rise to
power. By the early eighties, the Medellin cartel was funneling
cocaine into the United States at unprecedented levels.

In response, many in the Reagan administration believed the
key to dismantling the drug cartels' success would come through
diminishing the demand for the cartels' products in the United
States. It makes sense. After all, if there's no demand, there's no
incentive to supply. (Though, as I later argue in the book, the only
way to really curb drug violence is by destroying the incentive for
criminal activity through legalization.) Nonetheless, the thinking
went like this: if the Reagan administration could curb demand,
the cartels would lose power. There is only one problem. It's
awfully hard to curb the demand for drugs—and instead of actually reducing Americans' dependence on these substances, some
drug programs may have inadvertently increased it, as Ryan Grim
points out in his book *This Is Your Country on Drugs*.

According to an August 1999 article in the *Journal of
Consulting and Clinical Psychology*, twenty-year-olds who had
received D.A.R.E. classes a decade earlier were no less likely to
have smoked pot or cigarettes, drunk alcohol, used illicit drugs,
or caved in to peer pressure than the students who had never par-
ticipated in the program. In other words, D.A.R.E. didn't work.
Usage rates, it is concluded, went up, in part due to the D.A.R.E.
program's assertions that "drugs are everywhere," leading some
students to actually think they were more prevalent and "normal"
than they actually were while simultaneously reinforcing the
"forbidden fruit" theory (that kids are more eager to try something if they're told not to go near it). In addition, the dramatic

rhetoric of the Just Say No message may have even pushed students toward drugs in an attempt to fit in with the popular crowd. Whatever the reasons, the program was a failure. Meanwhile, as the administration aggressively sought to control demand, Perlowin only saw demand increase. According to him, "It was insatiable."

The day after first meeting and interviewing Perlowin in Oakland, I go out on the San Francisco Bay with him to better understand how he ran the maritime aspects of his massive marijuana smuggling operation. As we cruise out of the Marin Harbor and into the open waters, the sun beats down on us, but, in typical San Francisco fashion, the wind keeps us chilled. The jagged San Francisco skyline is viewable from one angle, the inverted orange-red arch of the landmark Golden Gate Bridge from another. To my left are hundreds of houses scattered in the Marin headlands. Back on the water, I note the dozens of boats.

From tiny racing sailboats to container ships, we're surrounded. "It's not like you're out in the middle of nowhere here," I point out. This is, after all, real civilization. Hardly the kind of place where you'd think there would be drug runners.

"No," he agrees, perched on the edge of the boat's hull. But that was okay. Blending in with the masses was part of his goal. "When our boats came in they looked a lot like fishermen coming back from a fishing trip getting ready to come into port."

To carry out the logistics of his smuggling routes, Perlowin recruited a small navy, hiring boat captains and their fishing vessels anchored in the San Francisco Bay town of Moss Landing, which had been hit by hard times. "They were fishermen until I came along and gave them a more lucrative business enterprise. They'd much rather fish for marijuana than fish for fish. It was way more lucrative." He pauses to think for a moment, perhaps debating whether he should say more, then smiles, "And *more fun!*" He paid his teams well; one captain and crew received several hundred thousand dollars for a run to Colombia and back.

Perlowin, as the brains behind the operation, managed never to put up a penny. Instead, his two partners put up the money, serving almost as venture capitalists. They would give him $300,000 for the "product." Ten dollars a pound for a thirty-thousand-pound load would go straight to the Colombians to buy the pot. Perlowin would handle all of the logistics, including the pickup of the drugs, the shipment via boat to the West Coast, and the offload. Perlowin got 25 percent of the profits for his work and split the 75 percent with the partners. "They would each split 37½ percent and I would get 37½ percent. Plus my 25." Somehow, even without putting up a dime, he always managed to come out ahead of everyone else. They went along with that arrangement, he says, because he was the one taking on the risk. He was the one with the relationships with the Colombians— after all, he had spent years working with them when he was back in Miami. His main contact in Colombia "was like my brother. You give someone millions of dollars over seven, eight years, and you have a bond." Perlowin was the one with the infrastructure of boats and crews to handle the mechanics of the deal—and he was the one who could face time in prison if it all went wrong. Chuck Latting, the special agent later in charge of investigating Perlowin, said Perlowin never put up any money himself. It was *always* other people's capital. He was quite a businessman.

Perlowin's marijuana supply came primarily from South America, namely Colombia, although he did bring some marijuana in from Thailand as well. His contacts in Columbia consisted of a main guy and a backup. So once Perlowin had established a route from Colombia's coast up to California, he began to send his fishing boats, one by one, down to a tiny village along the Latin American nation's west coast. The marijuana was flown into the coastal Colombian town by Perlowin's Latin partners from the country's pot-growing regions hundreds of miles away. They would load it on to planes, fly it over three mountain ranges, and drop it on the west coast of Colombia, where it would be gathered and stored in the village.

The boats loaded up along the docks in the Colombian village, then set sail up the Pacific Ocean, back into the San Francisco Bay. The route back was always significantly more difficult—mostly, Perlowin says, because his crews had a propensity to run out of fuel and he'd need to send another boat to their rescue. "I used to say, 'Don't you guys know how much fuel?'" Two boats would rush to their rescue—either to refuel them, he says, or to tow them in. Good thing he employed enough boats to make a small navy, with boats from the Panama Canal all the way up to Northern California. "I had them in San Diego; I had them down in Mexico. I had about twenty boats that were nothing but radio contact. To be rescue boats, if needed. That's all their job was," he remembers. In fact, he was so well fortified on the water that he boasted that if any boat went missing between Colombia and San Francisco, he'd be able to rescue it faster than anyone else.

Three weeks after making the initial trip south to Colombia's shores, Perlowin's boats would return to Northern California filled to the brim with marijuana and prepared to pass under the Golden Gate Bridge. The moment that boat passed beneath the bridge's landmark arches, for Perlowin, was the moment of truth. He takes me back through his old route, and as we near the Golden Gate, he points to his right. "This is almost exactly where the boats came in. Maybe two hundred yards that way," he tells me.

The infrastructure and logistics involved in his smuggling operation, to a layperson, are daunting. Perlowin had sixteen lookouts stationed throughout the bay area. There was one man whose sole responsibility was to radio and say, "What time is it?"—a code term to notify his team the moment he saw the fishing vessel pass under the bridge. There was a team on the water in Oakland. Another team watched the Coast Guard key points in the bay. Another group cruised up and down the bay on Perlowin's yacht, watching the fishing boat filled with pot. Every police station in the area was being watched, every scanner attentively being listened to, and there was surveillance on every boat on the bay. Perlowin's lookouts on land included several who played the part of tourists admiring the view with binoculars from a Marin cliff. They were all watching to protect the boat, its crew, and, perhaps most important for Perlowin, the boat's cargo, as it ventured home into the bay. They were there to make sure there were no problems. No police. No Coast Guard. No helicopters surprising them. It was a massive operation, and Perlowin spearheaded all of it from the loading dock.

Back on the bay, a small boat passes us, and Perlowin jumps up. "This is a lot like the boats I had," he tells me, pointing at the rusted, old fishing boat anchored in the water.

"Well, how much pot could you transport in something like this?" I ask.

He's quick to answer, and even after all these years, the numbers flow from the tip of his tongue. "Based on the size of the haul, you could put between sixty to one hundred thousand pounds in a boat like this."

"So, how much money are we talking?"

"Thirty million," he smiles, not missing a beat. *Thirty million dollars.* (Remember, that's in 1979 dollars.)

As we cruise under the Golden Gate Bridge, the memories are fresh in Perlowin's mind. Adrenaline in his voice, he warns me, "This is the time. If they're going to bust you, then this is the time. Everyone is on full alert; it's the moment of truth."

Recalling the events, he tells me how, at the precise moment the boat crossed under the bridge, Perlowin would start his stopwatch. He knew the route by heart; first a quick move around Angel Island, and within forty minutes the boat would be ready to pass underneath the Richmond Bridge. For just a few minutes, the boat would momentarily disappear from radar while in the radar shadow of the Coast Guard—and that's when it would veer left, making a quick move to pull into Perlowin's East Bay loading dock, an old ferry pier that he had purchased for half a million dollars. The dock was in a perfect location for him because it was close to the Richmond Bridge, and it was fairly desolate in that the next road was nearly a mile away. So, as he puts it, "If the police were planning to come and bust us, we had some warning because we had a lookout that stood at the top of the hill and could give us the signal." Perlowin also had two speedboats stationed under the dock that were ready and loaded in case his team needed to make a fast getaway.

As soon as the boat reached the dock, three men immediately jumped aboard and began lifting bales up from the hull onto the boat's deck. Another two men were stationed on the deck to lift the bales onto the dock. Two more men were on the dock, lifting the marijuana from the dock and into the twenty-four-foot-long truck. Three men inside the truck then stacked the pot tightly, as high as it could go, to the roof of the vehicle. It was like an assembly line. "Everyone's working as fast and as hard as they can. Nonstop," he tells me, remembering the scene. "We'd always change out the guys in the hulls of the boat, 'cause it was real hot there." Everything was done with precision—there was not a second to spare; $30 million worth of marijuana, the entire hull, needed to be unloaded and sent on its way in fifty-seven minutes. Meanwhile, as the boat was unloaded, the captain and his crew were busy refueling, getting the boat ready for its next "fishing" trip.

As soon as a truck was full, it left. Perlowin's workers radioed the guard at the gate (who was also getting a cut of the profits), the gate opened, and from the dock, Perlowin's men had a clear view of the Richmond Bridge and watched to make sure the truck crossed the bridge to its destinations.

No detail was overlooked; the men even wore heavy-duty, industrial-style overalls over their clothes in order to prevent the telltale smell of marijuana residue on them. As soon as they'd finish their last load, they'd take off the overalls and throw them in the back of the last truck. They'd have clean, fresh clothes underneath—"and no smell of the raw marijuana." These details were "all part of the planning," according to Perlowin. "All the months, all the hundreds of thousands of dollars that had been paid for the pot, for the trip, for the boat. It all boiled down to this. That moment had to work in perfect precision."

The marijuana would be driven to a stash house where Perlowin and his men would work all night, weighing the weed.

Although it came taped and wrapped, they weighed it again, put additional wrapping around it, and marked the weight on the exterior of the package. The next morning, the pot would be ready for distribution. Most went to Northern and Southern California, but a good percentage went to Oregon while some went to Michigan and Ohio. By the next day there was nothing left. That morning, Marianne, who was the girlfriend of Perlowin's brother (his own wife stayed away from his business and remained at their home in the Mendocino area), made the team breakfast. There was a big reason to celebrate—the entire load had been dispersed.

Perlowin always rushed to make sure he cleared out his inventory as soon as possible. This was important because, first and foremost, he wanted the money back from the trip (the money put up to buy the pot and the fuel and crew costs). Typically, he had three boats always in motion, with a fourth being staged. As one came up the coast from Colombia, the other went down. The third was going in either direction while the fourth would be getting ready for the trip.

Some trips went smoothly and others, not so smoothly. The trips to Thailand, he laments, were the worst. "The loads," he says referring to the marijuana his crew returned home with, "were either all wet or they were 'no high Thai.'" "No high Thai" was weed that you could smoke but wouldn't get high on. "It was terrible," Perlowin insists, but such are the struggles of a modern-day pirate. "Smuggling is fraught with all these problems because of this or that or something else." It's the same as any other import business—except that, as chief executive officer of an international smuggling ring, Perlowin had the added responsibility of trying to handle his illegal accounts.

9

WHEREVER YOU LAUNDER

How Prohibition Drains Money out of the Country

With $50 million in annual revenue, Bruce Perlowin became the biggest source for marijuana on the West Coast during the late seventies and early eighties. Smuggling massive amounts of marijuana right under the noses of federal authorities, Perlowin ran his business like a Fortune 500 Company—with himself as CEO. "In 1980 alone, I spent a half a million dollars every week. The entire year," he tells me.

That money went to everything from paying for the marijuana itself to buying stash houses, speedboats, trucks, docks, small planes, and anything else he could find that might make his business bigger and more sophisticated. For Perlowin, it was always about expansion. He was insatiable and constantly worried he wasn't growing his business fast enough. A thirty-thousand-pound run wasn't enough for Perlowin. He wanted to smuggle sixty thousand pounds. Then one hundred thousand pounds. His staff struggled to keep up with his manic and constant need for growth, and even his suppliers in Colombia had a hard time keeping up. He recognized that sometimes he asked too much. "If a guy's growing twenty-five plants every year, and all of a sudden you say, I want two hundred and fifty plants, he has to go through a process to gear up to that."

But as more money came in, so did the responsibilities. Being the King of Pot not only meant being the mastermind behind the West Coast's largest smuggling ring, which he dubbed "the Company," it also meant knowing how to hide and launder money. By the early eighties, Perlowin had $16 million stashed in bank accounts all over the world, including in Luxembourg, the Cayman Islands, the Netherlands, and Antilles. Every year, there was $50 million—actual cash dollars—that was being funneled into his business that he needed to "deal with," meaning he had $50 million that he needed to launder. Referring to his money-laundering efforts, he admits, "You need to create an entire business on just what to *do* with the cash." And he did. Perlowin had lawyers regularly flying money to the Cayman Islands for him. "In those days," he promises, "it was easy. We'd just rent a Lear jet and head to the Caymans. Everyone is going to the Cayman Islands with suitcases full of money. They [the government] didn't care." That wasn't the only place they were flying. His team was making regular trips to Las Vegas, where they'd gamble a bit in the casinos, then head to the cashiers' booths, where the tens and twenties would be changed into $100 bills. "One of the casinos knew that we were doing that. They were never really told it was marijuana money. We just told them it was fishing money." Some of these hundreds would wind up getting sent back down to Colombia to buy the pot, while others would be sent in suitcases to offshore destinations and placed in his accounts.

There were other creative ways to clean his drug money. For example, he'd make loans to Panamanian and Costa Rican corporations. One loan went to the setting up of a coffee bean plantation in Costa Rica; another went to create a several fisheries in

El Salvador (he dealt with the Sandinista government on that one, he says) and Costa Rica. "It turned out those were pretty good businesses—and they really helped our cover story," he says.

But still, this was $50 million that he needed to hide from the U.S. government, so he became increasingly ingenious. One way to clean his hundreds was to get a loan from a Cayman Islands bank (that he had money in) for a shell corporation, like "First Cabin, Inc.," that he had created to buy and sell boats. First Cabin would then lease the boat back from the company or even buy the boat. Thus, the loan from the Cayman Islands bank would provide a paper trail in the form of a loan document demonstrating how the money was wired. Without that loan, investigators would have questioned why half a million dollars was being wired into a U.S. bank account. "Getting loans from an offshore bank is pretty much the same as getting loans from a U.S. bank," Perlowin explains, "except it's my money—and I can't exactly put my money into a U.S. bank and say, 'Gimme a loan in this corporation so I can keep on smuggling.'"

"At some point, doesn't the United States say, 'Why do you have this much money in this Cayman Islands bank?'" I ask.

"But they don't know that it's me. That it's my money. They just know that there was a loan given from a bank in the Cayman Islands." Nor does the United States know that First Cabin, Inc., is his company buying or leasing the boat.

It's complicated. "And I'm just skimming the surface!" Perlowin states. "Each part of it is more intricate and detailed." In other words, running a fifty-million-dollar money-laundering operation wasn't easy. It really was like running a major company. "Of course," Perlowin says, laughing, "I had all these other crazy things that normal Fortune 500 companies don't have to do."

He didn't—and couldn't—run the money-laundering operation alone. So, he employed people whom he called his "generals." These were the guys who specialized in investing and money laundering; they were also the folks who specialized in the smuggling business. They staged boats and developed technology and radio communication, and knew a lot about surveillance. And Bruce Perlowin? He specialized in managing all of them. "It was complex what I did. It would have taken four people to replace me," he boasts, but he's right. He was involved in a multilayered, highly complex, high-stakes game. The question of how to invest his cash was the most demanding. "Do I start a coffee bean plantation down in Costa Rica? Do I buy the National Bank of Belize? Do I put money into other businesses, like fishing companies? These were big economic decisions," he reflects, admitting that he didn't have enough life experience to know which decisions would be most profitable.

The money-laundering efforts that Perlowin created stemmed from the reality that there was no way he could run around with that kind of cash and not attract attention. Another reality is that the U.S. economy was losing out on the multiplier effect. Every dollar that Perlowin could have spent in the United States would have generated more wealth for the overall U.S. economy, but instead it generated wealth for the economies of the Cayman Islands, Belize, Colombia, and wherever else he chose to invest. Perlowin's customers were in the United States. They bought the illicit drugs from him—but instead of him turning around and spending in his home country the money they gave him, he spent it in Latin America. Thus, Latin America was the real economic beneficiary of Perlowin's illicit enterprise. It's an example of how prohibition can quickly suck money out of the U.S. economy.

That said, while the majority of money wound up in offshore accounts, some of Perlowin's profits did find their way into the local economy. He, unlike many drug entrepreneurs I've met, has a flair for drama—and he liked to spend. The country was mired in recession, but Perlowin had no idea. "I was totally oblivious to the fact that the country was in a recession in 1980. I was doing great. I had all this money." That's because the demand for marijuana, even in a tough economic environment, didn't change at all.

In fact, Perlowin spent so much money in the town of Ukiah, California, where he settled with his wife, Becky, and their new baby boy that he became a legend. Even today, when you say his name, people know exactly who he is and even seem to revere him.

The next day, Perlowin takes me and my production team several hours north of the Richmond offloading pier to his former residence. The home is located at the dead end of a long, desolate street, miles from any real civilization in Ukiah. My producer had called ahead and spoken to the current owner of the property, who told us we were free to film the house—all we needed to do was ring the bell and the current renter would give us access. The owner promised to alert the renter. We had planned to have Perlowin provide us with a tour of the home he built during his heyday.

The King of Pot's former home sits on 246 acres and is more like an armored fortress than a house in the country. The home comes complete with a steel-lined, bulletproof, computer-controlled central command post, a complete automobile repair shop, a $100,000 gym, sixteen surveillance cameras with night-vision capability, a fourteen-line telephone system, and a spiral staircase, which can be electrified to repel potential intruders, leading to the master bedroom. (Perlowin was especially proud of that staircase. He described it to me in great detail but insisted he never had to use it.) The residence is shielded from the road by an eight-foot-high faded brick wall. You can't see in, and you can't (well, at least not that we were aware of) see out. We did manage to peer through a black iron gate at the end of the driveway and caught a glimpse of an overgrown front lawn. I also spotted four or five cars in the driveway, so it seemed someone was home—yet, there is no bell to ring, the shades on every window are drawn tight, and the iron gate is locked shut. All we can do is wait and hope that someone spots us.

Well, some*thing* spots us. After waiting by the gate for nearly ten minutes (with a frustrated producer repeatedly dialing the home's owner on his cell phone), a large dog charges toward us, barking wildly. Nearing the iron gate, the dog stands on the other side, his jaw gnawing on the rods. Moments later a good-looking young man, likely in his early twenties, with short blond hair and blue eyes, dressed in a polo shirt and tan shorts, walks slowly toward us. Remaining behind the gate, he asks what we want. My producer gives him the quick synopsis: We are here for a documentary on marijuana. We want to take some video of your home because it used to belong to the West Coast marijuana kingpin—the kingpin is here with us, and it might be nice because he can show you some of the home's special features. Plus, your landlord said it was okay.

The young man graciously smiles and in a thick southern accent explains it isn't possible. "I'm not renting a two-hundred-acre property in the middle of nowhere so that a TV crew can show up at my doorstep," he tells us, matter-of-factly. Reaching into his pocket, he pulls out a leash. Leaning down, he snaps it on his dog's collar, turns, and walks back down the stone driveway toward the house.

We decide it's worth at least shooting some video of the home from the street. (After all, the street is public property, so it's entirely legal, and the shot will be valuable to us as we recount Perlowin's story to the viewers.) We even have a special camera with us—known as a jib—which enables us to keep the camera on the street and move it high over the brick wall, thereby guaranteeing our shot. As the cameramen set up the gear, I stand in the road talking with the producer. Suddenly, just two feet to my right, I hear a crashing noise. Then another one, and another. Within seconds, we realize that someone on the other side of the wall is throwing heavy stones up and over in an attempt to hit us. If one of us gets hit in the head, the consequences will be serious. I move toward our van for protection. Opening the door, I hoist myself up onto the front seat, then, while clinging to the top of the door, I arch my body forward and stand on my tiptoes, struggling to see over the brick wall. There's only one way to describe what I see: bizarre.

A tall, thin man with long, gray hair and a scraggly beard is scaling the back side of the brick wall. I assume he is trying to hide from the camera's view. Occasionally, he stoops down to the ground and scrambles for a rock, which he then throws backward over the wall in an attempt to hit us. One of the cameramen shouts out, "Knock it off, that's not cool, man," but the gray-haired man is unrelenting. Perhaps hoping to get a better angle for his throw, he darts back toward the house and hides himself behind a tree. He leans out, preparing to aim. For a split second, our eyes meet. His are wide open—paranoid. He throws another rock, and I duck back into the van. The camera crew quickly disassembles their gear, and we vacate the premises. We did manage to get the shot, and Perlowin has a theory: "These guys have got to be growers. You don't get this upset unless you're hiding something." And he made another point: why would a southerner in his early twenties be renting his old fortress? "You put two and two together," Perlowin says, his lips curled up in a smile, "and it tells you there's something illegal going on here." He should know.

Perlowin built his $3 million fortress deep in a Mendocino forest. He used rare, exotic woods, including mahogany, teak, and rosewood that he imported from Belize. Who knows if it still has an entire automobile repair shop; voice-activated, electronically controlled drapes; a steel-lined, bulletproof, computer-controlled central command post; solid-gold bathroom fixtures; and carpeting worth $70,000, custom made by the same firm that made carpeting for the White House? He even planted thirty thousand Douglas fir trees on the hillside and installed an automatic sprinkler system to keep them watered. At the top of the mountain on his property, Perlowin created a heart-shaped garden. It was so steep to get there that the gardeners needed helicopters to fly the plants to the area. The garden was complete with an eight-foot deer fence that had a red ribbon woven through it to outline the heart along with red flowers that would bloom alongside it.

It's no wonder, with a house (or should I say castle?) as crazy as this one that Perlowin became a legend in Ukiah. He employed half the town just to construct the place. Interesting, Ukiah is now home to one of the biggest pot-growing regions in the country. It's no wonder Eric Sligh told me he grew up hearing stories of Perlowin. "Everyone looked up to him," he said. "I mean, he was the real deal. He was legendary—like a pirate."

Perlowin's business had no real competition at the time. He was the only game in town for dealers looking to supply their customers. But while Perlowin was raking in the cash, FBI agents at the San Francisco field office were startled by a sudden increase in the amount of pot on the streets.

Special Agent Chuck Latting was assigned to the case. You can't quite get more different from Bruce Perlowin than Chuck Latting. While Perlowin was an alternative, hippie-style outlaw, Latting was a clean-cut, broad-shouldered former marine. "We knew there was marijuana coming in. We knew it was on the street," he told CNBC in an interview for *Marijuana Inc*. "We knew there was somebody that was bringing it in. We had NO idea who it was or where it was." Still, Latting knew this smuggler was a major operator. "He was making a million dollars a month," Latting insists. "No question in my mind."

There was also no question in Latting's mind that Perlowin's operation was not as nonviolent as Perlowin tried to insist. According to Latting, Perlowin surrounded himself with questionable people—people who could be very violent in the event someone tried to rip off their dope.

There's also no question in Latting's mind that the wires in Perlowin's head didn't quite connect. According to Latting, Perlowin was nothing more than a first-class manipulator who tried to con people into believing he was going to make them rich. But he was, Latting concedes, an ambitious entrepreneur at a time when entrepreneurs could service the marijuana trade. But, "Bruce could never survive in that trade today," he insists. "Bruce would last a week or two until somebody just cut his throat or something." Latting's contempt for Perlowin is still strong after thirty years. Perlowin is the kind of guy who just gets under

Latting's skin. As Latting puts it, one of Perlowin's biggest problems was that he talked too much. He was a kind of Robin Hood legend in his own mind—paying poor people in Colombia to grow for him, paying out-of-work fishermen to make drug runs for him up and down the coast while simultaneously providing the California market with plentiful access to marijuana. On top of all that? Latting complains that Perlowin was just "too flamboyant." Remember the heart-shaped garden on top of the mountain on Bruce's property? Latting says that garden was the result of a marital squabble. According to Latting, "He spends fifty thousand dollars to have some gardeners come in and put a garden that you could see up on the hill." This garden sits on the hill to be admired, he says. "He wanted people to drive by and say, 'Well, look at Bruce. He's even put that up there for Becky Lynn.' Most guys would take their wife out to dinner if she were mad. So, to put a rose garden on a hillside in Ukiah, well, it tells you something about Bruce's mind."

Perlowin's operation would thrive for four years after he built that rose garden (he and his wife split up shortly thereafter), and every lead Chuck Latting tried to uncover on the West Coast's Marijuana Kingpin turned out to be a dead end. But soon, the authorities got their big break. It wasn't exactly the kind of break you'd think FBI field agents would anticipate getting.

Latting was working in the San Francisco field office one afternoon when he received a phone call from another FBI operative in Mendocino County. The agent told Latting that a notebook had been left behind at a local Denny's restaurant, and the notebook was packed with information on marijuana smuggling. Everything Perlowin was doing, from laundering money through his First Cabin, Inc., corporation in the Cayman Islands to his fisheries in Costa Rica and the Dominican Republic to his routes to and from Colombia and the location of various stash houses and distributors was listed in the small black notebook.

That notebook, Latting soon discovered, belonged to none other than one Bruce Perlowin. How's this for a cruel twist of fate and a rather un-James-Bond-like ending to Perlowin's *Pirates of the Caribbean* existence? The King of Pot had left his smuggling notebook at a Denny's in Mendocino County. It proved to be his undoing. It provided investigators with intimate details about his organization. "The book was the key to everything we found. It even had financial reports in it." What perplexes Latting is that he cannot imagine how anyone who was competent enough to be running such a major organization could walk away and leave his most prized possession sitting in a booth at Denny's. But Perlowin did, and the evidence sent him to federal prison for nine years. It was just one of fifty convictions in the case.

Latting was proud of his work on the case and says how happy he was that he arrested Perlowin, although, "I just wasn't happy that he got out."

Perlowin's smuggling routes are long gone, and Latting is retired. Perlowin, who got out of prison in 1991, says he's found a new line of work; he's started a business designed, he says, to take advantage of medical marijuana by providing "solutions"—though it's unclear what that means. His company is thinly traded on what's known as the "Pink Sheets," an over-the-counter market, not a stock exchange like NASDAQ or the New York Stock Exchange. Typically, volumes are so extraordinarily low in this market that if just one person makes an investment in the company, its stock can soar. These companies are closely held, extremely small, and barely trade (which means you may be able to buy stock in the company but forget trying to sell it), and there are no listing requirements. In other words, anyone can go out and get themselves listed on the Pink Sheets. Even a company started by a convicted felon. Still, you've got to give Perlowin this: after all these years, he's still trying.

"Knowing what you know now, knowing that you went to prison for nine years as a result of this, would you do it again?" I ask him as we look out onto the bay that both made—and broke—him.

"Even though it was illegal. I loved it. It was fun. It was a big rush." He pauses briefly, admiring the view. "Yes. I would live my life exactly the way I lived it. It's been an amazing run."

POT OF GOLD

Sizing the Potential Market

There is no logical basis for the prohibition of marijuana. It's absolutely disgraceful to think of picking up a twenty-two-year-old for smoking pot. Even more disgraceful is the denial of marijuana for medicinal purposes." College-age stoner? Worked-up hippie? Try one of the fathers of economics.

Nobel Prize–winning economist Milton Friedman, perhaps the greatest free-market capitalist of the twentieth century, was the economic thinker on the front lines of the United States' cold war with communism, having served as an economic adviser to President Ronald Reagan. He was also a lifetime dues-paying member of the Marijuana Policy Project and an advocate for ending marijuana prohibition for both fiscal and moral reasons.

At ninety-two years old, Friedman became the lead signature on a list of 530 economists from around the country publicly endorsing Harvard economist Jeffrey Miron's report on the potential economic gains of legalizing and taxing marijuana. *Forbes* magazine described Friedman's move as "[a] founding father of the Reagan Revolution has put his John Hancock on a pro-pot report."[1]

Alongside Friedman's are signatures of economists from such major universities as Cornell, Stanford, and Yale. They advocate for "an open and honest debate about marijuana prohibition," writing, "We believe such a debate will favor a regime in which marijuana is legal but taxed and regulated like other goods." The basis for their conclusion stems from Miron's work in which he calculates that ending marijuana prohibition would result in a nearly $14 billion savings for taxpayers. The savings would be generated through a $7.7 billion reduction in the amount of money law enforcement spends prosecuting, investigating, apprehending, and jailing marijuana users and $6.2 billion via new tax receipts generated from the sale of the product. Miron's study in 2010, examining the implications of legalizing *all* drugs, concluded that states that legalize marijuana could yield over $20 billion in tax revenues and reduced enforcement costs.

The Marijuana Policy Project, which funded Miron's study, calls $14 billion in taxpayer savings significant. But, in reality, across an economy as large as the United States', $14 billion, while significant, is a small dent in the national budget. Nonetheless, as Miron tells me, "It's *still* fourteen billion dollars. There's no reason to waste that kind of money. Especially now." Moreover, by fully legalizing marijuana, medicinal patients who need the drug would finally have easy and cheap access. (One dispensary owner whom I spent time with in Denver told me it was "heartbreaking" to have to charge patients who were scrambling to get by on social security and coping with a terminal illness. "It can run hundreds of dollars a week for some people. The one major benefit to legalization," she says, "is maybe their health insurance would help them cover the costs—and maybe the costs would become more manageable.")

Of course, in an era of widespread shortfalls in state budgets, some states don't want to look a potential gift horse in the mouth. As California spirals deeper and deeper into debt, marijuana advocates, lawmakers, and general citizens alike are searching for ways to meet the \$20+ billion shortfall. The budget woes in California (and a number of other states throughout the country) are primarily the result of poor economic planning. Local governments' budgets ballooned during good times, resulting in bigger salaries and benefit packages. Despite the worst recession since the Great Depression, some state governments, including California, are still on the hook for plenty of overhead. Meanwhile, in California, it is doubly hard to institute any meaningful changes to the government's budget, in part because of the political landscape. California voters dictate how state money should be spent through the referendum process. Ironically, the same ballot-box process that gave rise to medical marijuana usage in the state, and may even sanction full legalization, is a main reason the state is struggling to make ends meet—and thus, may even inadvertently be a reason the state is willing to turn to marijuana as a revenue source. The chief justice of California's Supreme Court, Ronald M. George, didn't hold back when he argued in an October 2009 speech before the American Academy of Arts and Sciences in Cambridge, Massachusetts, that the state's referendum process has "rendered our state government dysfunctional." He denounced the use of the voter-driven process of changing state laws as out of control, with voters deciding on how parts of the state budget will be spent to how farm animals are managed—and everything in between.[2]

Marijuana advocates have been building momentum toward legalization ever since California became the first in the nation to legalize the drug for medical use in 1996, and advocates are seeing their biggest opportunity yet thanks to marijuana's promise as a significant source of revenue for the state. California advocates insist legalization would be an even greater boon to state coffers than Miron suggests. In California, the National Organization for the Reform of Marijuana Laws (NORML), the lobbying group in favor of legalization, concluded that legalization could yield between \$1.5 billion and \$2.5 billion per year in California alone. That's a lot of cash—especially for a state with no clear path to fiscal health.

California's Dale Gieringer of NORML calculates his numbers based on consumption rather than the overall market value of the drug. The author's reasoning for this is clear: most analysts on both sides think the price of marijuana would fall if it were legalized. The idea is that the elimination of risk would reduce the price not only at the consumer level but also at the production level, sending the price of an ounce into freefall. After all, it's not especially expensive to produce, and larger, more professional farms and processing facilities could result in savings as well.

Of course, no one really knows. As we've seen from Denver dispensaries, real businesses have a much higher overhead than informal ones. Complying with regulations from the IRS, the FDA, the EPA, and others adds to the administrative costs. Nonetheless, a transparent marketplace would theoretically reduce those frothy profit margins on pot since there would no longer be the threat of jail time for a grower, a producer, or a seller. Although popular gourmet strains might still command relatively high prices, overall prices would have to decrease. Gieringer says that to determine how much money a state could make by taxing marijuana, one must examine the expected demand. He suggests a basic $1 "per joint" excise tax that would likely result in $1 billion worth of revenue to the state. (His assumption, based on household drug survey numbers, is that one billion joints would be sold annually.) Meanwhile, the total value of marijuana retail sales (which would include joints and raw bud for cooking and vaporizing) is estimated at between $3 billion and $5 billion, which would yield an additional $250 million to $400 million in sales tax.

Gieringer estimates marijuana leveling off at current Dutch prices. Even in the Netherlands, there is no legalization of production, and did you know that it is still technically illegal to sell pot in Amsterdam's numerous coffee shops? (It's merely tolerated.) As a result, Dutch prices are still artificially high. Only a fully legalized production, distribution, supply, and legal consumer market would drive prices lower. The Netherlands's system for marijuana distribution is similar in many ways to the systems present in California and Colorado, and thus, Gieringer's calculations on price may be accurate because dispensaries and production facilities, even if regulated and taxed by the state, are still vulnerable to federal arrest.

The Dutch permit a limited number of small, domestic producers to distribute marijuana, just as some production and distribution is permitted by U.S. states. For example, as I mentioned in earlier chapters, Colorado individuals are permitted to grow marijuana plants for their own medicinal use—and they're also permitted to grow for others, provided the pot is medicinal and the grower is a "designated caregiver." The Dutch growers complain that even though they're licensed and trying to operate as legally as they possibly can, they struggle in a similar way to state-sanctioned dispensaries and pot shops in the United States. That's because they're tolerated by local police but still not fully legal. Even though the marijuana industry appears out in the open (judging, at least, by the number of neon marijuana signs in Amsterdam), because marijuana suppliers are not officially sanctioned by the federal government, they complain that they are forced to operate partly in the shadows. The price they pay their suppliers for marijuana is artificially high because large-scale production is not permitted. In addition, coffee shop owners are still subjected to raids at the whim of the police. Many coffee shop owners point to the Checkpoint Café as evidence of the risks they take.

Checkpoint, the country's largest marijuana shop, was fined nearly $15 million for breaking the country's drug laws. Police seized more than two hundred kilograms of cannabis on the premises, more than the locally "tolerated" amount. According to current Dutch regulations, coffee shops can hold up to eighteen ounces of cannabis in the store at any time. When police busted Checkpoint, they found 440 pounds of cannabis, enough, authorities said, to qualify Checkpoint as a criminal organization.

Checkpoint, a highly popular spot located in the southern town of Terneuzen on the banks of the Westerschelde River, near the Belgian border (hence the name "Checkpoint"), sold drugs to three thousand people a day, making it the equivalent of a drug megastore. Many customers specifically crossed over the border just to buy Checkpoint's legendary marijuana and hashish. Signs (put up by the town) directed customers toward the infamous coffee house. The town was so seemingly tolerant that it even built a parking lot nearby to reduce congestion caused by the overflowing traffic. Despite all of this, the town's mayor came out against Checkpoint, saying that the verdict "underscores the importance of tightening the tolerance policy and administering it better."[3] In recent years, local residents had complained about the clientele Checkpoint was attracting to their neighborhood, and authorities, which had known about the shop for years, decided to take action.

The owner of Checkpoint, identified as Meddy W. (no last name as a result of Dutch rules on privacy) was arrested, along with fifteen staff members. The owner got sixteen weeks in prison, while the sentences for the other workers and suppliers ranged from warnings (for those who rolled joints) to six-week jail terms.

As a result of an illegal production chain (catering to cartels) and no actual laws protecting coffee shops (although they're allowed to hold eighteen ounces of marijuana on site, there are no official laws permitting them to exist in the first place), Dutch consumers pay inflated, black-market prices for pot. This kind of quasi-legal, quasi-illicit market caters to underground activity (including the bribing of officials to stay in business) and thereby doesn't give consumers a fair price for the product. As a result, it's important to remember that in a fully legalized environment for marijuana the price of the product would decline dramatically because there would be no clandestine production operations or cartels trafficking the drugs, and suppliers would not need to worry about being shut down.

The savings associated with enforcement is also factored into NORML's numbers, with a predicted $156 million in law enforcement costs associated with arrests, prosecutions, trials, imprisonment, and helicopter surveillance that would no longer be needed. Gieringer predicts that saving the cost associated with state prison for 1,400 marijuana prisoners ($25,000 per person annually) will result in a yearly savings of $35 million in California alone, while marijuana felony arrests cost taxpayers $8.7 million (12,000 arrests at $732 per arrest). Still, NORML is a little optimistic in its assumptions of savings from no-enforcement costs. After all, legal does not mean unregulated. Authorities would still need funding to ensure a fair marketplace and make sure that marijuana was not being distributed to underage minors. Illegal cartels and traffickers trying to sell "under the table" might be less incentivized to operate because their profit margins would be greatly reduced, but authorities would still need funding to pursue any holdovers that might exist. Additional funding would also likely need to be reserved for educational purposes to better inform the public of the risks of marijuana.

Some of NORML's other debatable numbers come from predictions of drug tourism, with Amsterdam-style coffeehouses generating jobs and tourism. It's unclear how much tourism and industry around marijuana would be generated in California. If additional states followed California's example and legalized marijuana, then it would become an increasingly competitive landscape.

Just as Las Vegas is the gambling headquarters of the United States, perhaps Oakland, San Francisco, or Los Angeles could make a run at being the "Pot Smokers' Paradise." But, would residents even want that? There would likely be pushback in most communities—Las Vegas grew up in the middle of nowhere for a reason. Moreover, it's unclear whether there would be a significant move toward marijuana "tourism." Although Portugal decriminalized drugs, there has been no surge in the number of tourists traveling to Lisbon or Madeira in order to get high. Although it's definitely questionable whether California would attract a drug-seeking clientele, the NORML study provides some interesting insight into what legalization might mean for an economy that has already nearly sanctioned it.

Should tobacco companies or pharmaceutical companies take over the marijuana market? What is the actual size of the national market? It's clear, as I mentioned, that there is a market for pain.

Twenty-five percent of the U.S. population is said to suffer from daily pain. But the market for marijuana (for both recreational and medicinal) use is debatable. There are estimates that suggest the current amount of marijuana being sold in a given year is worth as little as $10 billion and others that predict it more than ten times that, or over $100 billion. The way the market is calculated depends on how the market is approached. Do you measure the supply or the demand? They each provide different answers.

Judging marijuana from the supply end, it's clear that the market is huge. The supply is clearly huge. According to the DEA's National Drug Intelligence Center, more than seven million plants were eradicated in 2007, up 120 percent from 2004. Meanwhile, the DEA seized 1.5 million pounds of bud in 2008, up 149 percent from 2005. Let's assume that each outdoor plant yields, on average, about 7 ounces worth of pot (these aren't like the Mendocino pot plants that yield up to two pounds each) and the average indoor plant, which is generally smaller, generates an average of 3.5 ounces per plant. If marijuana were selling for $400 per ounce, then an outdoor plant would be worth $2,800, while an indoor plant might generate $1,400. Then, these numbers would indicate that the market is enormous. Consider this: $6,400 a pound times 1.5 million pounds means the DEA alone theoretically confiscated more than $9 billion worth of pot (although it's unlikely the marijuana the DEA confiscated was all good-enough quality to generate a $6,400 per pound price tag). Keep in mind, the authorities are only eradicating or confiscating a small portion of the total amount available, and yet they may also be eradicating wild marijuana or so-called "ditch weed" that no one is tending and would never make it to the market, thus, it makes it difficult to rely on these numbers. Nonetheless, using these supply-oriented estimates, the illegal marijuana market may in fact be worth $100 billion or more.

Another way to model the market is based on demand and consumption; how much marijuana do people ingest or smoke? For this number, it's critical to look at surveys like the U.S. Department of Health and Human Services Substance Abuse and

Mental Health Administration's National Survey on Drug Use and Health. According to the survey, 6 percent of the U.S. population (above the age of twelve) uses marijuana in any given month. Of those monthly users, 15 percent consumed marijuana on a daily basis. (These numbers may seem large, but an interesting comparison comes from alcohol and tobacco numbers; 52 percent of Americans over twelve consumed alcohol in a given month, while 28 percent have used tobacco.)

Based on this data (and a price point of roughly $6,400 per pound), the market is thought to be somewhere between $10 billion and $40 billion, although again, some see it as high as $100 billion. It really all depends on the price and the number of people smoking pot.

Per the aforementioned estimates on the number of Americans consuming alcohol and tobacco, a 2009 study by Standard & Poor's indicates that the alcohol and tobacco market is worth $263 billion—$188 billion for alcohol and $75 billion for tobacco. Some economists like to use these numbers to model out what a potential marijuana market might look like, because it certainly serves as a check on values. How could marijuana possibly be worth $100 billion when tobacco is worth just $75 billion? Well, in fact, while marijuana may be worth more now than tobacco, if cannabis were legal and allowed to be sold in a free and fair marketplace, it would be worth a whole lot less since the price of the produce would be seriously reduced. That's one reason, when states consider putting a tax on marijuana or if the federal government should ever consider putting a tax on marijuana, if they want to truly reap some cash, they would need to add a tax to each joint, or each gram of pot sold. It would be critical that they not overdo the taxation, however, because if they did, they would simply force the industry back underground.

If marijuana sailed past its legal and cultural hurdles, it's possible that the major agricultural and tobacco companies might consider a move into the pot business—becoming the Jack Daniels of weed. Archer Daniels Midland, ConAgra Foods, Philip Morris, and British American Tobacco already have agricultural infra-structure in place. Why couldn't fields of corn or fields of tobacco become fields of marijuana plants if the product is deemed profit-able enough? These companies certainly have the know-how to manage massive crops. The tobacco companies have the added benefit of already having access to delivery and distribution, and it's logical that many of the same stores that purchase their ciga-rettes would also purchase their marijuana joints. A bill in New Hampshire that would legalize recreational marijuana for adults over the age of twenty-one says that if a businessperson applies for a license to sell marijuana and the state does not issue a qualified applicant a license within thirty days, then the applicant—if he or she holds a valid *tobacco* license—"shall be deemed the retailer." A similar bill in Rhode Island pushing for full legalization requires that if the state does not provide a licensed distribution system within a year and a half of the bill's enactment, then tobacco retail-ers would be allowed to sell the product.

Although California already has licensed dispensaries, many believe the tobacco distribution system would work best for mari-juana should it be legalized.

Of course, a big question when considering legalization is, how might the nation's top pharmaceutical companies react to losing billions of dollars worth of market share for prescription painkill-ers? Probably not well. That is, unless they were the ones to secure the patent on a drug that could reshape how a nation treats pain.

Big Pharma has a history with marijuana. Prior to mari-juana becoming illegal in 1937, Eli Lilly sold marijuana as an herbal extract for use as a painkiller, antispasmodic, sedative, and "exhilarant." Until 1942, it remained listed in *The United States Pharmacopeia* (a reference book for drugs) despite seeing a decline in use in the late 1800s. Harvard psychiatrist Lester Grinspoon, who is considered the most eminent scientist on the subject of marijuana (and who says he has been smoking it for forty-four years), writes in his book *Marihuana: The Forbidden Medicine* that the decline was fueled partly as a result of more predictable and thus, effective, pharmaceuticals coming to the market (although many of them, he points out, later proved to have serious side effects) and because modern hypodermic syringes could deliver faster pain relief using opiates. (That's because opiates were soluble while cannabis wasn't and still isn't.)

Still, if marijuana becomes legal, it could discourage scientific studies of THC by Big Pharma because, after all, why bother going through the expense of trial testing, as well as the hurdle of FDA testing, if there will be no market because people choose to smoke weed instead of ingesting a synthetic version of the plant? Legal marijuana would be significantly cheaper than a synthesized, highly scientific, and researched drug and thus, Big Phama would theorectically have little incentive to research new possibilities. Given that fifteen states have already approved medicinal use, you'd think their incentive to study the effects of THC would have diminished, and yet, according to a National Institutes of Health report, the number of cannabinoid (these are the compounds found in marijuana) drugs under development in the United States climbed to twenty-seven in 2004 (the most recent data available) from just two in 1995. Clearly, they still see possibilities in the marketplace, despite the recent push for medical marijuana at the state level.

Some analysts speculate that a THC drug would have more appeal, especially among young people for whom smoking is often regarded as taboo. They believe a pharmaceutical company that can create a pill, a patch, or a spray in which dosages are controlled and can demonstrate fairly immediate effects would have a huge market. The biggest reason that Big Pharma keeps spending money on researching a pharmaceutical equivalent to marijuana is that they're hoping to discover combinations of the THC molecule that are even better than what's available through the underground market. Dr. Grinspoon told Shelly Schwartz in an article for CNBC.com's Special Report "Marijuana & Money," "If pharmaceutical firms could develop a product that reduced the [so-called] munchie effect through biochemistry or one that could be injected to patients intravenously, which is not possible today because marijuana is not water soluble, they would make a fortune."[4] Still, it might render numerous other pain medications obsolete, as the professor acknowledges. "They know that marijuana is so versatile in treating everything from Crohn's disease to nausea to premenstrual syndrome," he tells CNBC, "that once it can be produced in an economy of scale and it's free of prohibition tariffs it would sweep all these artificially expensive pharmaceutical products on the market aside."

Several synthetic THC drugs are in the pipeline, including Sativex—a medical cannabis extract made from the marijuana plant by GW Pharmaceuticals—which is already approved as an oral spray in Canada.

Let's assume, for a moment, that the United States is definitely on the road to legalization. You don't have to discuss the future of the pot market for very long before it's logical to assume large corporate players will be lying in wait to take over the market. One only has to look back to the history of alcohol to see how this has played out before. The next time you double down with a shot of Jack Daniels, you should know that the brand is owned not by a man named Jack in Tennessee but by Brown-Forman, a global company with revenue of more than $2 billion and worth more than $12 billion. Brown-Forman was in existence before Prohibition and actually survived those years by applying for, and being granted, one of only ten licenses given by the U.S. government during Prohibition to bottle alcohol for medicinal purposes. After Prohibition ended, Brown-Forman and other corporations acquired smaller distillers to create large conglomerates. Today it's hard to find an alcoholic beverage that's not part of a large company: you like bourbon but want to drink a more authentic brand—good luck. Jim Beam and Maker's Mark are owned by Fortune Brands, a large company that sells everything from bourbon to golf equipment and home construction supplies. Okay, so maybe you should swear off liquor and settle on wine. How much more authentic can you get than a quaint winery, maybe like one of my favorites, Stag's Leap in Napa. That's actually owned by

Altria, which owns the Marlboro cigarette brand, Copenhagen and Skoal chewing tobaccos, and some really great wines owned by its Chateâu Ste. Michelle business.

The point is simple: if consumers really care about something and are willing to pay for it, eventually it will turn into a big business opportunity. It is not, however, likely to occur with marijuana for a very long time. First, of course, the product is not legal for recreational use, and the medical marijuana market is too small to affect large corporate players. Second, even if the product were to become legal, it would still have reputational issues that would make it off limits for larger consumer-oriented companies for many years. This is a situation even different from that of alcohol following Prohibition, as alcohol had been widely used and accepted in mainstream society for all of its history, with the exception of the decade or so of Prohibition. Marijuana is still seen by many as unsavory and counter to accepted culture and would be likely to remain so for many years even if it were legalized.

What you might see is something similar to what happened in the distillery business. The most successful purveyors of marijuana might buy up competitors with strong brand recognition and keep the brand name intact. Over time, these large players would get larger and own more and more brands and, assuming marijuana were made legal, over time society will likely become more accepting of marijuana use. So what you might see in fifty years is a very large pure-play pot company offering their leading brands like Purple Kush and Sour Diesel, and run by a man in a suit whose main goal isn't catching a buzz but driving his stock higher on the New York Stock Exchange.

11

Downers

Not Everything Is Coming Up Roses

It's a dark, cool December morning in Clear Lake in Northern California, 2005. Shannon Edmonds and his wife and two teenage boys sleep soundly in their modest green-and-beige house on 11th Street. Shortly before 4:20, the sound of glass shattering awakens the household. Three men, masked and covered with hoods, have smashed through the glass in the downstairs sliding door in the rear of the house. The intruders rush inside. One clutches a shotgun, pointing it straight in front of him as he runs through the pitch-dark living room, with only the shimmering moonlight to act as his guide.

Edmonds's sons, who were sleeping in a downstairs bedroom at the time of the break-in, jump out of bed. They run to stop the men, but the intruders push past them, threatening to shoot. Running into the master bedroom, one masked man flips on the lights. Another reaches for the homeowner, Shannon Edmonds, pulls him up, and points the shotgun in the man's face, screaming, "Where's the fucking weed? Give us the motherfucking weed! Give it to us *now*!"[1]

The father grabs the barrel of the shotgun with both his hands and tries to wrestle it from the perpetrator. It's clear to him that the shotgun is not loaded. As the wrestling ensues, the third intruder jumps on the mother, knocking her out of the bed and throwing her to the floor. He punches her in the face, screaming, "Give us the weed! We want the fucking weed!" Terrified, the teenagers race into the parents' room; one is holding a baseball bat, poised for battle. The boy begins hitting his mom's attacker with the bat, desperate to get the man to stop punching his mother. The bat distracts the robber, and the boy succeeds in setting his mom free. Barely able to stand, she grabs a cell phone from her bedside table and escapes into the bathroom. Slamming the door behind her, she locks it and frantically dials 911.

As his wife was being attacked, Edmonds was still wrestling over the shotgun. He can barely hear the intruders amid their swearing as they repeatedly yell, "Where's the weed?" Out of the corner of his eye, Edmonds spots one of the intruders with the bat—the man had somehow managed to get it away from the boy. Edmonds watches as the intruder hits his stepson in the head with full swings. Once, twice, then three, four times.

His adrenaline surges. Mustering all his strength, Edmonds throws the intruder he has been wrestling to the floor. Jumping over the bed, he grabs the man with the bat and tosses him out of the bedroom. Edmonds runs to his gun safe and pulls out a nine millimeter, semiautomatic Browning pistol.

The terrified mother is still hiding in the bathroom. Crying to the 911 operator, she pleads, "Please help me! The guy's got a gun! We need an ambulance, they smashed my son's head in with a bat!"

Edmonds glances down at his gun. The magazine is partially in. He pushes it the rest of the way. Releasing the safety, he cocks it. The intruders are trying to push their way back into his bedroom, so Edmonds opens the door and points his gun straight at them, threatening to shoot. Immediately, they spin around and start running, their backs to the homeowner. He chases them through his house, and when they get to the living room Edmonds fires as the intruders try to escape out the glass slider. A bullet hits the door handle but misses the men. Edmonds, still running after them, slips on some shattered glass outside the slider. He falls, and the gun accidentally fires, hitting a nearby tree. Squinting his eyes, Edmonds struggles to see the intruders in the dark.

Edmonds pulls himself up and starts running down the street after the hooded men. He shoots two of the men in the back. Rashad Williams, age twenty-one, is hit twice. Christian Foster, age twenty-two, receives five bullets. Both fall to the ground. By the time the police arrive on the scene, Williams is lying dead in the middle of 11th Street and Foster is dying in the bushes, just twenty yards away. The third man, Renato Hughes, twenty-one, had escaped Edmond's range.

In the end, the teenage son wound up with permanent brain damage due to the head injuries he sustained while getting hit in the head. Hughes was sent to jail, and Foster and Williams lost their lives. The police confiscated the marijuana.

It was clear to Jon Hopkins, the district attorney who prosecuted this case and later recounted the details of that night to CNBC, that the three intruders had driven north from their homes in the San Francisco Bay Area with the intent to steal marijuana. The Edmonds family grew marijuana for medicinal purposes, and ultimately, more than five pounds of pot (with a street value between $15,000 and $18,000) was recovered from their house.[2]

"Somebody among these three men had information that there was marijuana in the home," Hopkins said. "I think they thought that there was a lot more."[3] This is often the case because many "medicinal" growers are growing far more than the state permits. Local authorities are either powerless to react or simply choose to look the other way. Some residents, like Larry Puterbaugh, are fed up with the community's tolerance for pot.

• • •

Puterbaugh, a resident of Mendocino County since 1974, has lived in his current house since 1991. According to Puterbaugh, his neighbor Memo Parker began growing marijuana in 2000. Parker, Puterbaugh insists, grew marijuana in such massive quantities that "the smell became quite intense. So intense that there were times where we could not even come out in our backyard. It was really sickening. We had to keep our windows closed at all times, even when we wanted fresh air."

Memo Parker's garden allegedly swelled to hundreds of plants. Marijuana leaves were even spilling over a six-foot-high fence into Puterbaugh's yard. "This guy was growing more than two hundred plants. And the plants that he was growing are not little plants. We're not talking plants," Larry emphasizes, "we're talking *plants*! Very large plants. Six-, eight-, nine-foot plants. Come on. The peace and love thing that we were all thinking of in the sixties, that's gone. It's now commercial dope growing. It's now commercial dope selling. It's drug dealing."

Eventually, the smell of weed (combined with the tempting sight of marijuana leaves spilling over Puterbaugh's fence) attracted a criminal element to their street. "He came right by our bedroom with a loaded gun," Puterbaugh says, referring to a would-be robber who attempted to steal Parker's marijuana in 2004. "He jumped over my fence in order to rip off my neighbor's crop!"

But the robber didn't succeed. In what has become a much-told story in this small community, the would-be robber and Parker got into an altercation, and the intruder shot Parker in the hand before running from the property.

Four years later, in 2008, authorities caught up with Parker and his garden for the second time. (In 2006 he was acquitted of charges of marijuana cultivation due to a hung jury.) This time, Parker was arrested for having almost three hundred marijuana plants growing in his house and more than thirty pounds of processed marijuana. Community members, including Puterbaugh, cite Parker's and Edmonds's cases as prime examples of the violence that accompanies marijuana growers. Yet, while these cases are being talked about, there are many more growers falling victim to robberies that are never reported. Growers, who are engaging in illegal activity themselves, are adverse to reporting crime because, as they know, the government will not be an ally in helping them recover an illegal drug.

While some people think the backyard nature of the industry is a good thing, it's clear there are plenty of negatives. Zoning happens for a reason: people don't want to live near anything other than residences. Think of the term NIMBY—not in my backyard. Pot growing, because it's illegal, naturally attracts a criminal element. There's no reason pot should take over suburbs.

Some Mendocino County residents worry about the growers themselves. A former military man and his wife, who requested I not use their real names because they feared retribution, told me they were so disturbed by their community's marijuana growers that they feared for their lives.

The couple is surrounded by growers at both their main house in Mendocino County and at their vacation house two hours north, also in Mendocino County. I spent an afternoon with them at their year-round property, a small, gray-shingled house located off a dirt road and nestled in one of the Emerald Triangle's beautiful valleys. As we stroll through their backyard garden filled with walnut trees, the sun beaming through the tree's branches, the sixty-five-year-old former serviceman (whom I will call John) gives me the lay of the land, so to speak, beginning with the house next door. "This is the house where they were growing," he says, pointing to the brown house on a hill to our immediate left.

"They" refers to a twenty-some-odd-year-old couple with a toddler who had moved in just over a year ago. Within three months of the family moving in, John tells me, they had set up their greenhouse. "It was ready, and it was loaded [with plants]. The lights were always on," he says, referring to the bulbs that power an indoor hydroponic grow.

"They were people from Washington State and they had cars going up and down the driveway, from Nevada and Utah, Washington and Oregon, Arizona." He pauses as he thinks back to that hub of activity, then adds with emphasis, "*All night long*." Pointing toward the gravel path alongside the brown house to our right, John says, "You can see that's the driveway right there—and you can see my bedroom's right there." His hand motions back toward his own house, which stands barely thirty feet from the grow house. "And these cars were going up and down. All night," he says again, shaking his head. Those out-of-state cars, John suspects, likely contained marijuana buyers who were there to purchase the couple's stash.

Not only could John and his wife see (and hear) their neighbor's greenhouse, they could smell it. The stench would leak out from the greenhouse and hover over their property on hot days, John remembers—that is, until his complaints to local authorities were eventually heeded and the neighbors were raided and arrested. The house is for sale now, and John is praying another grower doesn't move in. But, even with the new neighbors gone, John has a serious drug problem. Motioning toward the field at the far end of his property, he tells me that that neighbor, the one up on the hill, grows too and "you can smell his crop periodically" when the wind blows to the east. Still, these grows, he assures me, are nothing compared to the grows—and most especially the growers—at his ranch in the North Country.

"I have about eight growers that surround me up there. At every border of my property, there's a grower."

"Can you see it? The marijuana?" I ask.

"Oh, you can see it," he says, chuckling, then turns serious. "I have to drive *through it* to get to my place."

His place is a family ranch house about two hours north of the Ukiah area. John has been vacationing there since he was four years old. "We go up hunting, fishing, camping, swimming. We do a lot of barbecuing and sitting around, relaxing, enjoying things. The kids go in the river and swim."

But in the last few years, the area has morphed into a very different community from the one John knew growing up. One by one, his neighbors sold their land to marijuana growers until he was the only nongrower left. Some growers grow two hundred plants, some grow five hundred, and others, he tells me, including his next-door neighbor, who recently threatened to kill him, are growing thousands.

The threat, the former military officer explains, is a result of his refusal to sell his property as his seven other neighbors did. The grower moved to the area from Louisiana more than a year ago to develop a commercial marijuana farm, and according to John, "It wasn't a month after he had bought his property that he started making offers to buy my place." John's property is considered highly valuable to growers because it is home to the only water source in the vicinity, with a half-mile of river frontage. John's sister tried to explain to the Louisiana grower that the ranch was a family property and thus her brother would never sell. The grower's alleged response was, "I hope your brother does not come up to your place anymore, 'cause I have people from New Orleans here to take care of him." To John, that was a death threat.

"I went to the sheriff," he says, the anger in his face brewing as he recounts the story. "And the next time we visited the property, the deputy sheriff escorted me."

"He went over," he says, referring to the deputy sheriff, "and talked to the neighbor. The neighbor said he was only saying it to harass me and that he wouldn't really do it." Meanwhile, "he had over three hundred marijuana plants sitting there!"

"Well, what did the sheriff do about those?" I ask. (Three hundred plants far exceeded the then legal limit of twenty-five and would have made for an easy arrest.)

"He just kind of ignored it." John sighs. "He said they'd be back to get the marijuana later, but he never put the marijuana in his report." John speculates that the deputy sheriff chose not to document the three hundred plants because the grower was paying people off in his department.

John's refusal to sell his property means that life is increasingly difficult for him and his family at their homestead. It's so bad that he won't walk anywhere on the property without a gun. "I carry a gun because my life has been threatened. And I carry it because of the dogs." Indeed, his sister and he have both faced run-ins with the neighbor's Rhodesian Ridgebacks. There are also Pit bulls, Rottweilers, and Great Danes in the vicinity, guarding other growers' crops, and John is fearful that one of his young nieces, nephews, or grandchildren might be attacked by the vicious dogs that roam the nearby property. The fear and the threats have transformed his life. "You don't allow the kids to go off anywhere by themselves anymore," he explains. "They stay right there at the cabin unless you personally take them to the river and guard them." But even then there are problems. He tells me of the time his neighbor followed his sister and her three young daughters, all between the ages of four and twelve, to the river. While the group swam and played in the water, the Louisiana grower stood along the riverbank and disrobed. He then dove into the river—naked. "What kind of person does that?" John asks me, the disgust all over his face.

It's that kind of harassment that the former military man says has him rethinking his plan not to sell. "I've spent every summer since I was a kid up here. Our kids love the place. I can't imagine ever leaving, but if things continue the way they are, I'm probably going to have to." The reality is he'd stand to make a lot of money thanks to the new crop of choice. "The marijuana growers have driven the price of the land up, considerably. The land value is inflated thanks to the marijuana. But use-wise, it's made it difficult to use. I personally can't go up there without another person being with me anymore. I used to go up and spend a week at a time, walking, doing things. Can't do that anymore." His voice trails off as he looks toward the sun setting against the backdrop of the walnut trees.

While John and his family held their ground, others have had to move on. Literally. When I met Joy and Sam Tucker, they were in the middle of packing up all of their belongings. The parents of two young children, the Tuckers were fed up with their community and its dependence on pot. They had decided to move from Mendocino County to Sacramento to start a new life. Potter Valley, California—the picturesque, small, rural town in Mendocino County that they lived in and Joy had grown up in—had, quite literally, gone to pot. "I don't think people realize how open it is," Joy complains. "We were at a soccer game this fall, and you can look up in the hills and you can see the plants. When you drive back from town, off the freeway, you can see the plants. It's everywhere."

The plants are so common that residents joke about "another Christmas tree lot" when they spot a grow. Let's just say, there are plenty of Christmas trees for sale near the Tuckers. "We have thirteen gardens within a mile radius of our house," Joy tells me. And those are only the ones she could see and count.

If you had to pick an all-American type of family from a lineup, the Tuckers (complete with their two kids, a dog, and a cat) would probably be it. Sam was the plant manager at the local propane company, and Joy worked as the elementary school principal. The couple had hoped to raise their children and make a life for themselves in Potter Valley. Yet, despite good jobs, a beautiful home, and plenty of family and friends nearby, the couple had wrestled for months over how long they could remain in Potter Valley before marijuana—and the violence associated with it—would force them to leave. At the elementary school where Joy worked, she says it was increasingly common to open a child's backpack and immediately smell marijuana.

"It's disappointing," she says with a sigh, referring to her move south to California's state capitol. "I mean, my children were going to have the same teachers I've had going through high school, and there are a lot of good things that happen [here], but we're just not going to take that chance with the kids."

The couple lament that even some of their best friends, who swore they'd never be involved in the trade, have succumbed to the lure of huge profits. The temptation is as strong as the pot that's grown in Mendocino County. "Hey, it's profitable," Joy rationalizes. "They don't have to have the regular nine-to-five jobs, and they can make a lot of money doing it."

The Tuckers question how the prevalence of marijuana in Potter Valley will affect its children. "As adults, we can make decisions as far as whether we want to be part of that type [marijuana type] community or not," Joy tells me. "But the kids, they have to make decisions all the time for alcohol and drugs no matter where you live. We understand that. But the *amount*, and the *acceptance* of marijuana in this area. . . ." She trails off, shaking her head in disgust. Everyone is growing, she insists. "It used to be more of the lower class that dealt with it, and it was hidden." But now, "upstanding and prominent" citizens are growing.

Meanwhile, the increasing number of robberies and aggravated assaults tied to marijuana has convinced the Tucker family that Potter Valley is no longer a place to raise a family. According to statistics from the FBI, Mendocino County's 2008 crime rate hit its highest level in a decade with 551 violent crimes recorded, up from 2007's 544 recorded violent crimes.[4] The increase (which bucks the state and national trend) is attributed to marijuana-related violence, and authorities insist the recorded number represents a small fraction of the actual violence occurring in the region. That's because individuals who are engaging in illegal activity (growing more plants than the state allows, for example) are hesitant to report a robbery or any other drug-related crimes, so the actual statistics are misleading and reflect fewer crimes. The nearby community of Willits, California, in Mendocino County has a murder risk rate that is nearly twice as high as the rest of the country.[5]

The complexity of the laws surrounding marijuana in California is one reason the Emerald Triangle has become such a violent outpost. According to Mendocino County sheriff Tom Allman, who grew up in nearby Humboldt County, it wasn't always like this. Allman, a man of medium height with salt-and-pepper hair and a matching mustache, tells me marijuana was always just a part of life and "part of our culture." His father ran a small store in Garberville, and many of the customers, he admits, were probably marijuana growers. "We just didn't talk about it." That's how it was.

Of course, that was before pot became so profitable and there-fore so critical to the community's economy. Indeed, weed is so ingrained in the community's culture that nowadays "there's this perception that marijuana is *actually legal* in Mendocino County," Allman admits. "People say, 'Well, you can't arrest me, because it's Mendocino County. And I thought it was legal.'" He pauses, shak-ing his head. "We're not an island."

Still, the complexity of county, state, and federal laws has emboldened resident growers to feel as if Mendocino County, is, in fact, an island (or at least a county) unto itself. I remind him that county law enables residents to grow for medicinal or recre-ational use. "It sounds like it's fairly legal here to me," I challenge.

"Well, last I checked, Mendocino County is still part of California. And California laws are enforced in Mendocino County. So just because county voters think that you should be able to grow twenty-five plants recreational, that doesn't mean a state's not gonna come in and say, 'We're going to enforce state law here.'"

But California law allows growing, I remind him.

"Prop 215 is strictly dealing with medical marijuana in California," Allman counters, referring to the referendum passed by California voters in 1996 permitting the growth of six mature or twelve immature pot plants for medicinal purposes.

When I push him on federal law, he seems inclined to defend California. "A number of states allow marijuana in one way or another." And this is part of the problem. One law says one thing, another says something else—and another, in this case federal law, says another thing entirely.

So where does that leave Allman as sheriff? With a lot of leeway. Allman goes after some growers, but not others. "I'm enforcing the law on *commercial* growers," he tells me. "Commercial growers who are saying, 'Well I have six doctors' recommendations.'"

The ability to grow fairly openly, and quasi-legally, has meant an influx of out-of-towners flocking to the county like bees on honey. Allman complains that these out-of-towners are migrating for "get-rich-quick (on pot) schemes."

The get-rich-quick schemes involve massive grows—indoor, outdoor, and even below-ground grows. According to Allman, an increasing number of growers are going underground, literally, using twenty- to forty-foot cargo containers (similar to the containers hauled by eighteen-wheelers on the highway). According to authorities, an excavator typically digs a hole in the ground and the containers are buried, subsurface. In 2008, the Mendocino County Sheriff's Office found a large parcel of land, northeast of Willits, California, with more than five thousand marijuana plants growing on it—according to law enforcement, the grower was producing a crop every seven weeks, *underground*. The grower used expensive, powerful, and sophisticated generators to power the garden, Allman explains. "These were four-hundred-kilowatt generators. Cost over three hundred thousand dollars each. And he had two of them. They were running the lights."

The Sheriff's Office issued a warrant for the underground grower's arrest, but when I spoke to Allman, it was believed the grower had fled to Latin America with his family.

Sky-high profits are attracting not only people from all over the country hoping to strike it rich in California's marijuana boom, they're also attracting the highly organized and deadly Mexican drug cartels. The cartels have learned that it is easier to grow in California's Emerald Triangle than to smuggle pot across the border.

The lure of massive profits, combined with complex laws and an overwhelmed local, state, and federal government, is a drug trafficker's recipe for success. Moreover, the pot grow in Mendocino is considered superior to Mexican-grown pot in terms of both quality and, most important for these drug lords, profits. For example, a pound of weed grown in Mexico's Sinaloa state might earn a Mexican farmer $25 and sell on the streets of Phoenix for $550 a pound.[6] This represents a significant profit margin, but one hardly as grand as that of Northern California's bud. High-end marijuana grown in the Emerald Triangle or in

U.S. hydroponic grows yields as much as $6,500 a pound while costing perhaps a few hundred in upfront costs. Thus, the cartels have learned that it's more profitable to grow in the United States—they're closer to their end market, and there is no need to smuggle drugs across the border. It's a better product and a streamlined delivery system. Therefore, it's good for business.

According to government sources, cartels are sending workers to the region to set up and maintain massive grows. The workers hike inland for miles searching for a water source and open land to grow their plants. They create hidden, sophisticated irrigation systems that enable the marijuana plants to grow as high as twenty feet. In 2007, authorities seized more than five million plants, worth an estimated $20 billion in California alone—and a large percentage of these plants were being grown outdoors. According to authorities, 60 percent of the Mexican drug cartels' revenue comes from marijuana—and today, the majority of their marijuana is being grown on U.S. soil.

My documentary team visited one of these so-called Mexi-grows in Mendocino County with Butch Gupta, the county's deputy sheriff, who works under Allman. Gupta heads one of California's airborne "search and destroy" squads. He and his team fly in helicopters over the region's vast hillsides searching for hidden pot gardens in the rugged wilderness. It's dangerous work. "Somebody's gotta keep their head up all the time, looking around," he warns, "'cause you never know. If they're armed, if they're gonna shoot you."

Standing in the middle of a Mexi-grow, he points to the marijuana plants. Growers are "uncanny at finding water. Anywhere. It almost seems like they can find it in the desert," he says. The grows' irrigation systems are impressive. Despite the remoteness of the gardens, they're jerry-rigged with plastic tubing and fertilizer.

Clearing the brush with his feet, Gupta leans down and pulls out a black plastic water tube. "They'll run this poly-pipe for miles." It's common since the garden needs a regular water source. It's not unusual to find a pipeline that meanders for miles, hidden along a hillside, before it hits a garden.

Growers employ migrant workers or send illegal immigrants into the region where they'll live for months, tending (and guarding) the gardens. Campsites, or living quarters for the growers, are common and are most often made with pieces of plastic tarp. It's typical to see garbage strewn throughout the living quarters—empty cans of food (the labels all in Spanish), fertilizer bags, and even guns are sure signs a worker is living in the grow. In 2007, Gupta's team seized more than one hundred guns from outdoor grows.

"A lot of Hispanic growers will come in on these tracts of land that are not heavily used by the public and embed themselves by building these little camps and garden systems," Gupta explains. "They're the only ones that are willing to get out here, go the distance. They'll walk four, five miles to get to this place to set this up, because no one else is going to be here."

One thing legalization is supposed to do is move the whole industry into the light of day. Cutting Mexican gangs out of the equation is arguably the greatest benefit legalization could bring, but it hasn't happened yet. In some ways, they've just gotten bolder.

It's an issue the Bush administration's drug czar, John Walters, was trying to fight, and something that continues to plague the current administration. On a media tour of Mexican grows in the Sequoia National Forest, Walters complains, "This is a place that is supposed to be preserved wild habitat. It's being turned into a place that cultivates poison and pays for people who kill as a matter of doing business."[7]

Indeed, the cartels currently dominating the marijuana trade (including the Federation, the Tijuana Cartel, the Juarez Cartel, and the Gulf Cartel) are considered some of the deadliest in the world. In the three years since President Felipe Calderon declared a war on drug gangs in December 2006, more than eighteen thousand people have been killed in Mexico. These murders are being financed primarily through marijuana.[8] According to the White House Office of National Drug Control Policy, U.S. marijuana sales accounted for more than 60 percent of the cartels' annual revenue, totaling $8.6 billion out of $13.8 billion in 2006.

One of the most brazen and deadly drug-related attacks occurred on March 13, 2010, when a thirty-four-year-old American named Lesley Enriquez attended a child's birthday party in the El Paso border town of Juarez, Mexico, with her husband and infant daughter. Four months pregnant, Enriquez worked at the U.S. consulate in Juarez. Her husband, Arthur Redelfs, was thirty years old and a detention officer for the El Paso County Sheriff's Office. The family left the party in the early afternoon. Moments later, they were gunned down in a hail of automatic weapon gunfire emanating from a Ford Explorer that had pulled up alongside them on a main thoroughfare in Juarez. Enriquez and Redelfs died. Their baby girl was found in her car seat, crying but unharmed.

That same day, another guest at the same birthday party was gunned down in a similar fashion. Mexican citizen Jorge Salcido Ceniceros had an American wife who also worked for the U.S. consulate in Juarez. He was also assassinated in his car, while his two young children traveling with him were injured.

Authorities believe the drug gang Los Aztecas, the "enforcement arm" of the Carrillo Fuentes drug cartel, was behind both attacks. Luis Astorga, a leading authority on drug cartels at the National Autonomous University of Mexico, told the *Washington Post*, "Marijuana created the drug-trafficking organizations you see today. The founding families of the cartels got their start with pot. And marijuana remains a highly profitable business they will fight to protect."[9]

As drug traffickers scramble to protect their precious routes into the United States, Juarez has become one of the most deadly places on earth. More than 2,600 people were murdered there last year, and in the first three months of 2010, an additional 500 were killed.[10] This in a city of just 1.3 million people.

Herein lies the problem. By making pot illegal, authorities are effectively inviting violent cartels to do business in the United States. Huge profit margins to grow marijuana in this country, along with the economic incentives to protect markets and smuggling routes into the United States, mean that as long as pot stays illegal, the cartel-related violence on both sides of the border will not end. Think of it like this: With no regulation in place, the U.S. government has forced the marijuana industry underground. Since buyers, sellers, and producers get no protection from the law, they resort to violence to resolve their disputes. Cartels are experts at taking the law into their own hands.

It's no wonder that the cartels (and even some mom-and-pop growers) have no interest in seeing marijuana legalized in the United States. In fact, this is probably the one area in which the drug lords and the DEA are united. After all, if marijuana were legal, the Mexican drug cartels would have no reason to grow—and if marijuana were legal, the DEA would lose a huge portion of its budget and mandate. Legalized marijuana production means the profitability margins of pot would shrink, "real" producers would step in, and the violence associated with an illegal enterprise would be significantly reduced because cartels and illegal growers would be unable to participate in the real economy.

It's an argument that is gaining traction worldwide, including in the hometowns of the world's biggest drug cartels. In February 2009, former Mexican president Ernesto Zedillo, former Colombian president César Gaviria, and former president of Brazil, Fernando Henrique Cardoso, teamed up to advocate for the reform of the U.S. drug war, declaring that the war on drugs has failed. They advised the United States to break from its "prohibition" policies, arguing that making drugs illegal has only increased violence and resulted in crammed prisons. Urging the United States to legalize marijuana, they said legalization would enable the system to treat addicts, rather than punish them. In a report they issued, they recommended a move toward decriminalizing marijuana and said current policies are rooted in "prejudices, fears and ideological visions" that prevent real debate.[11]

Former Mexican president Vincente Fox took his critique of the war on drugs a step further in the spring of 2009, insisting that it is time to consider legalizing drugs. He called for a debate on taxing and regulating drugs as a strategy to deal with violence in Mexico. Strict controls and high taxes would be part of legalization, according to Fox, and although levels of drug use might remain at current levels, the violence that accompanies the drug trade would be significantly reduced, as the cartels would no longer control the supply. "I am not yet convinced that that's the solution," he said. But he added, "Why not discuss it?"

In fact, the legalization of marijuana is increasingly being discussed. Much as the prohibition of alcohol was repealed during the Great Depression in an effort to curb violence and gain some much-needed tax revenue, the federal mandate against marijuana is being called into question by more and more states.

Legalization is a move the Tucker family would welcome. Sam Tucker theorizes that if marijuana "were grown like vineyards grow grapes, if it were a USDA crop and completely legal, then that would work." But part legal, part illegal is the recipe for the current disaster. "It's still kind of hidden, yet not hidden. You can see it growing here and there, but there are all sorts of locked gates and fences."

12

FREE FOR ALL

The Great Portuguese Experiment

At the turn of the millennium, while the rest of the Western world was preparing to cheer in a prosperous new year, officials in Europe's Iberian Peninsula were seeking solutions on what had become an epidemic. By 2001, Portugal had fallen into crisis. Fully 1 percent of the country's population was addicted to heroine.

"We have ten million inhabitants in Portugal," Dr. Joao Goulao, Portugal's drug czar, explains as I sit across from him in his Lisbon office. "And in the middle of the nineties, we have one hundred thousand people hooked on heroin, with a lot of problems, infectious diseases, mainly AIDS." Addiction was so rampant that parts of Lisbon had become open-air heroin markets where drug users would shoot up in broad daylight on the streets. In 1985, when first lady Nancy Reagan visited Portugal to meet with leaders from the Association for Prevention of

Toxic Substances, Portugal's chief government drug expert, Dr. Maria da Graca Pocas, informed Mrs. Reagan that there had been "a spectacular increase in the use of heroin here in the last year and a half and a spectacular increase in the amount of drugs entering Portugal as well." Da Graca Pocas said that just two years earlier, in 1983, only 14 percent of drug users being treated at a Lisbon clinic were heroin addicts, but by 1985—just two years later, 83 percent were addicted. It was clear that heroin addiction had spun out of control, and the country's youth were the most vulnerable. At that time, the government estimated that at least eighty thousand young people between the ages of twelve and twenty-five were drug dependent, out of a total population of young people numbering two million. In the following years, the problem grew increasingly worse.

By 2001, Portugal had the highest drug addiction rate in Europe. European newspapers were running stories depicting the drug horrors of Lisbon's worst slums, with one ghetto in particular depicted as the "most shameful neighborhood" in all of Europe.[1] The ghetto in question was Casal Ventoso, a squalid mass of tents, smack houses, and shacks made from wood and ribbed pieces of iron, where an estimated eight hundred drug addicts lived on one of the city's seven hills. The ghetto's main street was known as Portugal's "Drug Supermarket," where anything and everything was for sale. Every day, up to five thousand people from all walks of life would pour into the community to buy their daily fix of heroin or whatever other drug they desired.

According to London's *Evening Standard* newspaper, the slum was "stinking of garbage and human waste, the shanty town is a labyrinth of filthy alleys winding past wood-and-metal shacks and grubby tents. A teenage heroin addict lies oblivious to the squalor, his head burying deep inside his jacket."[2] Six months later, in the summer of 2001, the government bulldozed the infamous Casal Ventoso ghetto, and literally and figuratively never looked back.

• • •

Why did Portugal develop such a significant drug problem in the first place? Many point to the abrupt openness of society and an increasing population of prisoners.

Prior to the country's revolution in 1974, Portugal had been a closed society. For more than half a century, the fascist, authoritarian dictatorship, known as the Estado Novo regime, had ruled Portugal. As a closed society, everything from travel to drugs was off limits. Dr. Goulao remembers how, "prior to the revolution in 1974, we had almost no problems with drug addiction and illicit drug use." One theory suggests that the moment the country was liberated from its oppressive regime, there was a sudden desire among the people to try new things, and with that came the onslaught of powerful drugs like heroin. In the coming decades, drug addiction would become the number one problem haunting the country, and the government began enacting harsh punishments against drug users in an effort to stem the epidemic. "People kept getting sent to prison, yet the problem grew worse and worse," laments Goulao.

Portuguese prisons were packed with addicts, as Alvaro Gil-Robles, the Council of Europe's Commissioner for Human Rights, reported on his 2003 visit. Gil-Robles concluded that prison populations and escalating drug use were connected, writing that "the conditions in Portuguese prisons have been a concern of the Committee for the Prevention of Torture (CPT) for some time, with visits in 1992 and 1995 already identifying shortcomings with respect to material conditions, drug abuse, and inter-prisoner violence in a number of Portuguese prisons."[3]

Regarding drug use, the report concluded that drug abuse was a serious problem, affecting 50 percent of the prison population.

> In addition to the security concerns that result (4 persons died as a result of inter-prisoner violence in 2002), the pervasive consumption of drugs is becoming a serious

health hazard. Some 300 persons are already known to be HIV positive and its further spread is inevitable unless attempts are made to address this problem. High suicide rates (20 in 2001) reflect these concerns.[4]

The study's author links the nation's drug problems to high prison populations, writing that "over-crowding in prisons ill adapted to the types of inmate detained, have made it difficult to control drug abuse and the resulting inter-prisoner violence." Referring to the drug problems, he says, "Many of these problems have their origins in serious over-crowding."[5] For example, there were 14,060 prisoners in Portugal's prison even though the country only had the capacity for 11,603 people, resulting in 21.2 percent overcrowding. Meanwhile, there were approximately 130 detainees per 100,000 inhabitants, meaning that Portugal's prison population was well above the European Union average of 80 per 100,000 inhabitants. "It is clear," Gil-Robles writes, "that policies to reduce the number of prisoners and increase the capacity of the prison service are necessary."[6]

The World Health Organization's (WHO's) Regional Office for Europe concludes that HIV/AIDS is linked to overcrowded prisons and drug use. The WHO says HIV infection rates in Portuguese prisons reached 11 percent of the inmate population in 2000 (compared with a less than 1 percent, on average, of HIV prevalence rates among prisoners in Western Europe). Dirty needles still made their way into open-air heroin markets in the country's most notorious slums. Thus, HIV and other infectious diseases continued to spread. Indeed, since Portugal began reporting its HIV cases in 2000, it has demonstrated one of the highest HIV rates in Europe. In 2004, the country reported 280.5 new cases per million people—more than any other Western European country. HIV rates were considered a direct result of massive drug addictions.

Despite the challenges Portugal was facing with drugs and HIV, the country was ahead of its time in connecting the dots and linking the idea that HIV rates, intravenous drug usage, and stiff penalties for addicts were all related. It may not seem like rocket science, but few governments are willing to acknowledge how drugs and prison are connected, let alone act on those assumptions.

Portugal did both. In 2001, Portugal decriminalized all drugs.

Back in Dr. Goulao's office, I'm thinking out loud, trying to understand why a government would roll the dice on decriminalization when there was so much at stake and so much to lose. "So, one hundred thousand people, *One hundred thousand people*," I repeat, "all hooked on heroin, and you guys decide to just *decriminalize* all drugs?" I ask. I'm impressed but also amazed. I want to know how Goulao managed to convince the government to go along with such a revolutionary idea. After all, decriminalizing all drugs had never been done before. It was counterintuitive. It was a serious gamble.

"Yes," he answers me simply, nodding his head and adjusting his glasses.

"A lot of people are probably thinking, 'my goodness, they just decriminalized all drugs. Are they crazy?'"

The doctor laughs as he remembers that yes, a lot of people were thinking exactly that. Indeed, leading up to the day the policy took effect, the rest of Europe was highly critical of the Portuguese gamble, calling the plan an example of "ultraliberal legislation." There was a tremendous amount of fear that Portugal would turn into Amsterdam on steroids and foreigners would flock to the Algarve to shoot up heroin, snort cocaine, and smoke marijuana. Paulo Portas, the leader of the conservative Popular Party of Portugal at the time, predicted the country would entice tourists with the promise of "sun, beaches, and any drug you like," and drug tourism would ruin the country. He insisted, "There will be planeloads of students heading for Portugal to smoke marijuana and take a lot worse, knowing we won't put them in jail."[7] Other politicians worried that the country would see huge spikes in drug usage resulting in a slow deterioration of society.

Even the British Embassy was worried about the implications. In an interview with the British Broadcasting Corporation conducted shortly after decriminalization took effect, a spokeswoman for the British Embassy in Lisbon voiced her fear. "We are concerned," she said, "that some people may see the new law as a license for a free drug holiday."[8] At the time, the embassy complained that it was actually fielding calls from young Brits wanting to know when they could come to Portugal to "shoot up."[9]

"We decided to do that because we had to change something," says Goulao. Translation? Portugal was so desperate that it was willing to try anything.

Decriminalization, the theory went, would enable the government to focus on reducing the demand for drugs rather than reducing (and policing) supply. Drug users were a critical group to target; by 1998, more than 60 percent of drug-related arrests were linked to personal use or possession rather than to the sale or possession to sale.[10] Money that was spent on law enforcement and prisons could instead be used for treatment and prevention education. In the late nineties, the country created the Commission for a National Drug Strategy, on which Goulao was a member. His Commission issued a report concluding that criminalization drove resources away from treatment, deterred people from seeking help for addiction, and thus contributed to increases in drug usage. For this reason, the commission suggested that Portugal implement a radical approach and decriminalize the use of all illicit drugs. Elected officials agreed. In 2000, the federal government's Council of Ministers, which had reviewed the Commission's study, issued a policy consistent with the report. On July 1, 2001, history was made. A new law came into being. Portugal became the first country to formally decriminalize drugs. This meant that personal possession of all drugs, including heroin and cocaine, would no longer be a crime (although selling or trafficking remains a criminal offense).

Goulao admits that he was somewhat surprised—although clearly pleased—that the federal government followed his recommendations pretty much in their entirety, especially given that they were, at the time, considered so drastic. The Portuguese government is lucky it listened to Goulao. The United States, when confronted with a similar opportunity in 1972 when President Richard Nixon's Shafer Commission recommended an end to marijuana prohibition, failed to follow researchers' recommendations.[11] Still, the legalization of all drugs is just not what people would intuitively think should happen.

It's two-thirty in the morning and techno music blares onto the crowded street outside a packed club in the heart of Lisbon. The road is dark, and the only light emanates from a corner street lamp on the cobblestone sidewalk. The air is cool despite it being the end of May, but that doesn't stop hundreds of young people from gathering outside, a drink in one hand, a cigarette in the other. These club goers are very young. As in thirteen, fourteen, fifteen years old. Welcome to the Saturday nightclub scene in Lisbon, Portugal.

A study commissioned by the Libertarian think tank the Cato Institute in 2006 found that in the first five years since the country decriminalized drugs, usage rates among teens in Portugal actually declined. In addition, the rates of new HIV infections caused by the sharing of dirty needles plunged. Although overall usage rates among the rest of the population increased, they did so only slightly. As a result, the study's author, Glenn Greenwald, concluded that the country's decriminalization policy "has enabled the Portuguese government to manage and control the drug problem far better than virtually every other Western country does."[12]

As I talk with a group of the teens on the dimly lit street corner outside the popular club, it's clear that although there may be an alcohol problem among Portugal's youth (and there is—so much so that Goulao has just been tasked with trying to stem the escalating rate of alcoholism in the country), most young people seem to draw the line when it comes to drugs, including marijuana—or *hashish*, as it's more commonly called in Lisbon.

"You've never tried it?" I skeptically ask a fifteen-year-old girl.

"Never. *Never*." She's emphatic, her voice rising over the pulsating beat of the music. "Drinking?" she asks me, laughing and shaking her big, red plastic cup filled with beer in the air, "Yes, I do plenty of that. But smoking hashish . . ." She grows serious. Scowling, she shakes her head, her long, dark hair moving from side to side. "I would *never*."

Her ardent dismissal of marijuana—as though it were heroin—is a common theme among her peers. I receive similar responses from the majority of young people I talk to outside the club. Drinking is okay, marijuana is not. (I do spot one group of teenage boys, however, sectioned off on a nearby street bench, drinking beer and rolling joints. They tell me it's only a weekend activity.)

According to the Cato Institute case study, which cites state research from the Instituto da Droga e da Toxicodependencia de Portugal's (the Institute on Drugs and Drug Addiction of Portugal's) annual report, since decriminalization took effect in 2001, lifetime drug usage rates—which measure how many people have consumed a certain drug (or drugs) over the course of their lifetime—in the country has decreased among several age groups, primarily among young teens. The most significant finding shows that for students in the seventh to ninth grades (between the ages of thirteen and fifteen years old), the usage rate decreased dramatically from 14.1 percent in 2001 to 10.6 percent in 2006. For young people in the tenth to twelfth grades (between the ages of sixteen and eighteen years old), the lifetime prevalence rate fell from 27.6 percent in 2011 to 21.6 percent in 2006. As expected, for some older groups (beginning with nineteen- to twenty-four-year-olds) there has been what Greenwald defines as "a slight to mild increase" in drug usage.[13] The slight increase, Harvard economist Jeffrey Miron tells me, is to be expected, because a group of people might be willing to use drugs if there is no risk of major penalties. However, "this is a small group, essentially on the margin," he points out, and indeed, the study confirms it. Regardless, Portuguese officials are clearly pleased with the country's progress.

Here's why: for drug policy specialists, a demonstrated decline in drug use among adolescents is considered to be critical. That's because the behavior of individuals in their early years tends to have a major effect on drug-related behavior in later years. In other words, if you can influence behavior in the formative teenage years, studies suggest those same teens, once grown, will be far less likely to try drugs. They have essentially missed the window of opportunity when it might be considered most interesting and are therefore less likely to seek out recreational drugs as adults. Greenwald points to "Toward a Global View of Alcohol, Tobacco, Cannabis, and Cocaine Use: Findings from the WHO World Mental Health Surveys" from *Public Library of Science Medicine*, a 2008 study detailing drug usage trends in seventeen countries on five continents in which researchers concluded that the late adolescent years are critical in determining future, lifelong drug use: "In most countries, the period of risk for initiation of use was heavily concentrated in the period from the mid to late teenage years; there was a slightly older and more extended period of risk for illegal drugs compared to legal drugs."[14]

This conclusion lends some credence to the gateway theory that suggests that the use of lesser drugs may lead to the use of more dangerous, hard drugs in the future. While the theory is controversial, Portuguese policy makers theorize that by decriminalizing drugs, they are taking away the appeal and the allure of drugs—marijuana, for example, is no longer a "dangerous" forbidden fruit and may even be considered a little boring. Miron tells me that prohibitions often have the opposite effect of what is intended. By increasing the idea of the "forbidden fruit," they can create desire, as consumers sometimes want what had been forbidden. Consider the Netherlands, where marijuana has been tolerated in pot "coffee" shops for years. Per government statistics, Dutch youth are actually less likely to smoke pot than Americans are. For example, 38 percent of American teens have smoked pot compared to 20 percent of Dutch teens. In fact, according to the 2010 U.S.-government-endorsed "Monitoring the Future" survey, which is conducted yearly and includes students from the eighth, tenth, and twelfth grades, marijuana use in the prior twelve months was reported by about 12 percent of the nation's eighth graders, 27 percent of tenth graders, and a third of the country's twelfth graders.

If you believe in the gateway theory, you would be encouraged by Portugal's declining marijuana usage and the Netherlands' smaller percentages of drug use among the youth. If young people are more likely to abuse hard drugs in the future by starting with soft drugs like marijuana early in life, then Portugal and the Netherlands are success stories.

Additional potential reasons for the Portuguese decline in usage among young people stem from both education efforts to discourage drug use and from the country's own history with drug use. It's no secret among teens that their parents' generation suffered through a serious addiction to heroin, and there may be an aversion to drugs as a result.

Portuguese officials also point to what they consider another major achievement: in the first five years of the program, the number of deaths from street drug overdoses fell from 400 to 290 per year, and the number of new HIV cases resulting from the use of dirty needles to inject heroin, cocaine, and other drugs plunged, from nearly 1,400 in 2000 to about 400 in 2006. Meanwhile, the number of people seeking treatment for drug addiction more than doubled, suggesting that addicts no longer feared punitive repercussions and were willing to seek the help they needed.

By decriminalizing drugs, the country was immediately able to make a meaningful reduction in the number of inmates populating the nation's prisons. Portugal also offered drug treatment programs, including clean needles, to help stem the HIV epidemic. A decade later, in July 2010, scientists at the International AIDS Society, the International Centre for Science in Drug Policy, and the British Columbia Center for Excellence in HIV/AIDS recommended via the Vienna Declaration ahead of the 2010 AIDS Conference in Vienna that governments adapt a scientific approach to illicit drug use. The declaration questions the effectiveness of the criminalization of injection drug users and concludes that law enforcement personnel, by carrying out destructive policies, are helping to spread HIV/AIDS rather than to curtail infection rates. The declaration states: "The criminalization of illicit drug users is fueling the HIV epidemic and has resulted in overwhelmingly negative health and social consequences. A full policy reorientation is needed." It also states that outside sub-Saharan Africa, "injection drug use accounts for approximately one in three new cases of HIV. In some areas where HIV is spreading rapidly, such as Eastern Europe and central Asia, HIV prevalence can be as high as 70 percent among people who inject drugs, and in some areas more than 80 percent of all HIV cases are among this group.

The Vienna Declaration is essentially a statement from the scientific community about the harms of illegal drugs in our society. Dr. Evan Wood, the chair of the Vienna Declaration Writing Committee and director of the Urban Health Research Initiative at the British Columbia Center for Excellence in HIV/AIDS in Vancouver, Canada, is a proponent of the Portuguese model. He says "People like myself, I'm a physician, I'm a public health researcher, we all kind of held our breath [when Portugal decriminalized drugs]."[15] Dr. Wood insists,

> This notion of a war on drugs and this over-emphasis on law enforcement does more harm than good. The war on drugs has failed to achieve its stated objectives in terms of reducing drug supply or use. And on the contrary, if you look at all the international surveillance systems, the prices of drugs continue to go up. And that's despite ever-increasing numbers of individuals that we're locking up.[16]

Meanwhile, the president of the International AIDS Society, Dr. Julio Montaner, concluded that the war on drugs policy is doing more harm than good.

These policies fuel the AIDS epidemic and result in violence, increased crime rates and destabilization of entire
states—yet there is no evidence they have reduced rates of
drug use or drug supply. As scientists, we are committed
to raising our collective voice to promote evidence-based
approaches to illicit drug policy that start by recognizing
that addiction is a medical condition, not a crime.[17]

Portugal figured all of this out a decade ago, concluding that
throwing drug users in jail would not result in a decline in usage
but would push HIV infection rates higher. Despite the government's aggressive crackdown on drug offenders, by the late nineties, Portugal had hit a 1 percent dependency rate.

Reviews by the European Monitoring Center for Drugs and
Drug Addiction concurred with the Cato Institute's findings.
As a result, Portugal has been flooded with inquiries from other
nations, including many Latin American countries long plagued
with violent drug gangs, seeking to employ similar drug policies.

Dr. Joao Goulao—the country's chief architect behind the current
policy—is not surprised by the program's success. A family doctor
originally, Goulao tells me he's "addicted to fixing people's addictions." He currently serves as Portugal's National Coordinator on
Drugs, the administrative body that oversees current drug policy, and was recently elected head of the European Monitoring
Center for Drugs and Drug Addiction, a post he considers a testa-
ment to the success of Portugal's program. "They would not have
appointed me if they didn't think our program was a success,"
he tells me as we sit down, facing each other across a small glass
table in his elegant offices on the top floor of a midsize building
in Lisbon's center. As we chat, Goulao sucks on a cigarette, leaning his head to the side as he blows plumes of smoke into the air-
conditioned room. I'm struck by the irony of the doctor who aims
to cure everyone else's addiction having an addiction himself. We
are, after all, only human.

The doctor seems very Portuguese in both his appearance (olive skin, brown eyes, and black hair) and the formality of his manner. Dressed in a dark suit, white shirt, and navy tie, he glances down at the Oriental rug under the table, then reaches to push his metal-framed glasses higher on his nose before lifting his head and locking his eyes on mine. He wants to emphasize the dominant theme behind his country's program. "Portugal now considers a drug addict a *patient*, like a sick person," he says softly, in heavily accented English, "and *not* a criminal." That shift from criminal to patient, he stresses, has been the key to the policy's triumph. "We have a broad offer" (I think he means "range" as he struggles slightly with his English) "of treatments now here. We have therapeutic communities, detoxification units, and also substitutions treatments and maintenance."

Goulao began his career in the eighties as a family doctor in the southern part of the country, where he was best known for his knack for treating addictions. Using a variety of methods including psychological counseling, medical support, and employing the use of synthetic drugs like methadone for heroine addicts when necessary, he opened one of the country's first government clinics for the rehabilitation of drug addicts in the early nineties in southern Portugal before creating a similar program on the national level.

As a doctor, Goulao confides that, prior to decriminalization, he was constantly at odds with the law. As a civil servant, he says, he had a problem. "A conflict," he tells me, folding his hands on his lap. He recounts how he would look into a patient's eyes, knowing that as a doctor he could not—as the law required him to do—refer that person to the courts or the police. "As a civil servant," he says, his dark eyes staring wistfully out the office window at the Lisbon skyline, "I had the duty to refer the person to the police. Not only did I *not* do that," he says, turning back around to face me, his eyes defiant, "but I would give him a syringe in the name of the government to keep using drugs."

It was a difficult position for Goulao and others like him to be in, but one that fortunately, he says, is obsolete today. "As a health professional, I felt very uncomfortable in those situations. As a doctor, the interest of the patient prevailed—but it was uncomfortable anyway. After decriminalization, everything is much clearer. More smooth. The Portuguese law pursues the disease and not the patient."

And therein lies the heart of the Portuguese approach. The policy is not a war on drugs but rather, a war on disease. "An addict," Goulao maintains, "does not belong behind bars but needs medical help." It's a dramatic departure from previous policies, but one Goulao insists the country needed to make.

"It worked," he says. It did. Critics who worried that Portugal would embark on a treacherous path, becoming a safe haven for drug tourists, were proven wrong. It did not happen. Foreign students did not fly to Lisbon for the chance to buy drugs and get high. In fact, 95 percent of those cited for drug charges in Portugal since 2001 have been Portuguese.[18] Neither did society deteriorate. Petty crime, such as pickpocketing, that had been linked to drugs has actually declined, while addicted people are voluntarily seeking treatment, thereby enabling the government to help treat (rather than jail) those with dependency problems. Finally, the number of people on methadone or other substitution treatments for drug addiction jumped 147 percent to 14,877 in 2003 from 6,040 in 1999.[19] This is significant, proponents of decriminalization argue, because prior to 2001 the biggest hindrance to drug addicts seeking the treatment they needed was their fear that they would be in trouble with the law.

Today, Portugal's drug use numbers are now more impressive than those of the European Union and the United States. Following decriminalization, Portugal boasted the lowest rate of lifetime marijuana use in people over the age of fifteen in the European Union: 10 percent. The most comparable figure in the United States is in people over twelve: 40.2 percent.[20] Proportionately, more Americans have used marijuana than Portuguese have used cocaine. Meanwhile, drug-related deaths have been cut in half.

On an early evening visit to a park at the top of one of Lisbon's tallest hills near the historic castle of São Jorge, I admire the sunset and the view of the Tagus River while studying the faces of the hundreds of locals that have come for a visit or a stroll. They're gathered with friends, sitting in groups of two to a dozen to share a beer, some conversation—and a joint. They are openly smoking marijuana and hashish. In broad daylight. Here, in one of the city's historic neighborhoods, everyone is orderly, and their actions are tolerated. The police look the other way as though the pot smokers were smoking cigarettes. Apparently, it's not worth the hassle of trying to apprehend anyone, because an arrest would occur only if there is a ten-day supply or greater on a person. If the individual had less than a ten-day supply, then he or she would merely be given a citation. Critics say this ineffectiveness of authorities to police marijuana usage and ensure treatment for offenders is troubling; others insist it's a step in the right direction. Why waste resources pursuing something people will do anyway? Nonetheless, some arrests—of those who are considered "traffickers"—result in the offender being put behind bars.

13

GETTING THE TREATMENT
How Decriminalization Works

In Portugal today, if you are found with a ten-day (or less) supply of any drug, from marijuana to meth, you are offered help. Not jail. The police will confiscate your drugs, and you'll be brought before what's known as the dissuasion commission. Dissuasion commissions are three-person panels run by the government and are typically made up of a psychiatrist, a social worker, and a legal adviser. The panel meets with the offender and makes a recommendation. If a drug user is deemed an addict, the panel recommends a government-sponsored treatment program. Police bring an estimated 7,500 people per year to the commissions.

Nuño Capaz, a tall, willowy Portuguese social worker with thick, dark hair to nearly his shoulders, dressed in a black T-shirt and khaki cargo pants, a black leather necklace roped around his neck, serves on a Lisbon dissuasion commission. He looks more like he's heading to a rock concert than to a day at the office. On the day I meet him he has just finished conferring with a blond, blue-eyed, twenty-something-year-old dressed like a skateboarder. The young man had been brought to the commission after the police caught him smoking marijuana. The commission decided he did not have an addiction, and he was sent home with a slap on the wrist.

A big proponent of the system, Capaz stresses that a drugless society is impossible. He says he's a realist. "By criminalizing the usage of drugs, eventually what you are trying to do is forget. And that's utopian. It's not doable. There has always been and there always will be drugs in a society."

Drugs are not a crime, but they're also not actually legal in Portugal, Capaz explains to me. Anyone found with more than a ten-day supply is considered a drug supplier or trafficker and is referred to the judicial system. But the boy smoking marijuana (or snorting cocaine) on the street corner is referred to the commission for evaluation and treatment, if needed.

"So, how do you get around that?" I ask. "I mean, how can it not be a crime but yet, not be legal?"

Capaz tells me to think of it as a traffic ticket, or a ticket for not wearing a seat belt. "It's an administrative offense," he says, shrugging.

In the vast majority of cases referred to a commission in Portugal—83 percent—the commissions suspend proceedings. Indeed, the commissions are required by Article 11(2) to "provisionally suspend proceedings" (not impose any sanctions) if an alleged drug user with no prior offenses is found to be an addict but "agrees to undergo treatment."[1] Meanwhile, if an alleged offender is deemed to be a nonaddicted consumer of drugs and has no previous offenses, the law requires that the commission "suspend proceedings." Even an addict can squeeze through the system without sanctions provided he or she agrees to a treatment program. In fact, the panel does not have the ability to require treatment, although it can recommend it. Sanctions that the panels can use include community service or fines (anywhere from twenty-five euros to the minimum national wage), although fines are rarely imposed and are considered a last resort.

Panels also have the ability to temporarily revoke a driver's license, if necessary.

Critics ask, why have commissions if they are essentially powerless? Isn't this just bureaucratic red tape? By the commissions' own admissions, 30 percent of those referred to them never show up for their first appointment. Meanwhile, many police officers are discouraged, and some complain that they are now less likely to issue citations to drug users because they believe it's essentially a waste of time (consider the aforementioned example of smokers in the park). Still, other officers say they are more apt to issue citations now because they know it will result in a person getting some help rather than a jail sentence. Regardless, it is evident from the data that since 2001 the volume of cases referred each year to the dissuasion commissions has grown.[2]

Per the same Portuguese report, "The National Situation Relating to Drugs and Dependency," in 2005 there were 3,192 commission decisions. Of those, 83 percent were "suspended," and there were no consequences for the alleged abusers. In another 15 percent of the cases, the commission imposed sanctions while the remaining 2.5 percent resulted in absolution. Meanwhile, of the 15 percent for which sanctions were imposed, most simply required the offenders to report to local treatment centers on a regular basis.

When I ask whether the policy contributes to more people using drugs by encouraging nonusers to try drugs (given that there are no repercussions), Capaz is adamant. "No," he replies, shaking his head. "Normally, the forbidden fruit is the better one." What he's trying to say (and gets a little lost in translation) is that young people are attracted to the forbidden fruit. When something is no longer a crime, it becomes less attractive to those seeking to test the boundaries and break the rules. "Saying that it's a crime to do drugs never prevented anyone from doing it. There might be other reasons, like it's bad for your health or you might have problems in the future if you do it too much. But saying it's a crime, I don't think that works as a prevention [technique] especially at a young age."

The decline in usage among teens may not just be a result of the forbidden fruit argument but may include several other factors, including the push to educate the public about the dangers of drugs and also the younger peoples' awareness of the difficulties their parents' generation faced as a result of heroin. Referring to heroin as "public enemy number one" in Portugal, Goulao says young people avoided the drug because they "saw what had happened to two or three generations of people."

It's noontime in Lisbon, and I clutch the handle dangling from the wooden roof of an old streetcar as it is slowly tugs up one of the city's steep, meandering cobblestone streets. I'm with my film crew for the documentary I'm shooting. The streetcar comes to an abrupt halt. It's a one-way, one-lane street, and apparently someone has parked a car in the middle of the street, thereby bringing traffic to an absolute standstill. We can't go up, and we can't go down. Glancing to my right, I make eye contact with a man seated on the wooden bench near me. He appears to be in his mid-fifties, and, after having heard me discussing Portugal's decriminalization efforts with my colleagues, he shyly tells me that this policy saved his life. A handsome man with short, gray hair and blue eyes, he admits that he still receives daily methadone treatments. "I wouldn't be here without that program. I wouldn't have lived," he concedes. "It's been nine years, and every day for nine years I've sought treatment. I've been able to reduce the amount of methadone I need gradually. It is a wonderful program. It has saved thousands of people. Including me," he tells me quietly before exiting the streetcar.

Tens of thousands of addicted residents just like him receive daily or weekly methadone injections—either from traveling clinics in vans that visit the neighborhoods to treat patients or at local hospitals where drug-addicted people can pick up their supply of methadone and needles. In addition to the methadone, some local treatment centers even offer individual and group therapy, art classes, computer classes—even a gym class. The goal is to enable patients to appreciate their bodies and thus not abuse them by taking drugs. Still, the Libertarian in me wants to know: why, if I were a Portuguese taxpayer, should I pay for someone's heroin habit?

Goulao has a compelling answer: you're going to pay for it either way. Either through greater enforcement expenses or higher state health care costs. "We are facing a disease," he tells me. His voice steadies, and his dark eyes grow intense. "A disease . . . like [type two] diabetes. It's a self-inflicted disease. It's a disease that results from bad elementary habits."

Still, isn't there a difference between eating too many cupcakes and shooting yourself up with heroin?

"Yes," he responds. "But the results are similar. You get the disease. When you are sick, you *must* be treated like a patient."

I pose the same question to Capaz at the local dissuasion commission.

Capaz turns my question around, suggesting I ask, "Is it fair for you, as a taxpayer, to pay for the imprisonment of a drug addict? Because it will also be your tax money that will be used for the addict's imprisonment. If that person is living on the street and has to go to an institution, it will also be your tax money that will be used. If that person has a health problem and goes to the hospital, it will also be your tax money." In other words, I'm on the hook no matter what option is used, and it's all a question of how to best allocate the funds. Capaz is convinced I'll get the most bang for my buck via decriminalization.

Portugal has essentially repurposed the money it spends. Instead of throwing millions of dollars at law enforcement, including jails, it spends money on treatment centers and dissuasion commissions. For example, there are outreach programs that target Portugal's youth.

It's nearly three on a Saturday night (or rather, Sunday morning) in Lisbon, and as I walk toward an anti-drug activist booth stationed outside a popular club, I'm convinced these activists will not be a welcome sight in this teenage community. It would be like having the D.A.R.E. representatives trying to hand out flyers in the middle of a high school keg party. Would anyone take them seriously?

Approaching the booth, I'm surprised and a little amused by the number of kids talking to the representatives and thumbing through flyers. Dozens of teens hover over the literature while slugging down alcohol in large plastic cups. They can barely read, because the only light emanates from a street lamp nearly a block away, and yet they appear genuinely interested in the multicolored pamphlets devoted to various topics like marijuana, heroin, and alcoholism. It's hardly what I expect, but the activists there tell me part of their appeal stems from their neutrality. They don't judge the kids. They say they are there simply to provide information, to help the teens in the event they are too impaired to get themselves home safety and in case they have questions. A basket of multicolored condoms sits on the edge of a large folding table as though it was a bowl of candy, and teens are encouraged to help themselves. It would drive many U.S. members of the religious right mad to see this—and as a new mother of two baby girls, I have a visceral reaction to seeing young kids drinking and thumbing through literature on sex and drugs. But the activists claim that by offering neutrality, it makes them relevant. There are many ways to help educate teens, they tell me, and this is one. If they appear as though they're judging them, they will immediately lose their audience.

"But, a lot of these kids look like they're *really* young," I tell one of the counselors. Petite, with short, brown hair, she's probably in her mid-thirties, although in the dark she could pass for an older sibling of one of the teens she's counseling. "Some look like they're twelve, thirteen," I stammer.

Nodding her head, she agrees, telling me many *are* that young. Their parents drop them off to drink with their friends, then pick them up at four or five in the morning. It's part of the culture. Her role, she tells me, is to offer support and to be a sounding board. The government encourages this kind of work, allocating funds for outreach programs to help educate young people.

Regardless of the country's alcohol issues (including underage drinking), it has managed to control its drug use and rate of new HIV infections. As a result, there are a growing number of countries that are looking to Portugal for guidance on how to manage their own drug problems. Goulao has received ambassadors from a series of countries, "in this very office" he tells me, as he makes a large gesture with his arms, including many in Latin America. They are anxious to learn whether decriminalization might also work on their own soil. "They come here, and talk with me and with my people. They take notes about our reality and prepare reports to send to their countries, to their governments in terms of recommendations." Portugal, he proudly says, is "inspiring other countries," including other European nations like the Czech Republic.

In 2008, the Czech government approved a drug decriminalization law and in 2009 set precise quantities of illicit drugs that are not considered a criminal offense. The list is as follows:

Marijuana	15 grams (or five plants)
Magic mushrooms	40 pieces
Hashish	5 grams
Peyote	5 plants
Coca	5 plants
LSD	5 tablets
Ecstasy	4 tablets
Amphetamine	2 grams
Methamphetamine	2 grams
Heroin	1.5 grams
Cocaine	1 gram

Possession of "larger than a small amount" of marijuana in the Czech Republic can result in a jail sentence of up to one year. For other illicit drugs, the sentence is two years. Trafficking offenses carry stiffer sentences.

By the summer of 2009, Mexico—one of the most notorious centers of drug trafficking in the world—followed Portugal's example, making the leap to decriminalize the possession of small amounts of all major narcotics, including marijuana, cocaine, LSD, meth, and heroin. The law outlines maximum personal use amounts for drugs. For example, the maximum amount of marijuana considered to be for personal use under the new law is 5 grams—the equivalent of about four marijuana cigarettes. Other limits are a half a gram of cocaine, 50 milligrams of heroin, 40 milligrams for methamphetamine, and 0.015 milligrams of LSD.[3] People detained with those quantities no longer face criminal prosecution, and instead are encouraged to seek government-financed treatment free of charge. If they are caught a third time, treatment is mandatory (although no penalties for noncompliance have been created). As of this writing, it's been almost a year since Mexico made its move, and like Portugal, perhaps what's most notable is that nothing has truly changed. It's still early, but drug usage has not soared, nor has Mexico become the Holland of North America for drug tourists.

Shortly after Portugal moved to decriminalize drug usage on August 20, 2009, Argentina's Supreme Court (having been presented with a case about young people being arrested for possessing a few joints) ruled that it was unconstitutional to punish people for personal consumption of marijuana, thereby decriminalizing personal use of marijuana. The Argentine administration had already been pushing for decriminalization. In 2008, at a meeting of the National Investigation into the Consumption of Alcohol, Tobacco, Psychopharmaceuticals and Illegal Drugs, Argentina's president Cristina Fernandez de Kirchner said, "I don't like it when people easily condemn someone who has an addiction as if he were a criminal, as if he were a person who should be persecuted. Those who should be persecuted are those who sell the substances, those who give it away, those who traffic in it."[4]

The Argentine high court ruled it unconstitutional to prosecute cases involving the personal, private use of marijuana. The decision struck down a 2006 lower court ruling that sentenced eight people to jail terms for carrying marijuana cigarettes. The Court concluded that smoking marijuana was a personal activity that did not put the state in danger and was therefore a matter of individual choice.

Goulao told me he had a hand in helping to influence the marijuana policy in Argentina. The Argentine government (with whom he had consulted) was instrumental in urging the Supreme Court to review drug possession laws. The government wanted to redirect state spending to prosecuting dealers, rather than consumers, and wanted to allocate funds for drug treatment instead of what officials called expensive prosecutions of thousands of smaller cases.

There are additional Latin American nations following Portugal's model. In 2002 and 2006, the powerhouse emerging market country of Brazil implemented legislation that resulted in the partial decriminalization of possession of drugs for personal use and is in the process of pursuing full decriminalization. Currently in Brazil, instead of prison, convicted drug users are sentenced with mandatory treatment and community service.[5]

Amid this trend toward decriminalization, critics worry that by not punishing drug users, governments are sending a wrong and conflicting message. They worry that policies like those of Mexico and Portugal are essentially legalizing, or at the very least legitimizing, drug use, thereby increasing the chances of individuals experimenting with addictive substances. After all, isn't the government effectively sanctioning a drug if it does not prosecute a user? Alvaro Uribe, the former president of Colombia (the country that once laid claim to one of the most dangerous drug criminals in history, Pablo Escobar), certainly thinks so. Despite a 1994 decision by the Colombian Constitutional Court that declared it unconstitutional to punish drug possession for personal use, Uribe, while in office, lobbied to recriminalize consumption. Currently, Colombian adults can possess up to 0.7 ounces (20 grams) of marijuana and 0.03 ounces (1 gram) of cocaine, among other substances, for consumption in their own homes and not face criminal sanctions. But the president sees this as inconsistent with efforts to curtail drug trafficking.

• • •

When I met President Uribe at the presidential palace in Bogota in 2007, I interviewed him about his efforts to reduce drug trafficking. His number one goal was to improve security in his country, and at that point he had already achieved considerable success. The kidnapping rates in the capital cities of Bogota and the infamous Medellin had plummeted by more than 80 percent to their lowest levels in decades. Despite Colombia's bad press and reputation as the murder capital of the world, the country's murder rate was lower than those of Washington, D.C., and Baltimore. Uribe had achieved this success, he told me, by being tough on drug traffickers. For a small man, he had big plans. He aimed to put Colombia's drug terrorists out of business and was willing to die trying. (He had already dodged seventeen attempts on his life.) Destroying Fuerzas Armadas Revolucionarias de Colombia (FARC), the leftist guerilla terrorist group that makes its money primarily from drug trafficking, was a personal goal of Uribe's. In 1983, Uribe's father was killed during a botched FARC kidnapping. Uribe has received (and spent) millions of dollars combating illegal drug production and trafficking under Plan Colombia—a joint U.S.-Colombia strategy to fight illegal drugs and organized crime—and although drug-related kidnappings and murders have declined, coca cultivation for the manufacturing of cocaine has remained relatively stable. According to estimates from the United Nations Office on Drugs and Crime, cocaine production varied little between 2000 and 2007.

Uribe tried five times, without success, beginning in 2003, to overturn the court's ruling and amend the constitution. Nonetheless, the Colombian Supreme Court recently reaffirmed the 1994 Constitutional Court ruling making it unconstitutional to punish someone for drug possession.

As many Latin American countries experiment with some form of drug decriminalization, the United States has said relatively little. The United States is examining the case study of

Portugal (and our Latin American neighbors) as it confronts escalating violence tied to drug trafficking here at home; however, it's unlikely the administration would ever entertain such a radical policy idea in the near future. Although the aggressive, hard-line war on drugs policy has failed and Americans' frustration with federal policies is growing increasingly evident on the state level, a drastic move like fully decriminalizing all drugs is unlikely to happen.

But maybe it should. Despite having some of the world's harshest penalties for drug users, the United States maintains some of the highest rates of cocaine and marijuana use in the world.

Opponents of decriminalization dismiss the Portugal case study, in part, because it was commissioned by the Cato Institute—the Libertarian think tank. The Obama administration's drug czar, Gil Kerlikowske, told me that he hardly thought much faith could be put in research conducted by a group with an agenda. "I don't buy any research study in which an organization has already stated the outcome, and then essentially conducts research to prove what they've already stated. I'm sorry. I think it's a little difficult for someone to say, 'We're going to do a study,' after already having stated their claims and what their outcomes should be, and then doing a study which essentially supports it." What he seemed unaware of, however, is that the research—including the graphs demonstrating the decline in drug usage among young people in Portugal, came not from Cato but rather the Portuguese government's own researchers. Thus, Glenn Greenwald, the author of the Cato study and a Portuguese speaker, was translating the Portuguese reports, and numbers are numbers. While he may have had a Cato spin on the subject, the data are real: there has been no huge spike in usage, no drug tourism, a decline in usage among the nation's youth, and a substantial drop in the number of new HIV infections. In addition, the European Numbers Information Gathering and Monitoring Association came to the same conclusion—that Portugal's decriminalization efforts were a success. When I pointed this out to Kerlikowske, he said, "I'd love to comment but I haven't read the study and I just don't know."

• • •

Several weeks after our interview, Kerlikowske followed up in a letter to CNBC, telling the network,

> I am very interested in learning about other nations' approaches to drug policy and I am watching closely what is happening in Portugal. To date, the impact of Portugal's changes are inconclusive and clearly insufficient grounds for adjusting drug policies in other countries. . . . I remain convinced that policies which eliminate or significantly reduce deterrents to drug use will result eventually in greater drug use and serious harmful consequences for drug consumers and their families.

Other critics insist that Portugal is an unrealistic model for the United States, given the differences of size and culture between the United States and Portugal.

There are some serious—and understandable—concerns about the message a country is sending its young people when it decriminalizes drugs. Critics fear that by not punishing drug users, a government is sanctioning drug use. It is more complicated than that, however. The government in Portugal is saying drug use is, for some, a disease and needs to be treated as such. Thus, in Portugal addicts are not prisoners but rather patients. It's also telling people that they are responsible for their own health choices. It's a theory that some U.S. politicians are paying close attention to. Senators Jim Webb and Arlen Specter have proposed that Congress create a national commission, similar to Portugal's, to address prison reform and overhaul drug-sentencing policy. While the United States is home to 5 percent of the global population, it is home to 25 percent of the world's prisoners, a stat that Webb highlights. The country spends $68 billion per year on corrections, yet one-third of those being corrected are in prison for nonviolent drug crimes. Perhaps most startling is that $150 billion is spent on policing and courts and nearly half, 47 percent, of all drug arrests are marijuana related. It's an example of U.S. taxpayers' dollars at work. Is it money well spent? Drug usage rates are escalating, and money is paying for prisons rather than treatment.

In part due to the frustration about the number of dollars spent, in part due to a shift in demographics, and in part due to research showing that the United States still has the highest level of illegal cannabis use in the world at 42.4 percent (followed by New Zealand at 41.9 percent), the decriminalization movement is gaining traction in the United States, with statistics showing that two-thirds of Americans support drug treatment instead of jail time for first-time drug offenders.[6]

In response, some politicians are pushing for the ability of states to make their own decisions on policing the most widely used illicit drug in the country—marijuana. Massachusetts Democrat Barney Frank sponsored a bill (along with Ron Paul, the Republican from Texas; Maurice Hinchey, Democrat from New York; Dana Rohrabacher, Republican from California; and Tammy Baldwin, Democrat from Wisconsin) to end federal penalties for Americans carrying fewer than 100 grams, or almost a quarter-pound, of marijuana. Passage of the act would provide state lawmakers with the autonomy to decide their own marijuana laws. It would also enable states to consider full legalization of marijuana for adults without federal interference. "The vast amount of human activity ought to be none of the government's business," Frank told lawmakers on Capitol Hill. "I don't think it is the government's business to tell you how to spend your leisure time."

Many policy analysts—impressed by efforts in Portugal—are asking whether decriminalization of drugs could work here in the United States. Might prevention programs targeting youth help cut down on drug usage in American youth? Economist Jeffery Miron, who received funding from the Marijuana Policy Project for his research, examines whether full legalization of marijuana would be economically productive for society in his 2005 paper titled "The Budgetary Implications of Marijuana Prohibition."

He calculates that in 2002, the U.S. government spent $2.6 billion on policing marijuana.[7] Miron tells me his numbers are actually highly conservative but that, in total, state and local justice costs associated with marijuana arrests now equal $7.6 billion, or approximately $10,400 per arrest. Of this total, annual police costs are $3.7 billion, judicial costs are $853 million, and prison costs are $3.1 billion. It may not seem like a ton of money in the grand scheme of things, especially when you compare it to the size of the national debt, but according to Miron and hundreds of other legalization advocates, every dollar counts.

14

LAW AND DISORDER
Navigating the Legal Maze
We've Created

J ane and Jon Smith, who requested I not use their real names in order to help protect them from being targeted by the feds, employ ten full-time workers and ten part-timers at their two dispensaries and grow operation. "I eat, sleep, and breathe this business," Jane tells me. "But I think any small business owner does that because it's their paycheck. And it's other people's paychecks: employees, insurance. Of course, we also have this whole layer of the unknown: What's going to happen with regulation? What are the local police thinking? Are we going to be able to get a permit?" Jane's voice trails off as she ticks off her list of industry woes, before summing it up with, "It's a little more complicated than your average small business." To say the least.

The Smiths are probably not whom you'd first think of when you think of pot growers. They're a typical American family, with two small children ages four and six. Jane, thirty-four years old, is the image of the all-American girl: blond hair, green eyes, high cheekbones with a few freckles scattered across her nose, plus a quick laugh and a quick wit. She moved to Colorado in 1998 to begin her MBA program at the University of Denver. Shortly after graduating, she met her husband, Jon, when he was tending bar at her favorite watering hole. "I had never hit on a guy in my life," she says, laughing. "But I was constantly trying to find ways to talk to him. I even became friends with his roommates just to talk to him!"

Jon didn't want to date her, Jane muses, because she was ten years his junior. Eventually, they worked through that, got married, and had two children. Jon suffers from severe back pain due to a degenerative disc disease. He's had several operations, and after struggling with drugs like Percocet and Oxycontin ("He was miserable on those and he was miserable to live with," Jane says. "I joke that marijuana saved my marriage."), he turned to pot. His surgeon actually recommended medicinal marijuana as a treatment, and Jon began growing it himself at home, mostly because it was too expensive to buy. "It was the best thing I could do. It was therapeutic—just the act of growing these plants," Jon tells me.

Soon, he realized he had too much supply, so he began selling his extra marijuana in an effort to help some fellow patients and yes, bring in a little extra cash. (He had left work years earlier on disability.) At the time, there were only seven dispensaries in Colorado, so the demand was huge. "The phone was ringing off the hook," explains Jane. "And Jon, with his bad back, was in the car maybe six hours a day, delivering to people." There were additional problems associated with the deliveries, she says. "To meet someone in a parking lot for what seems like an illicit drug deal, but is actually quite legal in this state, can be awkward and uncomfortable."

Meanwhile, Jane was working for the state, helping Colorado manage its municipal bond portfolio. It was a good job, but her goal was to work for herself. And then there was the issue of being a government employee. The last thing she needed was her husband being arrested for marijuana. "Just imagine the headlines," she says, laughing. So in 2008, eight years after Colorado had approved the growing and sale of medical marijuana, Jane decided it was time she put her MBA to work. Bigtime. She decided to make her husband's fledgling business official. She and Jon would open a dispensary and grow. Jon would be responsible for all aspects of growing, and she would handle everything else. It was a huge gamble. But it was the American dream. She'd have something of her own. She'd work for herself—and there was a chance that she and her husband could become very successful.

With their eyes on the prize, they cashed out Jane's 401(k) and took out both a second and a third mortgage on their home. "It took everything we had, including a lot of loans from friends and family, to rent this space and purchase all the equipment," she says as she leads me through the offices of her growing facility in an office park near Bolder. "It cost us two hundred fifty thousand dollars in initial investment, and let's face it: you can't exactly go to a bank and ask for a small business loan." No, you can't.

With five hundred patients, you'd think that making money would be easy for Jane and Jon. Think again. They've been in business two years and are considered one of the most successful operations in town, yet making payroll every week is a constant stress. "On paper, everything looks great," she explains. "The problem is our cash flow." Although she sells her product primarily at her two dispensaries (she's in the process of acquiring a third) and any leftover bud is sent to other dispensaries (the ones that don't grow their own crops), cash flow is still tight. Trying to get dispensary owners to pay on time is often an issue. For example, although Jane may have already sold her product, she often hasn't been paid.

"I'm constantly going over the accounts receivable on the ledger. Constantly." Scrambling for the money to pay her staff every week, Jane has been forced to cut corners in her own life. Case in point: for eight months, she and her husband didn't pay their mortgage. "I didn't have a choice. It was the business or the house. And we couldn't lose the business." She was on the brink of foreclosure when her mother came to her family's rescue, making two months' worth of mortgage payments, which was enough to keep the bank at bay. "It's hard," Jane admits, shaking her head. "You have all the headaches any small business owner has—and then you have all the extra problems that go with this industry."

Like the paperwork. "We have something new every day we have to deal with. The local jurisdictions are changing their rules, or the state is adopting this legislation." And then there are the things—which are actually fundamental to running a business—like finding a bank. "Every few months we get a note in the mail that they're closing our account, and suddenly I'm out looking for another bank." In their two years in business, Jon and Jane have had to switch banks five times. Banks are subject to federal regulations, and by allowing those that "traffic" in a Schedule I illegal substance to move funds through a bank's account, that bank is (in the eyes of the federal government) enabling the money to be laundered. Like many others, Jane could try to get around the situation by claiming the profits came from an alternative source; however, she is adamant about being honest and upfront. "When they ask what the business is, we tell them." And that's when it gets difficult. Still, Jane insists she needs the bank to run the business. Burying cash in the backyard, while it may exist in parts of Northern California, is not for Denver. "With the volume we're handling, with accounts receivables, with employees to pay, with equipment to purchase . . . you *have* to do all this through a bank. You couldn't operate on this kind of scale in cash."

But it's not just the banking system and payroll fears that keep this young mother of two toddlers up at night. Her real fear is whether she is putting her children at risk by not being fully compliant with all the changing rules and regulations.

"I'm always sick about it. I can feel it right here," she says, pointing to her stomach. "My stomach gets sick at night. All the time. The risk is enormous. I think of [my kids'] sweet, beautiful little faces, and it just makes me nervous. I know I have to do everything right. I have to protect them." She says she made a measured decision getting into this business. It was a financial risk and a personal risk, but one she had decided was worth taking.

"But the reality," I remind her, "is that you *could* go to jail. You *could* be arrested. The feds could bust in here tomorrow and take you out in handcuffs."

Much of the national conversation about legalization portrays it as an easy to way to greater freedom and big-time tax revenues, or a regrettably hedonistic free-for-all. But for everyone in the trenches it's a legal minefield that stretches as far as the eye can see. For decades the debate has been when pot will be legalized, but now we're shifting to *how* it will be legalized, and the answers aren't any clearer.

Jane thought about that and came to the conclusion that this was a risk she was willing to take. "If, God forbid, that were to happen, I do have wonderful family that could take care of my children if Jon and I were in federal prison. And at least they'd know that Mommy and Daddy were doing what they believed in. That we were trailblazers. I believe we're good role models for the kids," she tells me. "We emphasize that marijuana is medicine, it's something Daddy needs to make him feel better and it helps hundreds of people. The kids know what we do. Well, I don't know that at four and six you can completely comprehend what we do. But we do explain to them that we grow medicine for people and that not everyone agrees with it."

There's a line between marijuana as medicine and marijuana as a recreational drug, however, and it's one that Jane recognizes and worries about. The marijuana message, she complains, is confusing to children. "We'll be driving down Broadsterdam," she tells me, referring to the now infamous street in Colorado known for its pot shops, "and [the kids will] be in the car screaming, 'Mommy, look! Marijuana, marijuana, marijuana!'" she says, laughing. "And you have to say, 'Yes, that's a marijuana leaf,'" she nods and says in a voice that's used to talking to small children. "'So that's a medicine store.' But at the same time, it's not something we really approve of; it's not something we do at our place . . . advertise in that way."

She always tells the parents of her children's friends what she and her husband do for a living. ("I can't hide it from them, and at least so far, they've all been fine with it and let their kids come here to play with mine.") There's no growing operation in her home—that's all saved for the warehouse, where Jon arrives every morning at four to make sure the lights are on and the plants are watered. "I get up at three-thirty in the morning, and I come straight here," he tells me as we walk through one of his brightly lit grow rooms where hundreds of beautifully manicured, tall plants are lined up. They're all carefully labeled and even include the name of the patient for whom they are being grown.

Jane gets to sleep in. She's up at seven and gets the kids off to school before heading to the upstairs offices at the grow house. She's chief executive officer, chief financial officer, chief administrative officer, the head of human resources, and chief lobbyist for her company.

Standing together in the middle of the grow, Jon and Jane smile affectionately at each other. "I couldn't do this job without her," Jon tells me, looking at Jane with admiration. She returns his compliment, "I wouldn't have anything to sell without him. He is an incredible grower. I'm not kidding. There's so much to it. It's really an art. You could take the same plants with the same genetics and same grow equipment and give them to three people. I guarantee you Jon would grow the best marijuana. He's just intuitive. He has a real skill."

As I walk through Jon's grow house, I see evidence of that skill. In a warehouse in the back of his company's headquarters is a massive grow. The ceilings are over twenty feet high, and bright white lights leave me squinting as I make my way through the narrow paths in between hundreds of plants. Some Grateful Dead music blares in the background. Apparently, it's good for the plants. "We're not Deadheads. We just like the music," Jane clarifies for me. Everything in the room is meticulous—from the wiring to the irrigation system. The walls, the floor, the entire room is immaculate, and the plants seem to have struck a balance between hearty and delicate. Pointing to the cards with patients' names on them, Jane emphasizes that this "is part of dotting every i and crossing every t."

"Do you consider yourself a trailblazer?" I ask her once we reach the relative quietness of the hallway outside the music-filled grow room.

"I guess." She smiles. "You know, my mom said to me the other day that she was really proud of me. My *mom*! And she's the last person who would approve of this." (Jane was raised as a church-going Catholic girl in the suburbs of Chicago.) "But she told me, 'Your grandfather would be really proud of you, too.' I was like, 'Really. Mom. Are you sure?' And she said, 'Yes. You're taking a risk. You're doing something innovative. You're doing something you believe in and you're becoming successful. He would admire that risk taking. I definitely do.'" As much as Jane basks in her family's compliments, she carries with her, every morning and every night, the knowledge that she and her husband could go to jail for the business she runs.

It's not just the marijuana providers who are facing risks by walking on the wrong side of federal law—the users, even those who say they're in desperate need of marijuana, are also taking risks.

James Casias didn't work for a dispensary or grow cannabis; he worked at Walmart. Casias appears to have been a model and committed employee. He even earned an Associate of the Year award in 2008. Casias has also suffered from inoperable brain and sinus cancer for nine years and began using medical marijuana upon the recommendation of his oncologist. His illness is very serious; it has affected his ability to speak and causes him physical pain and nausea. Marijuana has greatly relieved his symptoms and given him an enhanced quality of life. There may be a universe of people who fake a medical affliction to get access to marijuana under medical use exemptions, but Casias is not one of them.

Medical use of marijuana is legal under Michigan law, where Casias was employed. He was given a drug test after injuring his knee at work and tested positive. When asked about his use of marijuana following the test, Casias told Walmart about his medical condition and presented a state-issued card that authorized his use of marijuana. The store terminated him anyway. Casias also says he didn't use marijuana at work or come to work under the influence of the drug; store management has not alleged otherwise.

Walmart is not the most sympathetic party. The company has long been under fire for providing workers with inadequate benefits and is routinely a target of labor unions and protectors of local businesses that cannot compete with the mammoth retailer. Walmart, it should be noted, has publicly acknowledged the difficulty of the situation and said that it is sympathetic to Casias's condition. It, however, is very aggressive about enforcing its policies and, if needed, litigating to protect what it sees as threats to its business. In an unrelated situation, Walmart is contesting a small fine after an employee was trampled to death by a crowd that charged at the opening of a store for a large sale. Walmart's position is that it disagrees that it was reasonably foreseeable that a crowd could be excited by a sale to the point where someone could be trampled to death. Conceding the point could open them to more litigation and penalties in the future. In this situation, Casias began drawing unemployment benefits after being terminated by Walmart, and Walmart is contesting his right to do so because he was fired for drug use. Presumably, Walmart is also concerned it will be liable for unemployment benefits for any employee it terminates for drug use.

This is about as close to David versus Goliath as you get, and it will soon play out in Michigan courts. In June 2010, the American Civil Liberties Union (ACLU) announced that it was suing Walmart for the wrongful termination of Casias.

While it's very easy to paint Walmart as Goliath and very clear that Mr. Casias has suffered greatly, the issue is not as simple as an insensitive employer acting without regard to the tragic situation facing a single employee. The litany of issues an employer must consider when dealing with employees is challenging:

- What laws need to be complied with in dealing with employees—federal, state, local? When the laws conflict, which applies?
- Will employee misconduct or negligence that harms the general public, customers, suppliers, or other employees expose the company to legal liability for the employee's actions? If so, how can that risk be managed?
- How can employers tailor employment policies and standards that are consistent and fair for literally millions of employees?

For a company with as many employees as Walmart, more than two million globally and one million in the United States, it becomes necessary to have general policies that can be applied across the board. When evaluating the risk to Walmart or another large employer of continuing to employ a person who is known to use a controlled substance, consider the following hypothetical situation:

Situation: A Walmart forklift operator has an accident in which he backs into a warehouse racking system, collapsing it onto a fellow employee and killing him. Walmart learned four months before the accident that the forklift operator used marijuana legally under a state law and decided to continue his employment under the condition that he would not use the drug while at work. After the accident, investigators learn that the forklift operator had marijuana in his system at the time of the accident.

Analysis: Walmart likely would be liable for negligent supervision of an employee and may be liable for the death of the employee and be open to economic damages to the survivors of the deceased employee. Walmart might also be liable to fines and other penalties for having an unsafe workplace under the Occupational Safety and Health Administration. It would also be open to criticism and reputational damage as a result of the death.

Perhaps this example is remote. However, with more than three million employees, the risks of having employees on the job under the influence of any mind-altering drug must be considered. Walmart could rationally conclude that the risk from drug use of its three million employees warrants a zero-tolerance policy.

Adding to the complexity of the situation, marijuana remains illegal under federal law—the outright ban of marijuana under the Controlled Substances Act was upheld in 2005 under *Gonzales v. Raich*—and companies that receive federal contracts are required to prohibit marijuana use under the Drug Free Workplace Act of 1998.

The legal analysis of the situation is of course complex. The issue has, however, been litigated in state courts, and thus far courts have not ruled in favor of employees.

The most recent decision was handed down in April 2010 in Oregon. In that case, Oregon passed the Oregon Medical Marijuana Act, which authorizes that people who hold a registered identification card can use medical marijuana. A temporary employee of a steel products manufacturer was terminated after telling his supervisor that he used medical marijuana in accordance with the Oregon law. The employee did this before taking a drug test that would have been required prior to gaining a permanent employment position. The employee later filed a complaint with the Oregon Bureau of Labor and Industries, alleging that the employer had discriminated against him in violation of an Oregon law that prohibits discrimination against an otherwise qualified employee because of a disability and requires employers to make reasonable accommodations for a person's disability. The Oregon Bureau of Labor and Industries agreed with the employee's position and filed a claim against the employer.

This situation didn't have quite the drama of the David versus Goliath situation facing Walmart in Michigan. The employee in this situation apparently had meaningful medical issues but not to the degree of Joseph Casias. In the Oregon case:

> Since 1992, the employee has experienced anxiety, panic attacks, nausea, vomiting and severe stomach cramps, all of which have substantially limited his ability to eat. Between January 1996 and November 2001, employee used a variety of prescription drugs in an attempt to alleviate that condition. None of those drugs proved effective for an extended period of time and some had negative side effects. In 1996, employee began using marijuana to self medicate his condition. In April 2002, employee consulted with a physician for the purpose of obtaining a registry identification card under the Oregon Medical Marijuana Act. The physician signed a statement that employee has a "debilitating medical condition" and that "[m]arijuana may mitigate the symptoms or effects of this patient's condition." The statement that the employee's physician signed tracks the terms of the Oregon Medical Marijuana Act. That directs the state to issue registry identification cards to persons when a physician states that "the person has been diagnosed with a debilitating medical condition and that medical use of marijuana may mitigate the symptoms or effects" of that condition. No prescription is required as a prerequisite for obtaining a registry identification card.[1]

While perhaps not as dramatic as the facts facing Walmart in Michigan, the facts and the law are similar and set the stage for an intersection of conflicting laws:

> The question that this case poses is how state and federal laws intersect in the context of an employment discrimination claim; specifically, employer argues that, because

marijuana possession is unlawful under federal law, even when used for medical purposes, state law does not require an employer to accommodate an employees' use of marijuana to treat a disabling medical condition.[2]

The Oregon Bureau of Labor and Industries argument was centered on an Oregon statute that required employers to make reasonable accommodations for employees with disabilities— essentially a state law version of the federal Americans with Disabilities Act. Both the federal and state laws contain provisions that the protections of the laws do not apply to protect an employee who uses an illegal drug. The Oregon law also contains a provision that mandates it be construed in a manner consistent with the federal law. Thus, the legality or illegality of marijuana in the state of Oregon became the central issue in the case. If marijuana was illegal in Oregon, the protections of the state law protecting workers with disabilities would not apply to a user of medical marijuana. If, on the other hand, marijuana were legal in Oregon, the protections of the law would be available to protect a worker with disabilities despite using marijuana.

The Oregon law gave detailed guidance on whether a drug was illegal or not:

> Illegal use of drugs means any use of drugs, the possession or distribution of which is unlawful under state law or under the federal Controlled Substances Act, but does not include the use of a drug taken under supervision of a licensed health care professional, or other uses authorized under the Controlled Substances Act or under other provisions of state or federal law.[3]

The Oregon Supreme Court determined that this provision of the state law put the question directly before them of whether the Oregon Medical Marijuana Act could be read consistently with the federal Controlled Substances Act—which banned the use of marijuana in all circumstances. The case was decided after

Gonzales v. Raich, which had held that the Controlled Substances Act would prevail over the California law permitting medical marijuana. Relying on *Gonzales v. Raich,* the Oregon Supreme Court found that by categorizing marijuana as a Schedule I drug for which there was no accepted medical use Congress had concluded that marijuana has no medical use. Therefore, the Controlled Substances Act and the Oregon Medical Marijuana Act were in direct conflict and that "to the extent that the Oregon Medical Marijuana Act affirmatively authorizes the use of medical marijuana federal law preempts that subsection leaving it without effect."

After making that determination, the Oregon Supreme Court rejected the Bureau of Labor and Industry's argument that marijuana was not an illegal drug in Oregon if used for medical purposes and that the employee was therefore not entitled to the protections of the Oregon law requiring employers to make reasonable accommodation to employees with disabilities.

The California Supreme Court reached a similar result in *Ross v. Ragingwire Telecommunications*, concluding that, despite California's authorization of medical marijuana, employers could conduct drug tests and could fire an employee for use of marijuana without being deemed to discriminate against an employee with a disability and that employers have no duty to those who use marijuana.

It is almost certain that litigation on this front will continue, although perhaps under different legal theories. Seven states have passed laws that specifically state that employees may be terminated for on-the-job marijuana use or impairment. It seems, however, that those laws would fail if a court applied the same logic as the Oregon Supreme Court—the laws appear to be in direct conflict with the Controlled Substances Act and thus would be struck down.

In the Michigan case involving Walmart, the ACLU appears to be positioning an employers' right to terminate an employee for following the medical advice of a doctor in conflict with the doctor-patient relationship. According to ACLU attorney Scott

Michelman, "No patient should be forced to choose between adequate pain relief and gainful employment, and no employer should be allowed to intrude upon private medical choices made by employees in consultation with their doctors."[4] This argument is interesting, because it may be an attempt to force a court to look at this situation under the framework applied by the Supreme Court in *Roe v. Wade*, which is the 1973 case in which abortion was made legal in the United States. There the Supreme Court found there to be a right to privacy that included the doctor-patient relationship and determined that the government could not intrude on that relationship by mandating what procedures the doctor could perform—with certain exceptions based on the gestational age of the fetus. In the Michigan case, the argument may be made that an employer who can terminate an employee for following his doctor's medical advice is tantamount to interfering with the doctor-patient relationship. The argument may, however, be a stretch, as the employer's action does not directly limit the doctor from prescribing a course of care to his patient.

It's not, however, a stretch to conclude that there is no greater conflict between federal and state law than as they relate to medical marijuana—fifteen states currently have laws providing for some use of medical marijuana, and that number is growing each year; meanwhile, marijuana is completely illegal under federal law, and the federal government still regards marijuana as a Schedule I drug with no accepted medical purpose. Making the situation more confusing is the directive from the U.S. attorney general's office that states that prosecution of medical marijuana cases won't be a priority, although that does not mean the government can't prosecute. Confusing, to say the least. The simple and fair answer would seem to be for a federal policy that recognizes there are legitimate medical uses for marijuana, which would then allow deference to state laws for the appropriate regulation of medical marijuana. This would allow the federal government (and the states) to exercise their normal power against illicit use and trafficking of marijuana as they do today for other drugs with recognized medicinal and illicit uses such as morphine and cocaine. This would provide clarity for medicinal marijuana users and suppliers so that they could be certain that their use, if compliant with state law, would not put them in jeopardy of prosecution under federal law or at risk of losing their jobs because their employers will not recognize the validity of medical marijuana under state law. If only it were so easy.

15

THIS IS NOT GAY MARRIAGE

Why Advocates Can't Turn
to the Courts for Help

Eight months after Eric Holder first shocked reporters by say-ing that the administration would not target medicinal users and cultivators of marijuana, the U.S. Department of Justice attempted to spell out the administration's stand on the subject by issuing its October 19, 2009, memo. David Ogden, deputy attor-ney general, writes on the "Investigations and Prosecutions in States Authorizing the Medicinal Use of Marijuana" in an effort to provide some much-needed clarification and guidance to fed-eral prosecutors in states that have enacted laws authorizing the medical use of marijuana. Under close examination, however, the memo may in fact only serve to make the law more confusing.

The government suggests that, although U.S. attorneys have full discretion to enforce the laws, they should not waste resources pursuing marijuana users and distributors in states that permit medical marijuana. The government clarifies its guidance in the following paragraph by explicitly discouraging U.S. attorneys from pursuing marijuana users and providers who are operating within state law:

> As a general matter, pursuit of these priorities should not focus federal resources in your States on Memorandum for Selected United States Attorneys individuals *whose actions are in clear and unambiguous compliance with existing state laws providing for the medical use of marijuana.* For example, prosecution of individuals with cancer or other serious illnesses who use marijuana as part of a recommended treatment regimen consistent with applicable state law, or those caregivers in clear and unambiguous compliance with existing state law who provide such individuals with marijuana is unlikely to be an efficient use of limited federal resources.[1]

Nonetheless, the Justice Department makes a distinction between medical users and providers and what it considers "traffickers." Major distributors are viewed as a problem and thus, Ogden is encouraging the attorneys to focus their prosecutorial and investigation efforts on large drug rings.

The prosecution of significant traffickers of illegal drugs, including marijuana, and the disruption of illegal drug manufacturing and trafficking networks continues to be a core priority in the Justice Department's efforts against narcotics and dangerous drugs, and the department's investigative and prosecutorial resources should be directed toward these objectives.

Perhaps the big takeaway for medical marijuana providers is that although you may provide cannabis to your patients, you can't grow your business too much or make too much money or you'll be at risk for some unwanted attention from the federal government, as the letter articulates.

The federal government also warns that ambiguous compliance and the "following characteristics" are indicative of illegal drug trafficking:

- Unlawful possession or unlawful use of firearms
- Violence
- Sales to minors
- Financial and marketing activities inconsistent with the terms, conditions, or purposes of state law, including evidence of money-laundering activity and/or financial gains or excessive amounts of cash inconsistent with purported compliance with state or local law
- Amounts of marijuana inconsistent with purported compliance with state or local law
- Illegal possession or sale of other controlled substances
- Ties to other criminal enterprises

But the Justice Department also covers itself—reminding everyone that federal law trumps state law. Of course, no state can authorize violations of federal law, and the list of factors above is not intended to describe exhaustively when a federal prosecution may be warranted.

Accordingly, in prosecutions under the Controlled Substances Act, federal prosecutors are not expected to charge, prove, or otherwise establish any state law violations. Indeed, this memorandum does not alter in any way the department's authority to enforce federal law, including laws prohibiting the manufacture, production, distribution, possession, or use of marijuana on federal property.

And just in case you were hoping that this letter sanctioned the use and sale of marijuana? The Justice Department wants you to know:

> This guidance regarding resource allocation does not "legalize" marijuana or provide a legal defense to a violation of federal law, nor is it intended to create any privileges, benefits, or rights, substantive or procedural, enforceable by any individual, party or witness in any administrative, civil, or criminal matter. Nor does clear and unambiguous compliance with state law or the absence of one or all of the above factors create a

legal defense to a violation of the Controlled Substances
Act. Rather, this memorandum is intended solely as a
guide to the exercise of investigative and prosecutorial
discretion.[2]

Ogden also reminds everyone that state law cannot be invoked as
a means of protecting someone who is producing marijuana for
recreational purposes.

Finally, nothing herein precludes investigation or prosecution
where there is a reasonable basis to believe that compliance with
state law is being invoked as a pretext for the production or distribution of marijuana for purposes not authorized by state law.
Nor does this guidance preclude investigation or prosecution,
even when there is clear and unambiguous compliance with existing state law, in particular circumstances where investigation or
prosecution otherwise serves important federal interests.

Are you confused yet? Thousands of marijuana providers certainly were (and still are). Chris Bartkowicz in Denver is hoping
this memo will enable him to avoid prison, but in truth, it provides a lot of leeway to the feds, thereby enabling the federal government to use its discretion in determining which growers, users,
and sellers they should pursue.

Eric Holder's February 2009 statement demonstrates a new
respect for, and tolerance of, states' rights. Prohibition was
repealed at the state level prior to being repealed by the U.S.
government, and there are many similarities between the prohibition of alcohol and the prohibition of marijuana. Lawmakers realized there was an economic advantage to taxing alcohol, just as
California's lawmakers are seeing a potential boost to state coffers.
Meanwhile, just as most doctors in the United States desire the
ability to prescribe medical marijuana to patients in need, medical
professionals in the twenties lobbied, along with the alcohol industry, of course, for repeal for medicinal liquors. In fact, Congress
even held hearings on the medicinal value of beer! As Prohibition
became increasingly unpopular, especially in the big cities, repeal
was eagerly anticipated. Eventually it happened. With public

sentiment in favor of legalization of marijuana for medicinal purposes and with poll numbers increasingly suggesting that a growing number of Americans are comfortable with full legalization of the drug, the question now is: Is it possible for marijuana prohibition to be repealed in the same fashion as alcohol prohibition? Marijuana advocates say yes. Time will tell.

A comparison to gay marriage may also seem apt here, as many readers may be thinking to themselves, "Can't the courts sort this out?" Unfortunately for states that legalized medical marijuana, the courts have already decided it. If the feds say it's not legal, it's not legal.

It may be useful at this point to take a step back for a civics lesson. At this point in our nation's history, the federal government has far more stature and power than states and municipalities. Think Barack Obama versus Bill Ritter. Who's Bill Ritter? He's the governor of Colorado and charged with enforcing, or not enforcing as the case may be, the laws of the state, including those Bartkowicz assumed would shield him from prosecution. The reason this is confusing to most people is that in the area of governmental authority, the exercise of power is not a simple matter of size, resources, or stature, especially when it comes to the powers of the federal government. While the federal government may appear omnipotent—it is, after all, the master of a $3.5 trillion budget, able to project military power globally and affect how we live our lives in ways large and small, from how fast we drive on the highways to how much tax we pay when we die—in reality the federal government is quite limited in its powers. If there is not a specified power in the Constitution, the federal government does not have it, at least in theory.

Let's start with the basics. When one thinks of the most important powers in the Constitution, people might think about the federal government's power to make war, collect taxes, and protect people from unjust treatment. All are clearly important, and all are provided for in one way or another in the Constitution or in the amendments to the Constitution. But what about all of the other things the federal government does? Is there a specific power in the Constitution that authorizes the federal government to pass speed limits? No. How about a specific law that enables the federal government to pass sweeping health care legislation? No. Environmental protection laws, aviation laws, kidnapping laws? No, no, and no. So how does the federal government accomplish all of the things it does if there aren't specific rights that grant them the ability to do so? The answer lies in eighteen words known as the commerce clause, which states that the U.S. Congress shall have power "to regulate Commerce with foreign nations, and among the several States, and with the Indian Tribes."

This simple clause has arguably provided the federal government with as much power as all of the other powers in the Constitution combined. The beauty of the commerce clause is that Congress has attempted to justify almost every law imaginable by simply saying that it has a direct or indirect effect on the economy. Anyone challenging a federal law in court has to prove that the law, or the lack of one, won't have any financial effect on anyone, which is nearly impossible to do.

The purpose of the clause was very straightforward: to create a central government that could facilitate commerce with other nations and among the states. The idea was to vest the authority over interstate and international commerce in the federal government to prevent the several states from pursuing protectionist policies that would over time weaken the overall economic power of the nation. This makes perfect sense, because one of the principal weaknesses of the Articles of Confederation was the lack of federal power over commerce. And in the early years the Supreme Court ruled in cases that established the power of the commerce clause, but in ways that were not far from what a simple reading of the text would lead you to believe the framers intended.

The most notable commerce clause case from the early years of the republic was *Gibbons v. Ogden*. In *Gibbons*, Chief Justice John Marshall issued a decision that struck down the attempt by the state of New York to grant a steamboat monopoly to Robert Fulton. Fulton later sold the monopoly to Ogden, and Ogden sued to establish the legitimacy of the monopoly. Marshall ruled that the power to regulate interstate commerce included the power to regulate interstate navigation. This clearly makes sense; it would be a rather empty power for the federal government if it could not regulate the means by which commerce moved from state to state—and navigation of the nation's rivers, lakes, and coastal waters was a primary mode of transferring goods and people.

Marshall, however, went further than that, saying Congress is only limited in expanding its power under the commerce clause by its ability to retain the support of the people at the ballot box. This line of thought would ultimately be relied on in future interpretations of the commerce clause to expand it far beyond obvious applications like that in *Gibbons*.

The commerce clause would take its largest leap forward during the New Deal. During the 1930s, Franklin Delano Roosevelt pushed several laws and programs through Congress aimed at reversing the miserable economic conditions of the Great Depression. Among these laws and programs were the Works Progress Administration, which employed workers in local improvement projects; the Social Security Act, which established social security insurance; the Fair Labor Standards Act, which established a minimum wage and hours; and the Agricultural Adjustment Act, which set limits on agricultural outputs. The last of these acts, the Agricultural Adjustment Act, provides a great place to illustrate how the Supreme Court has interpreted the commerce clause in modern times.

Bartkowicz makes a good case that he was shocked that the federal government would come after him for growing pot. But one has to think that somewhere in the back of his mind he must have been a little nervous that this was too good to be true—he had been arrested before for possession and growing a lot of pot, and selling it is something that's been illegal for a very long time. But, given the confusion surrounding Colorado's laws permitting medical marijuana and Eric Holder's memo, it's believable that Bartkowicz thought he wasn't running much of a risk by starting his grow. If you think he was surprised, imagine the shock at having the federal government come after you for growing—wheat! That's right, wheat—the grain, the kind you use to mill flour and bake bread. And, yes, some poor, unsuspecting farmer found himself on the wrong side of the federal government when his wheat crop ran afoul of the limits set pursuant to the Agricultural Adjustment Act of 1938.

The farmer's name was Roscoe Filburn, and the 1942 case was *Wickard v. Filburn*. The Agricultural Adjustment Act set limits on the production of wheat for the purpose of stabilizing the price of wheat in the national market. Filburn was a farmer, growing wheat on his own land, and he produced more than the amount allotted to him under the act. Filburn stipulated that he had grown wheat on 23.1 acres, which was 11.9 acres in excess of his permitted acreage of 11.1. This resulted in excess production of 239 bushels of wheat, and the federal government ordered Filburn to destroy the wheat and pay a fine. Filburn admitted to growing wheat in excess of the limits but argued that he had grown the wheat for his own consumption and that it could have no bearing on interstate commerce, putting his actions beyond the reach of the federal government. The Supreme Court, however, disagreed. it concluded that the power of the commerce clause did extend to Filburn's farm, because even though he had not put the wheat he grew into interstate commerce, by growing rather than buying wheat for home consumption, Filburn did affect commerce. Did it matter that 239 bushels of wheat could hardly have an effect on commerce, however defined? Not to the Supreme Court, which reasoned that while Filburn's individual act may be insubstantial, the cumulative effect of thousands of farmers taking the same action would become substantial.

The Supreme Court's adoption of this line of reasoning also makes it quite clear that for all practical purposes there may be no limits on the scope of the congressional power acting under the commerce clause, for almost any action taken could have some ultimate effect on interstate commerce, especially if that individual action is combined with the potential for thousands to take an identical action.

Following *Wickard*, the commerce clause predictably was held to be the source of congressional power in numerous areas. And, although the facts and holding of *Wickard* may be troubling to those concerned about the expansion of federal power, the end results were not all bad. The Supreme Court would use the power of the commerce clause to uphold congressional legislation that established many important policies Americans now take for granted. The most notable was the Civil Rights Act of 1964. It may be surprising that the power to enact the Civil Rights Act was not based on the explicit power to stop discrimination. Instead, Congress attacked the problem of racial discrimination by proscribing it in any place that is involved in interstate commerce. That is how Congress got the reach to stop discrimination in restaurants, hotels, stores, and other businesses. Eliminating discrimination in public places was certainly a great outcome for the country, and from a more technical perspective, the application of the commerce clause to businesses involved in interstate commerce appears to be much less of a stretch than pursuing a sole farmer for growing crops for home consumption.

It wasn't until 1995 that the Supreme Court would hold that Congress had overstepped its power under the commerce clause. The case was *United States v. Lopez* and involved a challenge to the Gun-Free School Zones Act of 1990, which made it a federal crime to carry a gun within one thousand feet of a school. Congress clearly had a noble objective in its attempt to make schools free from guns, but this would not carry the day with the Supreme Court. The Court rejected the government's claim that carrying a gun near a school was in any way related to commerce. The holding is significant not only because it was the first restraint the Court placed on Congress's use of the commerce clause in over four decades but also because it questioned the expansion of the powers sustained under the commerce clause:

> To uphold the Government's contentions here, we have to pile inference upon inference in a manner that would bid fair to convert congressional authority under the Commerce Clause to a general police power of the sort retained by the States. Admittedly, some of our prior cases have taken long steps down that road, giving great deference to congressional action. The broad language in these opinions has suggested the possibility of additional expansion, but we decline here to proceed any further. To do so would require us to conclude that the Constitution's enumeration of powers does not presuppose something not enumerated, and that there never will be a distinction between what is truly national and what is truly local. This we are unwilling to do.[3]

Five years after *Lopez*, the Supreme Court would strike down parts of the Violence Against Women Act of 1995 as exceeding federal power under the commerce clause. The parts of the law that were struck down provided victims of gender-based violence the right to sue their attackers in federal court. So by 2000, the Supreme Court was finally placing limits on the exercise of federal power under the commerce clause.

That new hesitance to follow Congress's lead, combined with the relaxation of attitudes toward marijuana use, at least for medicinal purposes, and outright legalization might have meant clear sailing for Bartkowicz. Except for one problem—the Supreme Court confronted the issue of marijuana possessed for medicinal

purposes in 2005 and ruled that the federal government could outlaw homegrown marijuana cultivated for medicinal purposes.

The facts of *Gonzales v. Raich* make it clear that the Supreme
Court still views the power of the federal government under
the commerce clause to be essentially unlimited for matters of
actual commerce. In *Raich,* two women, Angel Raich and Diane
Monson, sought to use medicinal marijuana within the bounds of
California's Compassionate Use Act, which allowed for the possession and use of medicinal marijuana. Monson grew her own marijuana and had six plants. In April 2002, county sheriffs' deputies
and federal agents from the Drug Enforcement Agency came to
Monson's home. After the plants were found, the county officials
concluded that Monson's possession and use of marijuana was per-
fectly legal under California law. The federal agents seized and
destroyed all six of her plants. Monson and Raich sued the government, seeking a declaratory judgment prohibiting enforcement
of the "federal Controlled Substances Act to the extent it prevents
them from possessing, obtaining, or manufacturing cannabis for
their personal medical use."[4]

The facts of *Raich* could not have been better positioned for
marijuana users. The women possessed a small amount of marijuana. The women were clearly very ill and were using marijuana
under a doctor's orders. And, they were doing so in California,
which had enacted the Compassionate Use Act that specifically
made it legal for them to possess and use marijuana for medical
purposes under California law.

The Supreme Court, however, held that under the commerce
clause, Congress had the authority to outlaw homegrown marijuana even in states that approve its use for medicinal purposes.
It was a 6–3 vote, and the decision made it clear that federal anti-
drug laws trump state laws—the Controlled Substances Act prevents the cultivation and possession of marijuana, even by people
who claim a medicinal need for the herb, and even in a state that
expressly authorizes medicinal marijuana.

While this decision makes clear that the logic of *Wickard* is alive and well, it also provides a rationale for its ruling that makes clear that the majority does place restraints on congressional power under the commerce clause. The Court explained that modern commerce-clause jurisprudence was based on a framework that identifies three legitimate areas in which Congress can exercise its powers under the commerce clause:

> First, Congress can regulate the channels of interstate commerce. Second, Congress has authority to regulate and protect the instrumentalities of interstate commerce, and persons or things and interstate commerce. Third, Congress has the power to regulate activities that substantially affect interstate commerce.[5]

The third category is the basis on which the Supreme Court upheld congressional power in *Raich*, with the Court holding that its task was merely to determine whether a rational basis exists to support the conclusion that private production of marijuana substantially affects interstate commerce. The Court referenced its earlier logic in *Wickard* in holding that private production and consumption could have substantial effects on interstate commerce:

> The parallel concern making it appropriate to include marijuana grown for home consumption in the Controlled Substances Act is the likelihood that the high demand in the interstate market will draw such marijuana into that market. While the diversion of homegrown wheat tended to frustrate the federal interest in stabilizing prices by regulating the volume of commercial transactions in the interstate market, the diversion of homegrown marijuana tends to frustrate the federal interest in eliminating commercial transactions in the interstate market in their entirety. In both cases, the regulation is squarely within Congress' commerce

power because production of the commodity meant for home consumption, be it wheat or marijuana, has a substantial effect on supply and demand in the national market for that commodity.[6]

The Court further explained the logic of the modern commerce clause case law by finding that Congress may regulate activity that substantially affects interstate commerce, even if such activity is not itself interstate commerce. This is found in the "necessary and proper clause," which provides that Congress has the authority to "make all laws necessary and proper" to enact its enumerated powers.[7]

The Supreme Court also explained that its holdings in *United States v. Lopez* and *United States v. Morrison* were distinguished from the facts of *Raich* in one very substantial way: neither the Gun-Free School Zones Act nor the Violence Against Women Act themselves regulated economic activity of any kind. The Controlled Substances Act clearly regulated the economic activity, or commerce, of manufacturing, selling, and buying controlled substances. Thus, the fundamental purposes of the Controlled Substances Act was to regulate interstate commerce, and the laws that were meant to support it could be deemed to substantially affect interstate commerce.

In reading the opinion in *Raich,* it also became apparent that in some ways it was even more of an extension of federal power than in *Wickard*. In reading *Wickard,* Filburn seemed to be the very epitome of a victim of federal abuse—the small farmer growing wheat on his farm to be consumed by his family. Not being very familiar with farm quantities, the fact that Filburn produced 293 bushels in excess of his quota didn't seem egregious to me. It wasn't until reading the discussion of *Wickard* in *Raich* that I realized 293 bushels equated to almost nine tons. That is a lot of wheat, and it becomes clear that if thousands of farmers exceeded their quotas by such a significant amount, it would ultimately affect interstate commerce. In *Raich*, the amount of contraband at issue was much smaller—six plants and a more limited universe of participant farmers versus medical marijuana users.

Justice Sandra Day O'Connor, in her dissent in *Raich*, stressed the need to enforce clear boundaries over the reach of the commerce clause: "We enforce the 'outer limits' of Congress' Commerce Clause authority not for their own sake, but to protect historic spheres of state sovereignty from excessive federal encroachment and thereby to maintain the distribution of power fundamental to our federalist system of government."

O'Connor went on to make two important points. The first is simple, the second more abstract, but perhaps more important. The simple point was that "the sphere of state sovereignty had always included police powers to define criminal law and protect the health, safety, and welfare of [a states'] citizens." By extending commerce-clause authority to this level there was virtually no police power that the federal government could claim authority over.

The more abstract point was that by limiting the state's ability to experiment we risked stifling policy innovations that may, over time, lessen one of the key strengths of our federal system:

> One of federalism's chief virtues, of course, is that it promotes innovation by allowing for the possibility that "a single courageous State may, if its citizens choose, serve as a laboratory; and try novel social and economic experiments without risk to the rest of the country." Relying on Congress' abstract assertions, the Court has endorsed making it a federal crime to grow small amounts of marijuana in one's own home for one's own medicinal use. This overreaching stifles an express choice by some States, concerned for the lives and liberties of their people, to regulate medical marijuana differently. If I were a California citizen, I would not have voted for the medical marijuana ballot initiative; if I were a California legislator I would not have supported the Compassionate Use Act. But whatever the wisdom of California's experiment with medical marijuana, the federalism principles that have driven our Commerce Clause cases require that room for experiment to be protected in this case.[8]

Justice O'Connor's respect for the role of local government in forging policy solutions that may be of value to the nation as a whole should not be surprising—prior to her appointment as an associate justice on the Supreme Court, O'Connor was a state legislator in Arizona.

In her dissent in *Raich*, O'Connor cited her opinion in *United States v. Lopez* (the prior medicinal marijuana case on record), where she invoked the common argument that the states are the laboratories of democracy. It's a good idea, in other words, to let different states try different policies because that's ultimately the only way to sort good laws from bad ones.

Meanwhile, Justice Clarence Thomas wrote a straightforward analysis arguing that it's not interstate commerce if a person never intended for his or her weed to leave his or her own backyard. He stressed that the commerce clause is inapplicable because:

> respondent's local cultivation and consumption of marijuana is not "Commerce . . . among the several States."
>
> Certainly no evidence from the founding suggests that "commerce" included the mere possession of a good or some personal activity that did not involve trade or exchange for value. In the early days of the Republic, it would have been unthinkable that Congress could prohibit the local cultivation, possession, and consumption of marijuana.[9]

In addition, Thomas argues that regulating the personal growing of marijuana goes far beyond the necessary scope of the federal government.

> If the majority is to be taken seriously, the Federal Government may now regulate quilting bees, clothes drives, and potluck suppers throughout the 50 States. This makes a mockery of Madison's assurance to the

people of New York that the "powers delegated" to the Federal Government are "few and defined," while those of the States are "numerous and indefinite."[10]

The reality is, under the current configuration of the Supreme Court it's unlikely the country will see state law trump federal law. This means that anyone in the industry who is caught by the feds, although he or she may be operating 100 percent in line with state laws, is going to have a hard time arguing a case. The law, as it now stands, is the law. Although the feds, via Eric Holder, may say they don't intend to go after medicinal users and producers operating in compliance with their states, they still have every right to do so—and once you're caught, you're caught. Perhaps the only real path to removing serious penalties for those involved in the medical marijuana industry is to change the schedule of the drug so that it is classified as a drug with medical value and can therefore actually be prescribed by a doctor rather than recommended. In the meantime, don't count on the courts.

16

SMOKE FREE OR DIE

Changing Minds in a
Hard-to-Change State

In New Hampshire, the state I grew up in, residents take pride in the state motto "Live Free or Die," which is plastered across every state license plate. New Hampshire has a Libertarian undertone to its politics, as Joe McQuaid—the longtime editor of the *Manchester Union Leader* newspaper—once told me years ago when I interviewed him about the New Hampshire primary. "People in New Hampshire don't want the government being too involved in their lives," he said, as we strolled through the newsroom. "It's one reason why we don't have a state income tax." It may also be a reason that many in the state are pushing for marijuana legalization. As McQuaid points out, New Hampshire residents don't want the government—and certainly not the *federal* government—meddling in their lives.

Not only does New Hampshire not have an income tax—it also has no sales tax. There's a fiscal conservatism that runs deep in residents' blood. I can't tell you how many times I've heard Granite Staters say, "What government has, government spends." Thus, the state government is kept on a tight leash both fiscally and politically. (New Hampshire is one of the few states that elects its governor every two years.) Although there are some property taxes, New Hampshire residents enjoy the second-lowest tax burden in the nation, after Alaska. But it does maintain a revenue source: New Hampshire actually makes quite a bit of money, tens of millions, on alcohol every year. The government has a near-monopoly on liquor, and bottles of some spirits can only be bought from state-owned stores. Don't misinterpret this, though, as plain conservatism. In the summer of 2009, my uncle, Paul McEachern, a state representative, introduced a bill legalizing gay marriage throughout New Hampshire. It was passed by the legislature and signed into law by the governor. New Hampshire is just one of five states (and the District of Columbia) to now allow gay marriage.

Some people have called marijuana legalization the new gay marriage, with its state-by-state approach and modest successes. Is that a fair way to look at it? Is New Hampshire the next state to loosen the rules about pot?

Matt Simon is on the forefront of the Granite State's marijuana legalization efforts. A former college English teacher, he had grown tired of seeing his students be arrested for marijuana. He spent time in Kentucky, a state where the gateway argument—the idea that if you try one drug, like pot, it will inevitably lead to other more harmful drugs—is believed very strongly. "By going after marijuana so hard, by putting so much effort into making sure young people don't smoke, students have turned to more dangerous drugs like pills and meth."

Kentucky actually produces more marijuana than any other state except California, according to officials at the Office of National Drug Policy's Appalachia High Intensity Drug Trafficking Area Program. Many of the small towns of remote Eastern Kentucky have had a long history of bootlegging moonshine. That tradition—coupled with high rates of unemployment and poverty—has helped fuel the marijuana trade. Much of the harvest is carried in car trunks to metropolitan areas like Pittsburgh, Cleveland, and Detroit.

In 2007, Simon left Kentucky and moved to New Hampshire to begin his marijuana campaign. In 2008, he worked to push a bill that would reduce the penalty for marijuana possession, lowering the penalty on amounts less than a quarter of an ounce. The current penalty is a few thousand dollars and time in jail, and the bill would have reduced that to just a $200 fine.

Originally sponsored by a Democratic member of the state House of Representatives, Jeffrey Fontas, HB 1623 passed that March 193–141. Simon and other advocates cheered the support but soon watched the bill die in the Senate. While various polls showed a majority of citizens backing decriminalization, opponents repeatedly claimed that passing a bill like this sent the wrong message to young people.

The irony about protecting our impressionable youths is that there's a strong correlation already between age and beliefs about cannabis. Some analysts attribute changing attitudes toward marijuana to the fact that younger people, who tend to have more liberal attitudes toward the substance, are now in positions of power. Case in point: President Barack Obama is now the third president in a row to acknowledge having smoked marijuana, and unlike President Bill Clinton who swore he "didn't inhale" and President George W. Bush who had to be rehabilitated from his addictions, Obama was rather matter-of-fact about his experimentation— saying famously in the campaign, "As a kid, I inhaled. That was the whole point."

Although there are numerous reasons for the shift in public opinion, one stems, rather simply, from the change in demographics. According to the National Organization for the Reform of Marijuana Laws's (NORML's) Dale Gieringer, the resistance is most significant among the over-sixty-five set. He says every study that his organization has conducted demonstrates that the most disdain for pot emanates from the oldest segment of the country's population. Indeed, a 2009 Gallup poll notes that 72 percent of seniors (age sixty-five and older) were against marijuana. But Americans over sixty-five would have been past college age and too old for Woodstock when it happened. Not surprisingly, the younger the group, the more favorable the attitude toward pot. For example, 50 percent of those Americans in the 18 to 49 demographic said they favored legalization, up from 39 percent in 2005, and 45 percent of the 50 to 64 set backed legalization, up from 37 percent four years earlier. Referring to the strength in the overall Gallup results, Gieringer tells me, "We've never seen numbers like that."

A poll by the Pew Center released in April 2010 showed that nearly three-quarters of Americans, 73 percent, are in favor of seeing their state allow the sale and use of marijuana for medical purposes if it is prescribed by a doctor, while 23 percent were against the idea. Younger Americans are more likely than older Americans to favor legalizing marijuana for medicinal use, although the majority across all age groups supports medical use. Sixty-one percent of Republicans favor permitting medical marijuana in their state, compared with 76 percent of Independents and 80 percent of Democrats. Conservative Republicans are the least likely to support legalization of medical marijuana—still, 54 percent of this group are in favor.

Still, they may grow even stronger in the near future. According to Gallup, "if public support were to continue growing at a rate of 1 to 2 percent per year as it has since 2000, the majority of Americans could favor legalization in as little as four years."[1] The reality is that as older generations (the parents of the baby boomers) gradually die off, the country is left with Americans who are increasingly tolerant of marijuana use.

This shift in public support has become a groundswell that is sweeping the country. Lawmakers from Rhode Island to Washington, D.C., to New Mexico are rethinking their attitudes toward marijuana. Fifteen states and Washington, D.C., have legalized medical marijuana, while another fifteen states are

weighing legislation or ballot initiatives that could legalize medical marijuana in the near future. Marijuana growers, dispensary
owners, and marijuana advocates—and their critics—all agree on
one thing: the movement toward legalization began, in earnest,
with Eric Holder, the fifty-nine-year-old newly appointed U.S.
attorney general.

It was February 2009 when Holder stunned the country by
announcing to reporters in a press conference that the Justice
Department would no longer raid medicinal marijuana clubs that
are established legally under state law. It was a major departure
from the policies of any previous administration and clearly the
polar opposite of the Bush administration's zero-tolerance policy
for marijuana (regardless of state law). But Holder's declaration was simply living up to campaign promises from President
Obama who, while stumping in New Hampshire, told voters that
he would not "have the Justice Department prosecuting and raid-
ing medical marijuana users."

Despite these comments on the campaign trail, the Drug
Enforcement Administration continued to (and still does) carry
out raids on medicinal clinics. At a February 2009 press conference, reporters asked whether the raids would continue. "No,"
Holder told them, "What the president said during the campaign,
you'll be surprised to know, will be consistent with what we'll
be doing in law enforcement. He was my boss during the campaign. He is formally and technically and by law my boss now.
What he said during the campaign is now American policy."[2] The
new attorney general then dropped this bombshell: "We will not
use our limited resources in the fight against the marijuana trade
against those people who are using it consistent with state law and
to fight serious illnesses, such as cancer or other diseases." The
wheels toward legalization, at the state level, had begun turning.
A month later they began spinning.

On March 26, 2009, interested online citizens were getting
ready to tune in, on their computers, to what would become the
first live online video town hall meeting by a U.S. president. More
than 100,000 questions were submitted, and online voters cast

more than 3.5 million votes for the questions they most wanted answered. One of their top picks: whether President Obama believed legalizing and federally taxing marijuana might help stimulate the economy.

The president, standing alongside Jared Bernstein (chief economist and economic policy adviser to Vice President Joe Biden) brought up the question himself, injecting a little comic relief into the video chat.

President Obama: Jared, before you ask the next question, just to say that we—we took votes about which questions were going to be asked and I think three million people voted or—

Dr. Bernstein: Three point five million.

President Obama: Three point five million people voted. I have to say that there was one question that was voted on that ranked fairly high, and that was whether legalizing marijuana would improve the economy—(laughter)—and job creation. And I don't know what this says about the online audience—(laughter)—but I just want—I don't want people to think that—this was a fairly popular question; we want to make sure that it was answered. The answer is, no, I don't think that is a good strategy—(laughter)—to grow our economy. [Applause.]

Dr. Bernstein: Thank you for clearing that up. [Laughter.][3]

Although laughter emanated from the live audience of teachers, nurses, and some business professionals in the White House's East Room, elsewhere in the country, marijuana enthusiasts did not see the president's acknowledgment of their question as quite funny, but it did give them something to smile about. They considered it a major turning point in their decades-long push toward legalization. "It was a serious tipping point" in the legalization debate, as Gieringertold me. Despite the president's definitive response, marijuana advocates say the mere fact that legalization was even being *discussed* in such a prestigious and public forum exemplified the growing momentum behind their movement. Gieringer, who has written some impressive economic analysis supporting marijuana legalization, later described the moment when he heard Obama mention the marijuana question in the town hall meeting as monumental. "I've been involved in this issue for twenty years," he said, "and when that happened, for the first time, I really began to feel that legalization is on its way. The public climate has changed." He maintains that although it may not happen in the next year, "it will definitely happen."

Earlier in the book I mentioned Richard Lee, the founder of Oaksterdam University; he sees this change as inevitable, too, if a slow process. "Federal prohibition ended in 1933," he tells me. "Kansas didn't legalize till 1946. Mississippi till 1966, thirty-three years later. It'll be a similar thing [with pot] once federal prohibition will fall. Then it will be up to each state to decide whether they want to legalize it. States like California will be legal twenty years before Florida or Louisiana."

But there's actually more of a movement than Lee gives the country credit for, at least when it comes to medicinal marijuana. In addition to the states that have liberalized their marijuana laws, a number of traditionally conservative states are making progress toward legalization. In the right-leaning South, for example, the state of Alabama has a medicinal use bill before the state legislature, Missouri has a marijuana bill pending in its House of Representatives, Arkansas has a proposed bill due for consideration in 2011, and North Carolina is debating whether to allow marijuana use for people with certain illnesses. Meanwhile, in the more liberal North Country, Vermont is weighing whether to allow state-licensed liquor stores to sell medicinal marijuana. Indeed, Lee may see his life's work realized. For better or for worse, the consensus is we're on the road to becoming a Marijuana Nation.

• • •

What is it, though, that is making the cause seem so urgent? For a state like New Hampshire, the costs of jailing for having a little pot start to run pretty high.

Nearly one million individuals were arrested for marijuana possession in the United States in 2006. In both California and New York, state fiscal costs dedicated to criminal marijuana law enforcement are estimated to annually total more than $1 billion for each state. The national total for marijuana probation totals $41 billion. This is money that could be spent on education instead of prisons. This is money that could help prevent a generation of young people from engaging in behavior that may, depending on whether they have an addictive personality, endanger their lives.

Jeff Miron, in a telephone interview with me in the winter of 2010, said full legalization makes sense from an economic standpoint, as it would result in a savings of $7.7 billion per year due to a reduction in government expenditure on the enforcement of prohibition. Miron also estimates that $5.3 billion of this savings would go to state and local governments while $2.4 billion would accrue to the federal government.

Miron's researching is an interesting glimpse into what a legalized marijuana industry might look like. He admitted to me that he was extraordinarily cautious, given that his funding came from a promarijuana group, and he was keenly aware that he might be criticized for appearing too enthusiastically in favor of legalization. Thus, he deliberately used the smallest estimates for drug production in the United States in an attempt to present unbiased research. Miron does not believe a legalized marijuana market would result in a huge uptick in marijuana usage. He estimates that usage rates, although they would likely increase slightly, would remain fairly stable, as demonstrated in Portugal. The reason for this, he contends, is that people who want to smoke pot will do so anyway—regardless of the law. Although there may be a few guarded individuals who do not smoke for fear of being caught and prosecuted (he described them as "executive types that worry about what being arrested might mean for their careers and image"), that number is fairly small. Thus, usage rates would, in his estimation, remain relatively stable.

Meanwhile, legalization advocates point out that until marijuana is fully legalized, communities will still be subjected to the violence associated with the underground and criminal element of the drug trade. That's because the profits are too good for criminals to pass up. In fact, as Dr. Evan Wood, chair of the Vienna Declaration Writing Committee, points out, "Any time that law enforcement has any success at taking out a drug dealer . . . that has a perverse effect of making it that much more profitable for someone else to get into the market."[4]

Back in Portugal, I asked Dr. Goulao, the so-called father of the decriminalization movement, whether full legalization may be in the works. He looked at me, eyebrows raised, and sighed. "It's doubtful," he concluded, pointing to the various treaties the United States has signed and saying, "We have signed [them] at the United Nations conventions and are obliged to penalize the use of these drugs." Then how can decriminalization even exist, I wonder, if governments are obligated to penalize? Apparently, it comes down to semantics. "Penalize is not the same as criminalize," says the doctor. "So, this is a good intermediary solution."

"But, why not take it a step further?" I press him. "Why not decriminalize the entire process, including supply, so that you don't have as much crime?"

Although he has "no difficulty in assuming that [legalization] can be a solution," it's a transnational solution, and the rest of the world simply isn't there yet. "It cannot be taken on by one single country or even a single region. There has to be a movement, a much more broad movement in that direction, to allow it to happen."

"Do you think full decriminalization, including a legalized supply chain, is something that could happen in the world in your lifetime?" I ask.

"In my lifetime? I have my doubts. But, eventually, I think it can be the solution."

As a physician, he has accomplished his goal in that he's trying to ensure that addicted individuals receive treatment rather than jail time. "I have been able to do a wonderful thing," he tells me, a smile on his face. Indeed, he has.

Doctors are coming around to the legalization side of things as well. The American Medical Association recently reversed a long-time position and urged the federal government to remove marijuana from Schedule I of the Controlled Substances Act, which equates pot with highly addictive, and potentially deadly, drugs like heroin.

The Controlled Substances Act (which federally governs all known drugs including marijuana) became law in 1970 under President Richard Nixon as part of the Comprehensive Drug Abuse Prevention and Control Act. The CSA determines the federal government's policy for the manufacturing, importation, possession, use, and distribution of regulated substances, and the Food and Drug Administration (FDA) and the DEA have the power to determine which drugs are placed in various categories or classifications, known as schedules. The criteria for the scheduling primarily involves the issue of whether there is a chance that an individual may abuse the drug and whether there is medical use for the drug in the United States. International treaties that govern the substance are also considered.

According to the CSA, the findings required for Schedule I are:

(A) The drug or other substance has a high potential for abuse.
(B) The drug or other substance has no currently accepted medical use in treatment in the United States.
(C) There is a lack of accepted safety for use of the drug or other substance under medical supervision.

Marijuana, as a Schedule I substance, is thus classified along-side the highly addictive drug heroin. Yet, powerful drugs like cocaine, methamphetamine, morphine, and oxycodone (the active ingredient in Oxycontin and Percocet) are classified as more tol-erated Schedule II drugs. In response to the growing number of states seeking to legalize marijuana for medicinal purposes, the FDA defended its stance against cannabis and support of mari-juana as a Schedule I drug in the Controlled Substances Act. In an April 2006 news release titled "Inter-Agency Advisory Regarding Claims That Smoked Marijuana Is a Medicine," it states, "A growing number of states have passed voter referenda (or legislative actions) making marijuana available for a variety of medical conditions upon a doctor's recommendation. These measures are inconsistent with efforts to ensure that medications undergo the rigorous scientific scrutiny of the FDA approval pro-cess and are proven safe."[5]

While activists like Matt Simon in New Hampshire and fed-eral officials like Eric Holder may seem like part of a movement toward legalization, it's important to remember that there are peo-ple like Gil Kerlikowske, the Obama administration's drug czar, standing firmly in the way. In an interview in the summer of 2010 with Kerlikowske (who admitted to me that it was part of his job to oppose the legalization of marijuana, saying, "the requirement is that we actively oppose legalization"), I asked him as we sat in a large conference room in his D.C. offices whether he thought it was fair to categorize marijuana as the same as heroine while cocaine was classified as Schedule II.

"Intuitively," I say, thinking out loud as the documentary cam-eras roll, "cocaine is a much more significant drug. Why would that [cocaine] be Schedule II and marijuana Schedule I?"

"Well, I think Schedule I says that there's no medicinal value."

"But," I counter, "You were just saying . . ." (I remind him of his comment moments earlier. I had asked him whether there might be some medicinal value to marijuana, and he had responded with, "I think the science has already pointed out that some properties of marijuana have some medicinal value.")

He nods his head in agreement, confirming his earlier statement. "There are properties," he concurs. "Science has said that
there are properties within marijuana that may have medicinal
value. I understand that the science is still going on and that's who
we should have address the problem, rather than popular vote."

But, that could be wishful—or even political—thinking, as it
is difficult to rely on science. The reason? Well, there are actually relatively few substantive studies on marijuana, primarily due
to the mass of legal hurdles a scientist must overcome to study
the plant.

In 2009, Simon resurfaced in New Hampshire and nearly suc-
ceeded in securing legalization for medicinal marijuana users.
The support throughout the state was significant, and nearly every
newspaper's editorial board, including the conservative statewide
paper the *Union Leader*, backed the legislation. In an editorial titled
"Pot Is Medicine: Let the Ill Use It," the editorial board wrote,

> Marijuana use can produce lots of outcomes that are not
> socially desirable. It also can alleviate horrible symp-
> toms of numerous chronic illnesses and, recent research
> is showing, actually fight some types of cancer. New
> research even suggests that although smoking pot while
> young increases the odds of testicular cancer in men,
> marijuana can kill lung and brain cancer cells.
>
> We understand the concerns of law enforcement offi-
> cials who oppose this bill. But at this point, withholding
> the proven medical benefits of smoked marijuana from
> those extremely ill patients who cannot be helped by any
> other treatment would amount to a cruel deprivation of
> necessary medical care. The Senate should pass the bill.[6]

"The bill got through both the House and the Senate," Simon
tells me, enthusiasm emanating through the phone line. (It was a
long time coming for the small but steely state. As I detailed in the

preface to this book, New Hampshire had wrestled with this issue since the early eighties.) "But then," he says with a sigh, "but then," he adds for emphasis, "the governor vetoed it." Governor John Lynch, a Democrat, disappointed many with his veto.

"That meant the bill needed to be overridden. We had two-thirds of the House for the override vote, but the Senate also needed two-thirds. We got a fourteen to ten vote." But he needed two more votes and fell short of the override.

Critics of medical marijuana argue that there's no *need* to legalize cannabis since it is possible for U.S. citizens to receive the psychoactive components of the drug without smoking a joint. Some cancer and HIV patients take a capsule called Marinol, made by the company Unimed. Marinol mimics THC—the psychoactive component of marijuana. The difficulty with Marinol, however, is that although it may stimulate a user's appetite, the drug can take as long as three hours to take effect. In comparison, smoking marijuana enables the THC to hit the body in such a way that a patient feels the effects almost immediately.

Even so, there are other health side effects to consider. The jury is still out as to what the long-term effects of smoking are on marijuana users. Advocates of cannabis insist pot smokers don't smoke joints in the same volume as tobacco smokers ingest cigarettes and thus it's difficult for marijuana users to harm their lungs as significantly. Supporting their argument, a 2006 study at the University of California, Los Angeles, by pulmonologist Donald Tashkin, who studied marijuana for thirty years, concluded that smoking marijuana, even regularly and heavily, does not lead to lung cancer. His study was the largest case control study ever done, and the results surprised even Tashkin himself, who said, "We hypothesized that there would be positive association between marijuana use and lung cancer, and that the association would be more positive with heavier use. What we found instead was no association at all, and even a suggestion of some protective effect."[7] Dr. Lester Grinspoon, professor emeritus of psychiatry at Harvard Medical

School and the author of *Marihuana: The Forbidden Medicine*, is considered to be one the most eminent scientists in the field of medical marijuana. He began his research in 1967, assuming he would be able to prove that marijuana was unsafe, only to discover the opposite. He calls it an "amazing medicine" and makes a poignant point when he compares the hazards of simple over-the-counter drugs with marijuana. "Aspirin," he says, "is 'safe'— although it claims between one thousand to two thousand people per year. With cannabis, it's been around for thousands of years. There has never been a death—never been a death. Is there any other substance in the pharmacopeia about which you can make that claim? I'm not sure there is."

Kerlikowske, as the former police chief for the city of Seattle, a city known for its liberal view on drugs (it is, after all, the host of the annual Hempfest) and experimentation with drug programs (it implemented a needle-exchange program in 2003, and voters passed an initiative making the enforcement of marijuana violations a low priority), is considered one of the more progressive drug czars to hold the position as director of the Office of National Drug Control Policy. He has indicated that the Obama administration is likely to deal with drugs as a public health issue rather than simply a criminal issue.

Although Kerlikowske is adamant that the government will not make a move to make changes to the Controlled Substance Act, he is less aggressive when it comes to the issue of pursuing marijuana growers who are within state guidelines. Referring to the Justice Department's memo, he says the mandate is to use finite resources to go after traffickers and financiers. "If you look back, you're very hard-pressed to find cases of the Drug Enforcement Administration or others going after medical marijuana patients." Of course, the key word is patients, since people growing for other patients have been raided, some of whom I've already detailed in this book.

Still, his mere indication that the DEA is backing off medicinal users combined with the attorney general's statements and the deputy attorney general's memo to U.S. attorneys does suggest that the tide is turning. Plus, he said this: "Marijuana is clearly a public safety and public health problem. I think the states are already approaching it in a very smart way. We're a federalist country, and states have a great deal of autonomy and have always had autonomy. That's why I think the attorney general issued some clear guidelines, which were needed, about federal resources and how they should be used."

Asa Hutchinson, the former head of the DEA, if anything, was even more convinced of the drawback of medical marijuana. In fact, he recently wrote on the potential for increasing societal problems in an editorial for CNBC.com. Ultimately, he maintained, legalized marijuana will neither save nor generate money but rather will cost society more in the long run. "Legalizing the drug will swell societal ills, and this outweighs the monetary benefits that might be achieved from its lawful sale," Hutchinson wrote. "For example, there will be a greater social cost from decline in worker productivity and school performance."[8]

However, the decline in productivity and school performance that Hutchinson worries about is doubtful given that usage rates are unlikely to spike. After decriminalization took effect in Portugal, usage rates ticked moderately higher among adults and actually decreased among teens.

Kerlikowske has attempted to discredit Portugal's success by calling it statistical smoke and mirrors. He insists that its results were clouded by the fact that the Libertarian think tank, The Cato Institute, authored the report. Essentially, he argues that Cato already "knows" its answer when conducting a study because of its Libertarian bias. All of the data accumulated by Cato came from *government* sources, however, and the independent European Commission on drug usage came to the same conclusion: Decriminalization (in this case, of *all* drugs) has a positive effect on society as it enables addicts to seek treatment, reduces the number of infectious diseases being communicated via dirty needles, and results in a decrease of usage rates among the nation's youth—all while not morphing into a narco-tourism hotspot or seeing a major spike in drug usage among the general population. As a society, we have condoned many potentially harmful activities, leaving the choice to individuals: alcohol, tobacco, motorcycles, firearms, small planes, deep fryers, and so forth. One major problem with outlawing marijuana is that by making possession and growing a crime, hundreds of thousands of young people are being sent to prison thereby creating a drain on the system and often ruining these individuals' lives. According to data from NORML, U.S. marijuana arrests jumped 165 percent during the nineties, from 287,850 in 1991 to 755,000 in 2003. Despite enhanced enforcement, NORML writes in a 2005 report that "increased arrest rates are not associated with reduced marijuana use, reduced marijuana availability, a reduction in the number of new users, reduced treatment admissions, reduced emergency room mentions, any reduction in marijuana potency, or any increases in the price of marijuana."[9]

According to an AP-CNBC poll, a good portion of people in the country have concerns about the health effects of the drug. More of the people surveyed believed marijuana would harm the overall health of the country (46 percent). Thirty-nine percent thought it would have no effect. And 13 percent believed marijuana legalization for any use would mostly improve the health of the people.

Although the majority of Americans support the legalization of marijuana for medicinal purposes, they remain unconvinced that full legalization, which would include the taxation and regulation of cannabis for recreational purposes, is a positive for the country. Nonetheless, a good number of people see revenue possibilities. Assuming the sale and possession of marijuana were actually legal, 62 percent of the 1,001 people surveyed by telephone in the early April 2010 poll favored taxing sales of the drug. Twenty-eight percent opposed.

The majority of Americans (46 percent) believe legalized pot sales would have no effect on the economy, although roughly one-third of the population disagrees, saying that marijuana would make the economy better. The majority of those polled also said marijuana would have no effect on the number of jobs in their communities.

Perhaps speaking to the public's general mistrust of government, more than half the country (54 percent) would prefer marijuana, if legalized, be sold by private businesses, while 36 percent would rather see the government handle it, based on the poll results.

The idea that marijuana is a "gateway drug" that pushes people on to harder, destructive drugs received some support in the poll (39 percent), although nearly half the country believes marijuana has no effect on whether people will use more serious drugs.

Interestingly, the country is nearly equally divided on whether marijuana should be regulated more heavily than alcohol. While 43 percent of the population believes marijuana regulations should be stricter than regulations for alcohol, more of those surveyed—44 percent—said that marijuana and alcohol should share the same level of regulation. Just 12 percent told pollsters regulations on marijuana should be less strict than those for alcohol.

Meanwhile, Kerlikowske remains opposed to marijuana. "If you legalize marijuana," he tells me, "which we know has a number of significant problems, the availability of that formerly illegal drug will make it more widespread."

A study released in July 2010 by the Rand Corporation supported Kerlikowske's fear that marijuana could become more popular and more widespread. According to the study, legalizing the production and distribution of marijuana in California could cause the price of pot to plummet as much as 80 percent while consumption could increase anywhere from 50 to 100 percent. "If prevalence increased by 100 percent," says the study, "then marijuana use in California would be close to the prevalence levels recorded in the late 1970s."[10]

It's hard to argue with the Rand Corporation's predicted price decline. After all, the reason pot is so expensive is not because it is difficult to grow but rather because it is illegal, and thus, a grower is taking on risk to provide it to a user. The grower must be compensated for that risk via a higher price for the good. (This is one reason drugs attract organized crime.)

Of course, some marijuana growers and distributors active in the marijuana market right now would lose out. So many I met in Northern California who were campaigning for legalization (marijuana wasn't just their livelihood but a political movement) insisted they wanted to see marijuana legal. "But this is how you make your living," I'd remind them. Still, they believe there will always be demand for "quality weed." These growers argue that they would become the "gourmet" growers who command a higher price for their product. Just like all of those successful mom-and-pop stores downtown, right? Not so fast.

If legalization moves the marijuana industry out of the underground and into the light of day, then just as the repeal of alcohol prohibition restored the traditional open-market alcohol industry, one would have to assume, the majority of the marijuana businesses would be forced into an open, transparent market. Prices for pot would likely plummet. A few outlets could keep a high-priced clientele, but most users would look for price, safety, and convenience. Most likely, the largest growers with the biggest economies of scale would prevail. Yes, in Napa Valley and Sonoma County there are some wineries that can charge a premium for superior product—but none of them are seeing profit margins like the marijuana growers I met. Jane Smith from Colorado had a more realistic exit plan for the day marijuana becomes legal on a recreational basis in her state (and she believes that will happen in the coming years). "That's when I pack up and sell," she tells me, her green eyes twinkling as she laughs. "I will welcome that day! Hopefully, I'll have the infrastructure to offer a big company that wants to come in and buy up a whole bunch of growing and distribution companies. Then," she says, smiling, "I'll finally get to retire." In the meantime, for Jane and the hundreds of other marijuana entrepreneurs trying to make a living in a treacherous field, it's business as usual.

• • •

Still, there is little evidence to suggest consumption rates will double. Perhaps the closest parallel to marijuana prohibition can be found in alcohol prohibition, also known as the Noble Experiment, from 1920 to 1933 in the United States. Despite the crackdown, per historical records, there was no evidence of a cutback on consumption of alcohol during Prohibition. Nor was there a significant uptick once Prohibition ended. In fact, according to the Shafer Report on marijuana in 1972, alcohol consumption levels remained consistent throughout Prohibition. Instead of buying alcohol through legal channels, Americans turned to the underground market. "Where legal enterprises could no longer supply the demand, an illicit traffic developed, from the point of manufacture to consumption. The institution of the speakeasy replaced the institution of the saloon. Estimates of the number of speakeasies throughout the United States ranged from 200,000 to 500,000."[11] Since Americans continued to consume alcohol despite the government ban during the twenties, the government effectively lost out on much-needed revenue while simultaneously contributing to the crime rate, because illegal gangs stepped in to fill the void that traditional liquor businesses could no longer fill.

Consider the Netherlands, where marijuana has been tolerated in pot "coffee" shops for years. Strolling through Amsterdam's cobblestone streets on a hot Sunday afternoon in August 2008, I watched families traveling by boat along the city's canals and spotted the occasional artist sitting with her easel along the street corner, painting the water. I witnessed a scene of happy American tourists dressed in T-shirts and shorts, drinking beer under the awning of a sidewalk café. Amid these densely packed streets amid the seventeenth-century buildings, are nearly three hundred so-called coffee shops—stores that sell coffee in front and neatly packaged plastic bags of marijuana in two- or three-gram servings in the dimly lit booths in the back. Some shops are obvious, attracting tourists with their large, neon-green marijuana-leaf signs, while others opt for the more subdued approach, displaying a small, white-and-green sign with the words "coffee shop" in their windows to indicate their line of business. Since 1975, these coffee shops have openly sold marijuana and hashish on the premises. Today, the shops offer a variety of marijuana strains to their customers, not "patients," because unlike in California, in Amsterdam marijuana consumers do not need to prove a need for the herb. In fact, selling marijuana is against the law in the Netherlands (although it is tolerated by authorities.)

Despite the ready availability of the drug, per government statistics, Dutch youth are actually less likely to smoke than Americans. As I explained in Chapter 12, while only 7 percent of Dutch teens have tried marijuana by age fifteen, in the United States more than 20 percent of teens have tried marijuana by age fifteen. In fact, according to the 2010 U.S.-government-endorsed "Monitoring the Future" survey, which is conducted yearly and includes students from the eighth, tenth, and twelfth grades, marijuana use in the prior twelve months was reported by about 12 percent of the nation's eighth graders, 27 percent of tenth graders, and a third of the country's twelfth graders.

Despite tougher drug policies in the United States, Americans are twice as likely to have tried marijuana as the Dutch. In fact, Americans were more likely to have tried marijuana or cocaine than people in any of the sixteen other countries, including France, Spain, South Africa, Mexico, and Colombia, that the survey covered.[12]

Thus, while many legalization critics worry that if marijuana is legalized in the United States, then usage rates might spike among the general population, there is little evidence that this would occur—case studies in the Netherlands, Portugal, and even Mexico (which decriminalized drugs in 2009 and has not seen a massive increase in usage rates) all suggest little increase. Harvard economist Jeffrey Miron, who wrote a study titled "The Budgetary Implications of Marijuana Prohibition" (how's that for peaking the interest of your Economics 101 students?) in June 2005, told me that with legalized drugs, "The number of people who might occasionally use marijuana could go up, but it wouldn't be drastic." That's because people who want to smoke weed pretty much already do. Although Miron admitted that some individuals might be willing to try it as long as there was no longer a social stigma attached (along with the risk of being arrested), in general, it's unlikely that legalization would have a major effect on behavior. This was certainly the case in Portugal. In Portugal, it was also predicted that drug usage would spike, but instead, while overall usage rates increased slightly, young people actually saw a decline in their usage rates, leading many to dub Portugal's experiment a resounding success.

In addition to the cost benefits (the amount of money saved on enforcement and the boost to state, and potentially federal, tax revenue) and health benefits, there are numerous other benefits to legalization. Although it's debatable whether we might actually see usage rates among the young plummet, we would definitely see a fall in the violence from Mexican drug cartels on both sides of the border.

Meanwhile, there might be another benefit of legalization for America's youth: law enforcement would have the ability to actually properly regulate the marijuana industry and keep it out of young people's hands. If marijuana were sold by licensed merchants who were required to check consumers' IDs (in order to ensure the age of a potential customer), then it would actually be easier to police. In the Netherlands, for example, marijuana is sold in regulated establishments to adults who must show proof of age. Clearly, any teen, as long as he or she has the money, can purchase drugs from a dealer. After all, a dealer does not check to see if someone is twenty-one years old. That said, nothing is foolproof, and we all know that there are plenty of bars that permit underage drinkers on the premises, so it's clear government would have to be vigilant in enforcing age restrictions. But at least government would have the opportunity.

Matt Simon and his group reemerged in 2010 with another decriminalization bill for New Hampshire. This one called for dropping criminal penalties against individuals found in possession of a quarter-ounce or less of marijuana. The crime would be reduced to a misdemeanor, carrying a maximum fine of $200. (At present, possessing a quarter ounce will land you a year in jail and a fine of up to $2,000.) In March, the bill passed the house (214–137) and now heads to the Senate. "Campaigning for medicinal marijuana really wore us out," Simon said. "[Marijuana advocates] are just fed up with the governor." Nonetheless, he has every intention of resurrecting the medicinal marijuana bill and now believes he has the votes to overturn the governor should the bill again be vetoed.

Three thousand miles from New Hampshire, in sunny and liberal California, home to the biggest cash crop in America, marijuana entrepreneurs began coming out of the woodwork, anxious for their chance to make money off an illegal, yet *legal,* drug. Attorney General Eric Holder's message that states would be permitted to operate medicinal clinics without the threat of interference from the DEA created massive buzz in the California medicinal community. Seemingly overnight, the number of clinics in Los Angeles ballooned from a couple hundred to an estimated one thousand. The city is now under pressure to curtail its exploding industry, and lawmakers are trying to limit the number of dispensaries to seventy, although hundreds that registered during a 2007 moratorium may be permitted to remain open temporarily. By May 2009, California's governor Arnold Schwarzenegger called for a debate on the topic of legalization and taxation as a means to stem the government's hemorrhaging budget (though he made it clear he would not support legalization), and San Francisco Democratic assemblyman Tom Ammiano sponsored a bill to legalize and tax marijuana. Known as the Regulate, Control and Tax Cannabis Initiative, the bill would legalize recreational marijuana use in California for adults over twenty-one and also allow state residents to grow their own pot in household spaces of up to twenty-five square feet. Ammiano's bill would impose a $50 per ounce state tax on pot made available for sale. It also would license private marijuana cultivators and wholesalers and give the state Department of Alcoholic Beverage Control authority over a legal retail marijuana industry.

Meanwhile, in the spring of 2010, a marijuana legalization initiative was officially added to the November 2010 ballot. Proposition 19 failed by a 9-point margin when voters went to the polls in November 2010; however, that hasn't stopped advocates' push to make California the first state in the nation to legalize marijuana for recreational use. Advocates like Richard Lee hope to see a regulated marijuana industry similar to alcohol, so that people over the age of twenty-one will be permitted to grow, buy, sell, and possess marijuana. "The state of California is in a very, very precipitous economic plight," he told *Time* magazine. Putting it even more bluntly, he added, "It's in the toilet. It looks very very bleak, with layoffs and foreclosures and schools closing or trying to operate four days a week. We've had the highest rates of unemployment we've ever had. With any revenue ideas, people say you have to think outside the box, you have to be creative, and I feel that the issue of the decriminalization, regulation and taxation of marijuana fits that bill. It's not new, the idea has been around, and the political will may in fact be there to make something happen."[13]

The small Southern California city of Maywood (which is 1.4 square miles and has a population of about thirty thousand residents, per California records, while being the third-smallest incorporated city in Los Angeles County) could certainly use a little extra tax revenue. To use Tom Ammiano's words, its budget is definitely in the toilet. The city has been forced to lay off its police force and is firing all public sector employees as a result of its major budget problems. The city plans to contract out all public services in an effort to save cash. Maywood is a small example of what the state of California (which has a $19 billion hole in its finances) and the rest of the country are facing. Mark Baldassare, president of the Public Policy Institute of California, says municipalities are facing a conundrum: "Local governments are so constrained by their budgets—they can't raise taxes and they have rising pension obligations."[14] California municipalities are struggling with a 40 percent drop in income thanks to falling sales and property taxes and thus, suddenly, Ammiano's drastic measure may not seem quite as drastic. In fact, Long Beach County is considering the idea that marijuana sales may enable the city to plug its $18.5 million deficit. Council members are considering a proposal to levy a 5 percent tax on gross receipts from medical marijuana businesses as well as a 5 to 10 percent tax on the sales of other marijuana-related businesses that may open up if marijuana is legalized for recreational use under Prop. 19 in the November statewide election.

Long Beach councilman Patrick O'Donnell put it like this: "We tax alcohol. We tax cigarettes. Why wouldn't we look at taxing marijuana? We're turning over every rock to find new revenues, and under one of those rocks may be marijuana."[15] The question is: will other states begin viewing marijuana as an economic opportunity? States are clearly suffering as a result of the economic downturn. Their combined deficit is projected to reach $112 billion by June 2011. Local government activities, such as funding police, school buildings, fire departments, parks, and social programs, are in the line of fire. Suddenly, marijuana may not look so awful.

According to NORML, more than 20,000 studies on marijuana and its components have been published. Of these thousands of studies, only about one hundred have looked into the therapeutic value on human subjects. For forty years, the federal government has hindered research by only allowing just a single source to cultivate marijuana. The University of Mississippi is the proud owner of the home to the only lab with a DEA license to cultivate marijuana. More recently, an established botanist at the University of Massachusetts was denied an application to create another growing facility by the Bush administration (despite a ruling by an administrative law judge determining that it should go forward), while Bob Winnicki, the Denver scientist who founded Full Spectrum Laboratories to test the quality of various marijuana strains, saw his facility raided by the DEA after he applied for a license. ("I innocently thought I could get one. I had nothing to hide," he told me on my visit to his lab, "and I thought I could do some interesting research and science. But they said it was completely illegal, and they took all of the samples we were testing." At least they didn't prosecute.)

Still, there have been some small studies, conducted by the Center for Medicinal Cannabis Research at the University of California–San Diego, showing that smoked marijuana can relieve pain in HIV and multiple sclerosis patients. Another study by the Fred Hutchinson Cancer Research Center in Seattle indicated that marijuana may increase the risk of developing testicular cancer. (The study found that current marijuana users were 70 percent more likely to develop it compared to nonusers.) Meanwhile, there are numerous laboratory studies that suggest marijuana may inhibit an enzyme that leads to memory-robbing plaque formation in the brain and may help in treating Alzheimer's disease and other diseases. Margaret Haney, a researcher at Columbia University Medical School, says that her research has proven that THC, the chemical compound in marijuana, can increase appetite and relieve nausea. Still, she worries about the harmful effects of smoking on marijuana users as well as the potential for addiction (though addiction rates are far lower than tobacco or alcohol.) "We don't really know enough [about] potential medical benefits," she tells me. "What people don't realize is that the scientific investigation of cannabinoids is really very young." She's right. There are very few human, placebo-controlled clinical studies as researchers need permission from the DEA, the proposed study must be approved by the FDA, and then the U.S. Public Health Service must conduct its own investigation to determine if the study is properly scientific and has merit. The entire process can take years and is compounded by the fact that marijuana is against federal law. Whether or not research continues to be thwarted, however, remains to be seen. Members of Congress are urging the attorney general to overrule the Bush administration's order preventing the University of Massachusetts scientist from receiving his license to study the medicinal properties of marijuana. If additional facilities are permitted to cultivate cannabis for research purposes, then the DEA and the FDA may have the studies necessary to reconsider the drug's current Schedule I listing.

As for Matt Simon's effort to legalize medical marijuana in New Hampshire, like anything, it comes down to politics. While he may be able to get the state legislature on board (no easy task, given that with 424 members New Hampshire has the largest state legislature in the world), he needs the governor to be on board as well. One thing in Simon's favor: New Hampshire governor John Lynch, a Democrat, was reelected in a year that prove to be a challenge for his party. He defeated the former Health and Human Services commissioner John Stephen, Republican nominee, overcoming a strong anti-incumbent sentiment that characterized the 2010 elections. Stephen is a family friend, and I have known him to be pretty conservative on most social issues. However, if he's conservative enough to believe in a state's ability to decide its destiny outside the confines of federal law, then he may decide to uphold any decision on medical marijuana or decriminalization on which his legislature votes. One thing is certain: This is a battle that is playing out not only in the tiny Granite State but also across the country, and it's clear that the momentum favors legalization.

ACKNOWLEDGMENTS

First and foremost, I want to thank my husband, James Ben, for all of his encouragement on this project. I'll never forget that on the day after I signed my contract to write this book, we learned I was pregnant with twins. Talk about an intimidating proposition. But James insisted I could do it and was supportive throughout the project, as he always is. Meanwhile, my beautiful infant daughters, Alexandra and Elizabeth, were surprisingly patient as I tried to care for them while scrambling to meet my looming deadline, often writing and rewriting chapters between feedings in the middle of the night.

This book could not have been written without the hard work of many at CNBC who contributed to the success of the documentaries *Marijuana Inc.* and *Marijuana USA*. Much of the primary reporting, done for the documentaries, contributed greatly to this book. Thank you to Jeff Zucker, who was president of NBC Universal at the time the documentaries aired, for all of his support. I'd also like to thank CNBC president Mark Hoffman who had the foresight to recognize that the *business* of marijuana would prove to be a fascinating investigation, and I want to thank him for championing such a controversial project. Thanks to Ray Borelli, CNBC vice president of long-form programming, for pushing the development of these television hours. Mitch Weitzner, who led the production teams on *Marijuana USA* and

Marijuana Inc., was a huge part of the editorial process, oversee-ing the development of story lines and helping to fine-tune the documentaries in every way. Former colleagues Josh Howard and Jonathan Wald were enthusiastic about *Marijuana Inc.* from the very beginning and helped the project get off the ground. Senior producer Jonathan Dann, with Lauren Farrelly's help, worked tirelessly to identify characters and story structures to help reveal the inner workings of this industry for the production. Dann's dedication to the original documentary was enormous, his enthu-siasm was contagious, and his ability to connect with people was inspiring. In *Marijuana USA*, Na Eng, Nina Alvarez, and Morgan Brasfield spent months developing compelling story lines relating to the emergence of dispensaries as businesses, locating the new entrepreneurs within the marijuana industry, and lining up inter-views to better understand Portugal's experience as a pioneer in decriminalizing drugs.

I'd like to note that while I conducted the majority of the inter-views, the production teams in the field (primarily producers Jonathan Dann and Nina Alvarez) interviewed some of the char-acters profiled in this book. The producers on both projects were hugely instrumental in developing sources and finding people willing to talk on camera with me.

Thank you to Jeremy Pink, who runs CNBC Business News, Nik Deogun, Managing Editor at CNBC, and to my producer, Rich Fisherman, who oversees the daily CNBC program I cohost, *The Call*, for their support and willingness to let me disappear to California, Colorado, Portugal, and wherever else I needed to go to conduct my interviews and investigations. Thanks as well to my cohosts of CNBC's *The Call*, Melissa Francis and Larry Kudlow, for holding down the fort, providing encouragement, and helping me to promote the documentaries and this book on *The Call*. (I want to also thank Larry, as someone who has admi-rably abstained from all substances for more than fifteen years and is passionately against the legalization of marijuana, for always being such a good sport when the subject of marijuana comes up.) Thank you to Tom Clendinin, Frank Piantini, Brian Steel, Amy

Zelvin, Meredith Stark, Steve Smith, Jennifer Dauble, William Imboden, and Stephanie Marchese for marketing the documentaries and helping to drive *Marijuana, Inc.* and *Marijuana USA* to become the most highly rated original programs in the network's history. No pun intended.

This book could also not have happened without the support and expertise of my talented editor, Eric Nelson, who was enthusiastic about this project from the beginning and had a remarkable ability to help me to synthesize several related but distinct story lines into an interesting narrative. My agents, Henry Reisch and Mel Berger, were very encouraging and connected me with Eric, which was so critical to this book's development.

This is also probably as good a place as any for an admission: I've never smoked marijuana and haven't ever been particularly close to anyone who has. I point this out not to protect my image, but to demonstrate that I came to this project with little sympathy for marijuana and little understanding of the prevalence of marijuana use among very regular and normal people and many who are using pot to treat truly debilitating illnesses. Clearly there are many people who abuse marijuana; substance abuse of any kind is a significant problem in our society. This book shouldn't be taken as glorifying the abuse of marijuana or condoning its illegal use. I do hope, however, that it raises awareness that attitudes toward marijuana are changing at an amazing rate, that state and federal policies are confusing and typically in conflict, and that marijuana is subjected to a moral standard that alcohol and tobacco have somehow managed to escape.

NOTES

All quotes are from conversations with the author or the production crew for the CNBC documentary *Marijuana Inc.* unless otherwise noted.

Introduction

1. Eileen McEachern, "New Pot-Cancer Bill Is Filed," *Boston Globe*, January 25, 1981.

1. Potholes: The Challenges of the Marijuana Business

1. The United States Attorney's Office, District of Colorado Web Site, www .justice.gov/usao/co/press_releases/2010/February10/2_15_10.html.

4. Cannabusiness: Those Who Can, Teach

1. Rebecca Cathcart, "Schwarzenegger Urges a Study on Legalizing Marijuana Use," *New York Times*, May 7, 2009.

2. Ibid.

3. "Supporting Research Into The Therapeutic Role of Marijuana," American College of Physicians Internal Medicine, 2008, www.acponline.org/advocacy/ where_we_stand/other_issues/medmarijuana.pdf.

4. California proposition 215, section 1A: "To ensure that seriously ill Californians have the right to obtain and use marijuana for medical purposes where the medical use is deemed appropriate and has been recommended by a physician who has determined that the person's health would benefit from the use of marijuana in the treatment of cancer, anorexia, AIDS, chronic pain, spasticity, glaucoma, arthritis, migraine, or any other illness for which marijuana provides relief."

5. Mike Harvey, "California Dreaming of Full Marijuana Legislation," *Times*, September 28, 2009.

7. Seed Money: Making Money Supplying Suppliers

1. Daniel Chacon and Tom Roeder, "El Paso County Considering Medical Marijuana Regulation," *Colorado Springs Gazette*, December 15, 2009, www.gazette.com/articles/county-90862-marijuana-medical.html.

2. Jim Spellman, "Colorado's Green Rush: Medical Marijuana," December 14, 2009, CNN.com, http://articles.cnn.com/2009-12-14/us/colorado.medical.marijuana_1_medical-marijuana-dispensaries-supply-and-demand/3?_s=PM:US.

3. Jeff Brady, "Colorado Tightens Medical Marijuana Rules," NPR, June 8, 2010, www.npr.org/templates/story/story.php?storyId=127547295.

4. J. M. McPartland, "Microbiological Contaminants of Marijuana," *Journal of the International Hemp Association*, 1994, www.hempfood.com/iha/iha01205.html.

8. Modern-Day Pirate: The Price of Prohibition

1. Rudolph J. Gerber, *Legalizing Marijuana: Drug Policy Reform and Prohibition Politics* (Westport, CT: Praeger, 2004), 2.

2. Patrick Stack, "Medicinal Marijuana: A History," Time online edition, October 27, 2002. http://www.time.com/time/covers/1101021104/history.html.

3. www.nida.nih.gov/PDF/DARHW/033-052_Kendall.pdf.

4. Morris B. Hoffman, "The Drug Court Scandal," *North Carolina Law Review*, June 2000, 4, http://www1.spa.american.edu/justice/documents/2459.pdf.

5. Larry Sloman, *Reefer Madness: A History of Marijuana* (New York: St. Martin Griffin, 1998), 27.

6. Ibid.

7. Gerber, *Legalizing Marijuana*, 3.

8. Thomas Pinney, *A History of Wine in America from Prohibition to the Present* (Berkeley: University of California Press, 2005), 26.

9. *Marijuana Inc.*, CNBC, 2009.

10. Pot of Gold: Sizing the Potential Market

1. Quentin Hardy, "Milton Friedman: Legalize It!" *Forbes*, June 2, 2005.

2. Jennifer Steinhauer, "Top Judge Calls California Government 'Dysfunctional,'" *New York Times*, October 10, 2009.

3. Mike Corder, "Cannabis Café Convicted of Breaking Dutch Law," Associated Press, March 25, 2010.

4. "Business Model Debate: Big Tobacco vs. Big Pharma," May 4, 1010, www.cnbc.com/id/36177544/Business_Model_Debate_Big_Tobacco_Vs_Big_Pharma.

11. Downers: Not Everything Is Coming Up Roses

1. As described by the prosecution in an interview with the producers of *Marijuana, Inc*.

2. Patricia Yollin, "Families Agonize over Bizarre Murder Case," *San Francisco Chronicle*, February 7, 2006.

3. CNBC documentary research, details of break-in from production team interview with District Attorney Jon Hopkins.

4. Linda Williams, "Violent Crimes Up in the County," *Willits News*, January 29, 2010.

5. Willits, California, 95490 Crime Statistics, www.clrsearch.com/RSS/Demographics/CA/95490/Crime_Statistics.

6. Steve Fainaru and William Booth, "Cartels Face an Economic Battle," *Washington Post*, October 7, 2009, www.washingtonpost.com/wp-dyn/content/article/2009/10/06/AR2009100603847.html.

7. "Northern California High Intensity Drug Trafficking Area Drug Market Analysis," National Drug Intelligence Center, June 2008, www.justice.gov/ndic/pubs27/27504/production.htm.

8. Steve Huntley, "Decriminalizing Pot Would Devastate Cartels," *Chicago Sun Times*, March 20, 2010.

9. Steve Fainaru and William Booth, "Cartels Face an Economic Battle," *Washington Post*, October 7, 2009.

10. Olivia Torres, "Mexico Detains Suspect in Killings of 2 Americans," Associated Press, March 29, 2010.

11. Stuart Grudgings, "Latin America Ex-leaders Urge Reform of U.S. Drug War," Reuters, February 11, 2009.

12. Free for All: The Great Portuguese Experiment

1. Colin Adamson, "Welcome to the Worst Drug Ghetto in Europe," *Evening Standard,* January 17, 2001.

2. Ibid.

3. Report by Alvaro Gil-Robles, Commissioner for Human Rights, on his visit to Portugal, May 27–30, 2003, https://wcd.coe.int/ViewDoc.jsp?id=99093&Site=COE.

4. Ibid.

5. Ibid.

6. Ibid.

7. "Treating, Not Punishing, Portugal's Drug Policy," *Economist*, August 29, 2009.

8. BBC News, "Portugal 'Not a Drug Haven,'" July 18, 2001.

9. Ibid.

10. Mirjam van het Loo, Ineke van Beusekom, and James P. Kahan, "Decriminalization of Drug Use in Portugal," American Academy of Political and Social Science, July, 2002, https://litigation-essentials.lexisnexis.com/webcd/app?action=DocumentDisplay&crawlid=1&doctype=cite&docid=582+Annals+49&srctype=smi&srcid=3B15&key=2e7cc2b7f4b29cd582be7851c6b96e7b.

11. In 1972, President Nixon commissioned a study to examine marijuana. The commission was headed by Raymond Shafer, the former governor of Pennsylvania. That spring, the commission presented a report to Congress titled "Marijuana: A Signal of Misunderstanding," which favored ending marijuana prohibition and adopting other methods to discourage use. The commission recommended that marijuana be decriminalized, but instead President Nixon dismissed their findings and launched the war on drugs. Decades later, marijuana use has increased, and our own prisons are crowded with pot smokers.

12. Glen Greenwald, "Drug Decriminalization in Portugal: Lessons for Creating Fair and Successful Drug Policies," http://store.cato.org/index.asp?fa= ProductDetails&method=&pid=1441428.

13. Ibid.

14. "Toward a Global View of Alcohol, Tobacco, Cannabis, and Cocaine Use: Findings from the WHO World Mental Health Surveys," *Public Library of Science Medicine* vol. 5, no. 7 (2008), www.plosmedicine.org/article/info:doi/10.1371/journal .pmed.0050141.

15. Joe DeCapua, "HIV/AIDS May Be Fueled by War on Drugs," Voice of America, June 28, 2010.

16. Ibid.

17. Ibid.

18. "Treating, Not Punishing; Portugal's Drug Policy," *Economist,* August 29, 2009.

19. Caitlin Hughes and Alex Stevens, "The Effects of Decriminalization of Drug Use in Portugal: What Can We Learn from the Portuguese Decriminalization of Illicit Drugs?," http://bjc.oxfordjournals.org/content/50/6/999.full.

20. "2004 National Survey on Drug Use and Health," http://oas.samhsa.gov/ nsduh.htm.

13. Getting the Treatment: How Decriminalization Works

1. Glen Greenwald, "Drug Decriminalization in Portugal: Lessons for Creating Fair and Successful Drug Policies," http://store.cato.org/index.asp?fa= ProductDetails&method=&pid=1441428.

2. Instituto da Droga e da Toxicodependencia de Portugal, [The national situation relating to drugs and dependency], 2006 Annual Report, 35.

3. "Mexico Legalizes Drug Possession," Associated Press, August 21, 2009.

4. "Argentine President Calls for Decriminalization of Drug Use," Cnn. com, August 1, 2008, http://articles.cnn.com/2008-08-01/world/argentina.drugs_1_ decriminalization-traffickers-drug-users?_s=PM:WORLD.

5. Coletta A. Youngers and John M. Walsh, "Drug Decriminalization: A Trend Takes Shape," *Americas Quarterly,* Fall 2009.

6. United States Has Highest Level of Illegal Cocaine and Cannabis Use, *Science Daily, July 1, 2008,* www.sciencedaily.com/releases/2008/06/080630201007.htm.

7. Jefferey Miron, "The Budgetary Implications of Marijuana Prohibition," June 2005, www.prohibitioncosts.org/mironreport.html.

14. Law and Disorder: Navigating the Legal Maze We've Created

1. *Emerald Steel Fabricators, Inc. v. Bureau of Labor and Industries*, www .publications.ojd.state.or.us/S056265.htm.

2. Ibid.

3. Ibid.

4. Stephanie Chen, "ACLU Sues Wal-Mart for Firing Employee Using Medical Marijuana," June 29, 2010, CNN.com, http://articles.cnn.com/2010-06-29/living/ medical.marijuana.walmart.lawsuit_1_wal-mart-officials-medical-marijuana- associates-and-customers?_s=PM:LIVING.

15. This Is Not Gay Marriage: Why Advocates Can't Turn to the Courts for Help

1. David W. Ogden, "Holder Memo," Memorandum for Selected United State Attorneys on Investigations and Prosecutions in States Authorizing the Medical Use of Marijuana, October 19, 2009, http://blogs.usdoj.gov/blog/archives/192 (emphasis added).

2. Ibid.

3. William Hubbs Rehnquist opinion in *United States v. Alfonso Lopez, Jr.*, 514 U.S. 549 (1995).

4. *Gonzales, Attorney General, et al. v. Raich, et al.*, Certiorari to the United States Court of Appeals for the Ninth Circuit, no. 03—1454, argued November 29, 2004, decided June 6, 2005, www.law.cornell.edu/supct/html/03-1454.ZS.html.

5. *Gonzales, Attorney General, et al. v. Raich et al.* Certiorari to the United States Court of Appeals for the Ninth Circuit, No. 03-1454. Argued November 29, 2004, decided June 6, 2005. http://caselaw.Ip.findlaw.com/scripts/getcase.pI?court=US&vol=000&invol=03-1454#concurrence1

6. Wickard v. Filburn, 317 U.S. 111(1942). 317 U.S. 111. *Wickard, Secretary of Agriculture, et al. v. Filburn* No. 59 Reargued Oct. 13, 1942, decided Nov. 9. 1942. http://caselaw.Ip.findlaw.com/cgi-bin/getcase.pl?court=US&vol=317&invol=111

7. U.S. Const. art. I, sec. 8.

8. Citing Justice Brandeis writing in dissent in *New State Ice Co. v. Liebman*, 285 U.S. 262 (1932), argued February 19, 1932, decided March 21, 1932.

9. *Gonzales, Attorney General, et al. v. Raich et al.* Certiorari to the United States Court of Appeals for the Ninth Circuit, No. 03-1454. Argued November 29, 2004, decided June 6, 2005. http://caselaw.Ip.findlaw.com/scripts/getcase.pI?court=US&vol=000&invol=03-1454#concurrence1.

10. Ibid.

16. Smoke Free or Die: Changing Minds in a Hard-to-Change State

1. Karl Vick, "Support for Legalizing Marijuana Grows Rapidly around the U.S.," *Washington Post*, November 23, 2009.

2. Bob, Egelko, "U.S. to Yield Marijuana Jurisdiction to States," February 27, 2009, http://articles.sfgate.com/2009-02-27/news/17190325_1_medical-marijuana-marijuana-advocacy-group-medicinal.

3. "Remarks by the President at 'Open for Questions' Town Hall," www.whitehouse.gov/the_press_office/Remarks-by-the-President-at-Open-for-Questions-Town-Hall.

4. Joe DeCapua, "HIV/AIDS May Be Fueled by War on Drugs," Voice of America, June 28, 2010.

5. FDA News Release, April 20, 2006, www.fda.gov/NewsEvents/Newsroom/PressAnnouncements/2006/ucm108643.htm.

6. "Pot Is Medicine, Let the Ill Use It," April 16, 2009, www.unionleader.com/article.aspx?headline=Pot+is+medicine%3A+Let+the+ill+use+it&articleId=55abc179-1932-4d4a-ab27-7ffbf0e19af1.

7. Marc Kaufman, "Study Finds No Cancer-Marijuana Connection," *Washington Post*, May 26, 2006.

8. Asa Hutchinson, "Legalizing Marijuana Not Worth the Costs," cnbc.com, April 20, 2010, www.cnbc.com/id/36267217/Legalizing_Marijuana_Not_Worth_the_Costs.

9. Jon Gettman, "Crimes of Indiscretion: Marijuana Arrests in the United States," NORML Foundation (2005), executive summary by Allen St. Pierre, executive director NORML/NORML Foundation, http://norml.org/index.cfm?Group_ID=6474.

10. "Legalizing Marijuana in California Would Sharply Lower the Price of the Drug," www.rand.org/news/press/2010/07/07.

11. Lee, 1963: 68, commissioned by President Richard M. Nixon, March 1972.

12. Louisa Degenhardt, Wai-Tat Chiu, Nancy Sampson et al., "Toward a Global View of Alcohol, Tobacco, Cannabis, and Cocaine Use: Findings from the WHO World Mental Health Surveys," Public Library of Science, June 2008.

13. Alison Stateman, "Can Marijuana Help Rescue California's Economy?" *Time*, March 13, 2009.

14. Matthew Garrahan, "U.S. State Budget Crises Threaten Social Fabric," *Financial Times*, June 28, 2010.

15. Tony Barboza, "Cash-Strapped Long Beach Considers Taxing Marijuana," *Los Angeles Times*, July 7, 2010.

INDEX

251